W9-BIK-385

International Banking in an Age of Transition

International Banking in an Age of Transition

Globalisation, Automation, Banks and their Archives

Edited by

SARA KINSEY and LUCY NEWTON

Ashgate

Aldershot • Brookfield USA • Singapore • Sydney

© Sara Kinsey, Lucy Newton and the contributors, 1998

All rights reserved. No part of this publication may be reproduced, stored in a retrieval system, or transmitted in any form or by any means, electronic, mechanical, photocopying, recording, or otherwise without the prior permission of the publisher.

Published by
Ashgate Publishing Limited
Gower House
Croft Road
Aldershot
Hants
GU11 3HR
England

Ashgate Publishing Company
Old Post Road
Brookfield
Vermont 05036–9704

The authors have asserted their moral right under the Copyright, Designs and Patents Act, 1988, to be identified as the authors of this work.

British Library Cataloguing in Publication Data

International Banking in an Age of Transition: Globalisation,
    Automation, Banks and their Archives.
    (Studies in Banking History)
    1. Banks and banking, European.   2. Banks and banking,
    International.
    I. Kinsey, Sara.   II. Newton, Lucy.   III. European Association for
    Banking History.
    332.1'094

Library of Congress Cataloging-in-Publication Data

International banking in an age of transition: globalisation, automation,
    banks and their archives/edited by Sara Kinsey and Lucy Newton.
        (Studies in Banking History)
        Includes index.
        1. Banks and Banking—Europe—History. 2. Banks and banking—
    Technological innovations.   I. Kinsey, Sara, 1969–   .
    II. Newton, Lucy.   III. Series.
    HG2974.E89   1998
    332.1'094—dc21   97–45890
                                                                          CIP

ISBN 1 85928 384 5

This book is printed on acid free paper

Typeset in Sabon by Manton Typesetters, 5–7 Eastfield Road, Louth, Lincolnshire, LN11 7AJ and printed in Great Britain by The Ipswich Book Company, Suffolk

Contents

Part I   Bank Archives of the Future

Part II   Concentration and Internationalisation in Banking

List of Tables

List of Figures

Preface

This book contains the papers and comments that were presented at the Symposium in honour of Dr Wilfried Guth, held at Deutsche Bank, Frankfurt am Main on 2 November 1995. We would like to thank the hosts, Deutsche Bank, and Sir Evelyn de Rothschild and Hilmar Kopper for their opening addresses to the morning and afternoon sessions. Additionally, we should also like to thank all the speakers, panellists and the two session chairmen, Dr Wilfried Feldenkirchen and Dr Herman van der Wee. The symposium was also notable for the presentation of the first ever prize for young scholars working in European banking history, which was awarded to Lucy Newton and Boris Barth. We would like to thank the judging panel for all their hard work.

Gratitude must also be extended to Manfred Pohl and everyone at the European Association for Banking History for the organisation of the conference, and the initial rounding-up of the papers. Special thanks are due to Emma Johnston for her continued and invaluable assistance. We are also grateful to a number of people for their support and encouragement: Edwin Green, Rachel Huskinson, Phil Cottrell, Geoff Jones, Tom Bucke and Chris Wright.

Foreword

This volume contains the papers and comments presented at the conference 'The Archives of the Future' and 'Concentration and Internationalisation in banking' in Frankfurt in 1995. This event marked the fifth anniversary of the European Association for Banking History e. V. (hereafter EABH), but also, more importantly, honoured the commitment to the EABH of Dr Wilfried Guth who stepped down from the position of chairman of the association's Board of Patrons in 1995.

In recent decades Europe has been looking towards unification both financially and culturally. Countries of various political and social systems are anticipating a time of closer interaction with their European partners. However, many countries also wish to retain their identities whilst still taking an active part in the European sphere of commerce and exchange. The history of each country is therefore important for their future role in Europe and the banking world as a whole, and the history of banking in each country is inextricably linked with the economic development of that country and its people.

With this background, the idea of founding an organisation which would coordinate different facets of European banking history originated in the mid-1980s. The original sources of this history differ from bank to bank and from country to country, and it became clear that an organisation would benefit bank archivists by providing a tightly knit network which would enable them to exchange ideas and practices. Additionally, historians in the field wished to promote the serious study of banking history in Europe. Both archivists and historians thus took part in the initiative of founding what was to become the EABH. Bankers were also aware of the importance of the historic records of banking and of the value to a bank of establishing and maintaining an archive, and thus its own corporate memory and identity. Bankers, historians and bank archivists of the EABH may have differing roles to play but they all wish to recognise the importance of research in banking history.

In 1988 I approached Wilfried Guth (at this time chairman of Deutsche Bank's Supervisory Board), about a proposal for the planned association for the history of banks, an idea which he greeted with enthusiasm. Having been involved for nearly four decades in the banking profession, his knowledge of this community and his personal judgement were greatly valued by me.

Wilfried Guth has been one of the outstanding bankers of his generation. After only five years in the profession, he had already managed to make a name for himself when he was elected as the successor to Dr Otmar Emmingers as the West German Executive Director at the International Monetary Fund at the age of 39 in 1959. This rapidly rising career is more impressive when one considers that, having entered military service in 1937, he remained in the German army, was taken prisoner in Stalingrad and not released until 1949. Following this, he studied at the universities of Bonn, Geneva, Heidelberg and the London School of Economics and entered the banking profession in 1953. His first position was with the Bank Deutscher Lander, the predecessor of Deutsche Bundesbank. He was responsible for producing monthly reports for the economics and statistics department; in 1958 he was promoted to head of his department.

After working at the International Monetary Fund, Wilfried Guth returned to Germany to become a member of the Board of Management of the Kreditanstalt für Wiederaufbau in 1962. In this position he concerned himself with the developing countries, the long-term financing of exports and structural policy.

Wilfried Guth reached perhaps the peak of his distinguished career in 1976 when he became co-speaker, along with F. Wilhelm Christians, of Deutsche Bank. During this time, along with his colleagues on the Board of Managing Directors, he led one of the most influential and prominent banks in Germany.

Upon his appointment as co-speaker of Deutsche Bank there was some speculation that he would become a contender for the presidency of the Deutsche Bundesbank. In an interview with *The Times* (May 1976), which named him as the leading currency expert among German bankers, he mentioned that he was also interested in maintaining the means to bring about the goal of European integration and desired 'closer economic and monetary contact ... with countries which do not belong to the currency block'. As co-speaker of Deutsche Bank, the Dusseldorf-based Christians was the dominant figure in the bank's domestic business, and Frankfurt-based Guth generally took charge of its international dealings.

Wilfried Guth is greatly respected by many both within and outside the banking community. An indication of this high esteem apeared in an article 'The rise of Deutsche Bank' in the magazine *Institutional Investor* (October 1977): 'While no single individual could be given the credit for Deutsche Bank's emergence as one of the world's great international deal-makers, this highly competitive mountain-climber comes closest to getting the honours.'

In 1980 *Industriemagazin* (December 1980) chose Wilfried Guth as their manager of the year. In 1981, in recognition of the commitment of the co-speakers of the bank, Wilfried Guth and F. Wilhelm Christians were voted Bankers of the Year by the magazine *Institutional Investor* (August 1981). One prominent London banker spoke of Wilfried Guth in relation to Hermann J. Abs, an enigmatic figure in German banking history, as being 'Abs's bricklayer, the man who laid the foundation and implemented Abs's policy decisions. Guth took the platform that he had helped to construct and built a rocket on it.'

In 1985 Wilfried Guth became chairman of Deutsche Bank's Supervisory Board. He has also held honorary posts with many different business organisations such as Chairman of the Board of Management of the Gesellschaft zur Forderung des Unternehmensnachwuchses. His interest in international economics and currency politics is apparent through his posts on international bodies, for instance, as Chairman of the Stiftungsrat des Japanisch-Deutschem Zentrums Berlin and Board of Trustees. He is also a member of cultural organisations like the Gesellschaft der Freunde der Alten Oper Frankfurt.

Wilfried Guth's experience within the banking world more than qualified him for the position of Chairman of the Board of Patrons of the EABH. With his support the EABH was founded on 29 November 1990 in Frankfurt am Main. Representatives from 23 European banks were present at the inaugural meeting. The principles of the EABH were set down at this meeting: the wish to promote dialogue amongst historians and representatives from banks, to encourage the establishment of archives and to encourage historical research within existing bank archives.

It was not only for his knowledge as a banker that Wilfried Guth was cherished by his associates in the EABH but also for his knowledge acquired from outside the financial world. He himself has said that 'when I have my next life, I would like to be a publisher … I love books, love language, love people, to discover people'. This was apparent in Wilfried Guth's participation within the EABH; he was not just an honorary figure but someone who became involved in the organisation, took an active interest in its affairs and offered advice on its direction.

Manfred Pohl
Deutsche Bank, Frankfurt am Main

PART I
Bank Archives of the Future

CHAPTER ONE

Bank Archives of the Future: Introduction[1]

Sara Kinsey

The end of a century is traditionally a time for predicting the features of the next; the end of a millennium is an opportunity for even wider, and perhaps wilder, prophecies. Pundits who have sought to second-guess the twenty-first century have usually concentrated on the changes that will be wrought on everyday life by the advances in technology. In the field of banking this has led some commentators to claim that the next century will herald the arrival of the 'virtual bank' as branch banking becomes obsolete and armchair banking the norm. Will the twenty-first century also mean the appearance of the 'virtual bank archive'? As people become used to ordering their groceries and running their bank accounts through their home computers, will they also demand that the services of an archive should be accessible from the comfort of their own offices or homes? What will be the impact on archives of new demands and new media and will we need to develop new methodologies and new skills to cope with the new challenges? The contributions in this volume confront the obstacles and opportunities that lie ahead for bank archives and the various authors, being bankers, historians and archivists, demonstrate the differing viewpoints and priorities that each profession brings to the issues.

The three developments that will probably have the greatest effect on banking archives in the near future are the changing formats of records from paper-based to electronic media; the evolution of new delivery channels to transmit information about archives and their whereabouts (and in some cases versions of the archives themselves), in response to user-driven demands; and lastly the continuing drive towards standardisation within the archival profession.

Electronic records

Within the archives profession the debate surrounding the issues of electronic records has given rise to three particular concerns. First, the practically minded have pointed out the dangers inherent in keeping electronic records: it is impossible to predict with any great certainty how long a floppy disk, CD-ROM or laser disk will remain readable. Moreover, keeping information in a machine-readable format necessarily entails keeping the machine which is able to read it and, with the plethora of software and hardware available, this could result in the archivists' storeroom resembling a retirement home for computers.

Second, the proliferation of non-paper forms of communication, for instance e-mail and voice-mail, poses particular problems for the archivist. Although it is likely that these types of communications may contain information of value to the historian of the future, they are preserved on exactly the kinds of media that are rarely, at present, subject to any records-management policy and therefore will be discarded according to the memory demands of a computer system or the whim of the user. Some historians have already made dire predictions of a 'black hole' appearing in the historical record and archivists are becoming aware of the need to control such situations.

Third, the creation of large volumes of information in an electronic form has made it possible to keep for posterity the kinds of information that hitherto would have been discarded because of the low informational value of each individual record – the importance being in the sum rather than the parts. For instance, many banks now create and use very large databases (VLDBs) which analyse their customers' lifestyles, income and expenditure patterns, and details of individual transactions in order to retain their existing customers and increase the range of products sold to them. The potential of these forms of electronic records for recording new types and volumes of information has long been acknowledged by archivists and historians alike, but the theoretical and practical considerations in transferring such electronic records to the archives have so far postponed any mass accessioning of databases.

How are we to approach these problems, bearing in mind the traditional principles of the archive profession, the new capabilities and technologies at our disposal and the potential demands of our users in the future?

The problem of technological obsolescence is already being tackled by the emergence of platform-independent systems and software, and I suspect that this trend will continue in the next century as more and more countries and individuals will join the information age and their machines will need to talk to each other. It is likely that archivists will have to manage programmes of migration between systems and media, but they can take solace in the fact that they will not be alone in this. Nor is this principle new: archivists have long been transferring records to microfilm or microfiche. Archivists may have to update their own knowledge along with the formats in their care, but with the right guidance and advice this should not be an insuperable problem.

Electronic records have yet to conquer the world. Piers Cain's chapter in this volume (Chapter 6) illustrates the kinds of information that are being created in banks on new media and that are not as yet subject to any retention rules. To ease the mind of the anxious archivist, he reassures us that at the moment we are in a state of transition from paper media to electronic media. Thus those records that are still perceived to be worthy of permanent preservation are retained on paper, and these are usually exactly the kinds of records that archivists need to transfer to the archives. Studies of modern companies have shown that management information still relies on traditional media, not least because of the requirements in some cases of company law. Campbell-Kelly's study of information within businesses has led him to conclude that there is a pyramidal structure of information, the apex of which is strategic information such as board papers and reports which, he concludes, 'is generally modest in volume, of the highest importance to the business historian and is generally well preserved on paper media ... the impact of electronic media is likely to be slight, since the printed paper form will probably persist into the foreseeable future for both cultural and practical reasons' (Campbell-Kelly, 1993). However, it may be the case that once past the age of transition from paper-based to electronic media, it will be the statutory records that continue to be kept on paper and all others that are kept electronically. For instance at the moment the board minutes of a bank, the corporate backbone of an archive, are governed by company law which states that they must be kept in perpetuity.[2] In practice, this requires their retention on paper and will continue to do so until the law comes to terms with new media. The board papers, which contain reports and policy recommendations, and which are circulated to the directors before or at the meeting, are not governed by company law. It is not impossible to envisage a time in the future when they are created in a report form on an executive's computer, sent through an intranet (an internal company network) to the company secretary who then distributes them to the directors via e-mail. As a result they may not survive within the bank in a paper format. This is especially worrying; while board minutes have become increasingly formulaic and uninformative during the last hundred years, they may be the only records that are passed to the archives.

Archivists will need to be aware of how the records-keeping practices of their employing organisations are changing. If we assume that the well-organised archivist already has a clear documentation strategy whereby certain series or classes of records are transferred to the archives at specified time intervals, then it will be obvious to them when those records either appear on different media, or do not appear at all. In these cases the archivist must remember that it is the informational content, not the media, that is important. Where certain records are not earmarked for preservation in the archives it may be the case that the archives will lose out if they are stored electronically. For instance, at present when a director or an executive retires he or she may clear out his/her paper files by sending them to the archives. However, at the moment there is not the same inclination to copy this practice with computer files. They are somehow seen as more private and either deleted or downloaded on to disk and taken away with the individual. Cultural changes within the organisation may be required. The tendency is to associate archives departments with old books, ledgers and paper, and to associate the information technology department with anything regarding computers. Archivists must ensure that this misunderstanding does not prevent them from staking a claim to modern electronic records.

In addition to the kinds of records that archivists have tended to keep (the minutes, accounts, reports, policy documents etc.) there is also the problem of the creation of a new type of record in database form, to which I referred earlier. Historians have pointed out that in addition to the huge quantities of data kept in the database itself, some computer work systems also generate new varieties of information – for instance keeping the records of bank back-office processing will not only preserve the information on customers but will also produce information on the productivity and work flow within the processing area by bank staff. From the archivists' point of view it has been surmised that, as electronic records take up less storage space than traditional paper archives (in theory), they therefore offer greater possibilities for keeping series of records which hitherto were judged too bulky to keep. This is especially true of those series of records where each item possesses small informational content and previous solutions had necessarily involved some kind of sampling technique.

But just because we now have the capability to keep these records, does this mean that we should? The practical difficulties are many. These types of databases create, modify and destroy data each day. If the archives were to keep a copy of all versions of the system they would soon swamp the archive. Additionally, these systems, especially those used by banks, will hold confidential material on customers. Many countries now have in place legislation designed to protect an individual's right to see all information kept about them on computer systems. In Britain at present this takes the form of the Data Protection Act which states that every detail kept on computer on an individual must be for a stated and registered purpose and that the people who can access and use this information must also be stated and registered. Bank departments may be very reluctant to hand over to the archives records and/or databases which they have created and which are covered by such legislation. They will be concerned that they will be used for non-registered purposes by non-registered users, i.e. for historical research by archivists and historians.

Issues such as these have prompted some archivists to suggest that they should be involved with the creation of such records from the very beginning of their lives – 'the archivist will have to be an instigator of records creation rather than just a selector or custodian of records' (Higgs, 1992). In reality, however, enthusing non-archivists with this concept is not the easiest task. In banks it is even more difficult, given the cautious nature of these institutions, evolved from years of looking after other people's money. In practice, archivists of the future will need to cooperate with record-creating departments within their employing banks, and especially with their information technology departments, to discover what is practical and to resolve such issues.

When archivists discuss the issues of electronic records they must not forget the need to document the changes that the use of such systems has made to banking.[3] The introduction of new data processing techniques in the back office, of computerised information and management systems within bank offices and branches, and the advent of electronic forms of cash and smart cards, will all have their place in banking history. Archivists must always have an eye to what they consider will be potential research topics in the future and the impact of information technology will no doubt be a subject for much study. Historians will want to know how systems were designed and by whom, how they were introduced and when, what they were intended to do, who used them, how they saved money and time, improved margins and profitability and many other such questions. Jürgen Rebouillon's chapter in this volume (Chapter 4) touches on these questions and archivists can be sure that this will be a 'growth area' in years to come.

Delivery channels

There is no doubt that the users of the future will expect the more modern sections of the archive to be kept in electronic formats. One historian has written, 'the proportion of records reaching archives that are computerised will soon expand ... dramatically. The truth is that we are not looking at a trickle but a tidal wave that will reach our shores very soon' (Zweig, 1993). In some cases historians have already begun to speculate on the kinds of research that will be possible in the future –

'the potential for retaining huge quantities of communications and records suggest[s] opportunities which even the historian of the nineteenth century can never have' (Morris, 1993). Not only will users be expecting to use electronic records, but they will be expecting to use them via electronic delivery channels. Library catalogues have been mounted and searchable on the Internet for some time now, and many academics have been accustomed to searching for information in this way. Demand for a similar service for archives on the Internet already exists and can be expected to grow. In October 1995 the National Register of Archives in Britain became searchable via the Internet and by January 1996 their site had registered around 14 000 visitors.[4] A sample of European banking historians was recently asked if they would like bank archive catalogues to be available via the Internet: 100 per cent of respondents replied positively. In contrast, a simultaneous survey carried out on bank archivists discovered that none of those questioned had placed any of their finding aids on the Internet and only one had plans to do so (Kinsey and Newton, 1997). In Britain, at the time of writing, only one bank archive, that of the Bank of England, has a page on the Internet. In Europe many banks have used historical information and illustrations from the archives to enhance their company's Internet pages, but very few actually have detailed information on the work and holdings of the archives on the Internet.[5] However, the experience of North America, where use of the Internet is much more widespread and more accepted within business, suggests that this situation will change by the next century. Australian archivists have led the way in unifying information about all their archive repositories on one site, which contains links to each individual archive site, and these already include Australian bank archives. Perhaps the greatest advantage of the Internet will be the ease with which information, previously dispersed and time-consuming to collect, can now be gathered.

The ultimate progression of this trend is, of course, scanning either actual documents or transcripts of them into the computer and making them available via the Internet so that researchers can download at their end and study the documents at their leisure, without having to come to the archives in person. One historian has written recently of his vision of electronic archives 'which will allow us to download facsimiles of documents directly to the computers in our offices ... furthermore, archives will be able to change the texts: embedded interpretations or provenances will lie under specific words or phrases creating links with other documents, in the same or other archives' (Bradley, 1997). This has obvious advantages for the researcher in saving the time and money needed to travel to the archives – this is especially pertinent in the case of the archives of multinational and international companies which will have a worldwide constituency of users. Although there are benefits to the researchers, there are drawbacks to the archivist. First, the scanning in of documents and preparation of transcripts will be a time-consuming and tedious task requiring many hours that could more profitably be spent on other activities. Second, the process of scanning may be damaging or detrimental to the documents. Third, banks may be very uneasy at the thought of uninhibited access to their archives. Business archives, especially those of banks, rarely operate an open house policy with regard to access to their archives. Researchers wishing to use them usually have to state at least the subject and aims of their research and often need to provide references. Mounting documents on the Internet would mean that the archivists, and the bank itself, would lose control over who was actually reading and using them. However, as with most problems regarding the Internet, there is a technological solution to this problem: documents could be encrypted before being placed on the Internet, and the key to read them would only be available from the archivists to whom the potential researcher would apply and have to fulfil the approved conditions for access.

Standardisation

The Internet will also influence the work of archivists by allowing greater comparisons of professional activities and practices between repositories and countries. Not only will it be easier to read and download the professional literature from other countries, we shall also be able to join international discussion groups and, most importantly, have greater opportunities to see how other repositories work through their Internet sites: 'we will be more directly open to ... our colleagues and peers who will have easy and normal access to our material, we will be much more aware of what is standard' (Cook, 1997). The use of computers in cataloguing and the potential for electronic information exchange has already galvanised the archival profession in attempts to find some common standards for these activities. The search for common cataloguing rules has stimulated much debate and in 1993 The International Council on Archives formally adopted and published the *General International Standard Archival Description* (ISAD(G)), which is slowly being adopted throughout the archive world. A recent Danish survey concluded: 'the majority of archives in Europe are heading in a direction where ISAD(G) ... will become the used standard' (Steinmark, 1996).

   Much work has also been undertaken in the field of electronic exchange of information. In 1993 the Berkeley Finding Aids Project began collecting and comparing archival descriptions to find common elements. This work culminated in the Encoded Archival Description (EAD) projects that are now running at many American universities including Yale, Harvard and the University of California,[6] in addition to archives and university archives in the UK. All these projects use Standard Generalized Markup Language (SGML), a platform- and application-independent way to encode data and text to describe archival holdings.[7] These projects are still in a testing phase but the Library of Congress in America is supporting EAD as a standard. The advantages are obvious: the data themselves will be stored in a platform-independent format, the international standardisation of archival finding aids will allow searching and indexing across all those on the Internet, and researchers will be able to discover from a short session with a terminal where sources on their particular area of interest are kept, the extent of such sources and how to access them. At the moment, searching on the Internet is an exercise which requires time, patience and a good temper on the part of the researcher, as search engines do not distinguish between the important and the trivial. As the use of the Internet increases, so will the sophistication by which information on the net is used and processed.

For the archivists, the spread of common standards should encourage the adoption of best and consistent practices. However, archivists have invested much time and resources in the systems which they already use and there will be an inevitable time lag before uniform systems are adopted. Moreover, bank archivists work in a very cost-conscious environment and their main source of enquiries is often internal, from within the employing organisation, not external, from academic researchers. Although we do not want to dawdle behind the rest of the archival profession, we need to acknowledge that in business the time and costs are paramount considerations and, at the moment, the time taken to learn how to rewrite our finding aids using SGML and according to the rules of EAD may not justify the savings these may make in the future. I suspect that, as with most technology, as EAD becomes more widely used, so it will become more user-friendly and easier to learn and implement. Although bank archivists may not be in the vanguard of developments in this field, we should certainly ensure that we are aware of current progressions and tailor what we are doing now with an eye to what we could be doing in the future. In my view, it is likely that archive information on the Internet will be as diverse as the archives themselves for some time to come, but this information can be gathered together at a host site, for instance a page belonging to the European Association for Banking History, where access to bank archive information will become easier than at present.

Conclusion

Bank archivists and their users predictably have different opinions on what will be the major issues facing bank archives of the future. Archivists themselves are concerned with survival, both of their units and of the records themselves, as the mass of documentation of late twentieth-century banking activities continues to grow. Archivists face the challenging task of appraising different types of information and different types of media already touched on in this chapter. Banking historians remain preoccupied with issues of accessibility and also with the potential of electronic records for research purposes. Questions of access revolve around, first, access to closed records and, second, access to the archives of those banks which still have no archive provision. Youssef Cassis in this volume (Chapter 3) comments that 'the question of accessibility ... remains the crucial point for banking historians' (page 28). Although there has been a boom in the supply of archive services in financial institutions in the last thirty years (the history of which is recounted and examined in Green's chapter in this volume – Chapter 2), those banks with archives still remain in the minority. The overview of the state of European bank archives given at a conference of the European Association for Banking History in 1992 makes for depressing reading: Spain had only the archives of the Bank of Spain (Tortella, 1992); in Switzerland 'there are no guidelines for the safekeeping of records ... there are hardly any archives' (Bucher, 1992); and even in Germany 'the situation of bank archives ... is rather desolate' (Teichmann, 1992). The only European countries where the archive position seemed optimistic at the time of this overview were the United Kingdom, Italy and the Netherlands. The position has improved in the last five years but one of the biggest hurdles to be jumped by banking historians and archivists in the future will remain the problem of persuading banks of the value of their historical archives. Green's examination of the establishment of archive units in European banks shows that there is no one simple reason that has proved the decisive factor in providing an archive service, and this will probably continue to be the case in the next century. However, we now have a new set of weapons with which to strengthen our armoury of arguments.

First, the increasing accountability of financial institutions towards their customers, past and present, is a feature of today's banking scene. Growing numbers of customers are willing to resort to litigation in disputes with their banks and in such cases banks are required to produce reams of documentation on products and procedures. A particularly important and sensitive extension of this has been the search by survivors of the Holocaust, or their relatives, for money or valuables deposited in banks before the outbreak of war in 1939. Banks must be able to produce evidence not just of what happened to individual accounts, but also of historic procedures and regulations. Undoubtedly not all banks will be able to produce all the evidence required and will retrospectively learn the value to the organisation of keeping archives. It is to be hoped that some banks will take these lessons to heart and establish archive units to ensure that proper documentation of their activities is conserved for the future.

Second, the collapse of the communist system in Eastern Europe has had profound effects on financial systems as previously state-owned banks become private institutions. The question of what will happen to the archives of former government-run and -owned banks should open up a debate regarding the importance of such archives and their continuity now that the banks operate under different market conditions. This awareness of living through historical changes provides a third argument: banks should be aware that they are playing a large part in 'making history'. As Eastern Europe grapples with the problems of evolving market structures, so Western Europe wrestles with the concept of the single currency and a European bank. Bank archivists and, in a coordinating role, organisations such as the European Association for Banking History need to tackle the problems of documenting such transformations and modifications to the financial system.

The growth of concentration and internationalisation in banking, two of the themes explored in the second half of this volume, have their own implications for bank archives. As an organisation grows larger and sprawls geographically, so it needs to evolve methods of communication between the core and the periphery to ensure similarity of policy, methods and procedure. The growth of intranets within business makes it more likely that the primary route for communicating information and instructions will be via electronic channels. As we approach the twenty-first century, so it is the banking sector which is becoming increasingly multinational. The archives units of global banks could be directing collection and appraisal policies in countries on the other side of the world, and dealing with enquiries from any part of the organisation wherever they may be located: greatness is being thrust upon us. Bank archivists of the future will need clear documentation strategies when faced with the scale and scope of business development. Not only are we facing more information creation than ever before, but this information and its users will not necessarily respect national boundaries. Bank archivists in the next century will continue to be concerned with the capture of information, methods of keeping information and its use in a managed environment. The information itself, the strategies for its preservation and how it is made available and utilised, will all be subject to change. The bank archivist must be able to provide a flexible response to any mutations, modifications and alterations to existing practice. Although we are concerned with what is past we must also be prepared for what is to come.

Notes

1. I am grateful to my colleagues Edwin Green and Rachel Huskinson, and to Lucy Newton for their comments on early drafts of this chapter.
2. I am grateful to Nigel Barker, assistant secretary, HSBC Holdings plc for his comments on this issue.
3. This section owes much to a discussion with my colleague Rachel Huskinson.
4. The site can be found at http://www.hmc.gov.uk
5. An honourable exception that I know of is the Banca Commerciala Italiana, whose site can be found at http://www.bci.it/storia/astorica.htm
6. Reports on these projects can be found at http://Webtext.library.yale.edu (Yale); http://hul.harvard.edu/dfap/ (Harvard); http://sunsite.berkeley.edu/ finding aids (Berkeley)
7. For a good description of how this works in practice see R. Higgins (1997), 'Standardised languages for data exchange and storage: using the encoded archival description and SGML to create permanent electronic handlists', *Business Archives Principles and Practice*, 73, May.

References

Bradley, James (1997), 'From Peter Payne to Hydros – reflections on the use of computers in business history', in Allan, A. (ed.), *Proceedings of the Annual Conference of the Business Archives Council*, London.

Bucher, Silvio (1992), 'Rapport sur la situation des archives des banques cantonales en Suisse', in Pohl, M. (ed.), *The Situation of Bank Archives in West European Countries*, Frankfurt am Main, European Association for Banking History e. V.

Campbell-Kelly, M. (1993), 'Information in the business enterprise', in Higgs, S. and Ross, E. (eds), *Electronic Information, Resources and Historians: European Perspectives*.

Cook, Michael (1997), 'Changing times, changing aims', *Journal of the Society of Archivists*, 18 (1), April.

Higgs, E. (1992), 'Machine-readable records, archives and historical memory', *History and Computing*, 4 (3).

Kinsey, S. and Newton, L. (1997), 'The archivist, the historian and research co-operation', in Pohl, M. (ed.), *Bank Archives and the User: European Colloquium on Bank Archives*, Vol. 6, Lisbon.

Morris, R. (1993), 'Electronic documents and the history of the late twentieth century – black holes or warehouse – what do historians really want?' in Higgs, S. and Ross, E. (eds), *Electronic Information, Resources and Historians: European Perspectives*.

Steinmark, C. (1996), 'The use of Information Technology in the European Searchroom', *Journal of the Society of Archivists*, **17** (1), April.

Teichmann, Gabriele (1992), 'The situation of bank archives in Germany', in Pohl, M. (ed.), *The Situation of Bank Archives in West European Countries*, Frankfurt am Main, European Association for Banking History e. V.

Tortella, M. T. (1992), 'Les archives bancaires espagnoles à l'heure actuelle', in Pohl, M. (ed.), *The Situation of Bank Archives in West European Countries*, Frankfurt am Main, European Association for Banking History e. V.

Zweig, R. W. (1993), 'Electronic fingerprints and the use of documents', in Higgs, S. and Ross, E. (eds), *Electronic Information, Resources and Historians: European Perspectives*.

CHAPTER TWO

Bank Archives in Perspective

Edwin Green

> If it be asked on what ground we claim for banks this intimate and exceptional knowledge of other people's affairs, it might be sufficient to reply that we make no exclusive claim to the information. We seek it for ourselves, it is true, but we have no desire that it should be withheld from everybody else, nor from a single person who has a right to know it. (Rae, 1885)

When George Rae was giving this advice to would-be bank managers over a century ago, he was pointing to one of the great dichotomies of the banking profession. He understood and respected the requirement for confidentiality; bankers have access to particular and privileged information. At the same time, as a practising and highly successful bank manager in his own right, he recognised that such information could often be of most help to the bank, or to its customer, if it could be shared with other bankers, with suppliers and with professional advisers. The 'good opinion' of a banker was – and is – a powerful ingredient in the business community. Rae was anxious that succeeding generations of bankers and customers should come to a sensible and pragmatic understanding about the exchange of information.

Rae's ideas were framed in a traditional banking context but they also serve as a motif for the modern archivist. In business archives, and in banking archives in particular, there is this same delicate balance between confidentiality and the practical educative value of sharing information. This is an issue on which the European Association for Banking History has already made significant contributions, especially in its conference debates (Teichmann, 1994a: 35–42; Cameron, 1996). Looking ahead, it is also an issue where the Association is in a unique position to bring a common approach to the question of access to business archives. The Association's remarkable alliance of bankers, historians and archivists is ideally placed to establish workable standards for the use of bank archives in the years to come.

In order to set an agenda of this kind, we need to put banking archives into perspective. This chapter approaches the subject in four ways:

1. through a wide-angle view of banking archives in the very long term;

2. through taking a shorter-range view of banking archives over the past twenty to thirty years;
3. through taking a close-up view of the work of the European Association in its first five years; and
4. through picturing the needs and opportunities for bank archives over the next decade.

Bank archives in the long term

The archives of business and commerce have a long and distinctive pedigree. The churchmen and landowners of medieval Europe were managers of complex businesses which required a framework of financial and legal records. Their business activities are also well documented in their dealings with the state, especially in the voluminous heritage of taxation and customs records in the principal state record offices of Western Europe. The middle ages also produced the first recognisable records of businesses in their own right, that is to say, individuals or firms whose sole activity was industry or commerce. Perhaps the most spectacular example of these forerunners of business archives is the Francesco Datini collection. In 1870 the records of this Italian merchant, who was conducting a Europe-wide business in the late fourteenth century, were discovered bundled in sacks under the stairs of his house in Prato. The Archivio Datini contains the staggering total of 140 000 letters, 500 ledgers and 30 other documents (Melis, 1954; Origo, 1957: appendix).

Banking, if it cannot lay claim to the oldest examples of business archives, can certainly claim to have yielded the largest and most continuous sets of business records. The Italian banks, in particular, are the custodians for the archives of some of Europe's pioneering banking institutions. The Monte dei Paschi at Siena, which itself dates from 1625, holds records of the Monte Pío of Siena from 1472 to 1511 and its successor body from 1569 onwards. The Istituto Bancario San Paolo di Torino preserves the records of its ancestor Compagnia di San Paolo from 1563 to 1853; similarly the archives of the Banco di Santo Spirito, forming a continuous series from 1605 to 1892, are maintained by the Cassa di Risparmio di Roma (Benedini, 1992: 45–9).

Further north, there are also a number of remarkably long runs of banking archives. In England, the ledgers of Edward Backwell describe the transactions of the greatest of the 'goldsmith bankers' between 1663 and 1672. Backwell's business ranged from simple safe-custody arrangements to contracting for government loans. Also in the United Kingdom, there are continuous sets of records of the Bank of England from 1694 and the Bank of Scotland from 1695, placing them among the longest-established corporate archives in the world.

It would be wrong to claim that the survival of these very old sets of records was the result of the banker's love of history. There were simple practical reasons for their survival. The duty of 'safe-keeping' of money and valuables is inherent in the fiduciary tradition of banking. The custody of possessions required the retention of contracts and other records through several generations of customers, as the archives of Childs, Coutts and other private London banks can demonstrate.

As deposit banking developed from the mid-seventeenth century onwards, banking was increasingly identified with long-term customer relationships and long-term transactions, often in connection with mortgages, insurances and other durable securities. The confidentiality of banking relationships has meant that bankers have always insisted on the care and safety of business documents, especially where they have had legal significance. Proper records management also has a long pedigree in banking. The concept of 'inspection' (as the internal audit or policing of the company) is ingrained in banking and it places a high priority on the verification and safety of bank documents. In the 1870s, for example, the rules of the London Joint Stock Bank required that:

> There shall be a fire-proof apartment in the bank to be called the 'Library' in which shall be arranged in convenient order for reference such of the Books as have been disused for six years and under, and another called the 'Repository' for such as have been disused more than six years and are to be kept a longer period.[1]

The rules also laid down specific and varying retention periods, including perpetuity for the board minute books, private ledgers and letter books. The archivist and the historian are forever grateful for such instructions.

In practice, banks have proved to be relatively long-lived institutions. The demography of modern companies suggests that over the last 150 years banking has been less vulnerable to failure or exhaustion than other corporate sectors. Of nearly 400 banks extant in 1914 analysed by Philip Cottrell, for example, over half were already over 47 years old.[2]

These practical considerations explain the high survival rate of banking records in the very long term. There remains a great distance, however, between the existence of large quantities of records and the propagation of a banking archive. This gap could only be bridged by the banks themselves through the deliberate development of archive units and history projects. Without that conscious effort, the survival of banking records would have remained a 'locked-up' asset for the banks. When did European banks begin to make this effort?

There is evidence that banking archives were being listed at the Monte dei Paschi as early as the seventeenth century. This inventory was the basis for Federigo Melis's survey of the Monte Pío records (Benedini, 1992: 46). Nevertheless, it was not until the early years of this century that record-keeping units were created within European banks. Early examples included the Bank of England, where a repository was established before the First World War and an 'archives committee' was formed in 1938, and Crédit Lyonnais, where a records centre was established at Lyons early in this century (Nougaret, 1995: 63).

This process was given impetus by the growing popularity of bank history projects in the interwar period. At Midland Bank, the consolidation of the bank's archives was seen as a vital consequence of the centenary history project; it was a great blessing that the historians, Wilfrid Crick and John Wadsworth, were devotees of the original sources. In a bank which by then had acquired over 20 other banks by direct amalgamation and another 100 banks indirectly, this consolidation was no mean achievement (Green and Kinsey, 1996: 87–99). In similar style, collections of historical records were brought together at the Banque Nationale de Belgique (1936) and, as part of another proposed history project, at the private bank of Sal. Oppenheim & Co. (1932) (Teichmann, 1994b: 73). Later formations, delayed until after the Second World War, included the 'historical records' section of the Bank of England (1946) and the archives departments of the Banco di Napoli and the Istituto di San Paolo (1963).

Bank archives in the last thirty years

In many of these examples, banks have smiled upon their archives as an essential part of their history projects. By the mid-1960s, however, some of these collections were in effect 'homeless' within their own parent banks. Their links to other departments were not clearly defined and, more seriously, few of the collections had full-time housekeepers, whether professional archivists or not. In the United Kingdom, for example, there were no more than three bank archivists in post.

The situation has changed radically since then. Again in the United Kingdom, there are about thirty professional archivists in the banking sector. In Europe as a whole, the European Association's archives colloquia can support an attendance of between forty and seventy archivists and curators each year; the five colloquia held since 1991 have attracted a total attendance of nearly 300. In most cases these delegates to events represent units of more than one archivist and it is likely that the total constituency in the banking sector now numbers about 150 archivists in Europe.

What has brought about and sustained this change over the past thirty years? Bank history projects have helped to concentrate collections and give them a role in management information. In recent years such projects have been much more ambitious than their forbears in the 1930s and the 1950s. Examples include the multi-volume histories of the Bank of England and the HongkongBank and the new multi-author history of Deutsche Bank (Sayers, 1976; King, 1987–91; Gall et al., 1995). The archives of the National Bank of Greece were established in 1970 and closely linked to the research activities of the banking history committee.[3] These are projects on a greater scale, needing whole-hearted support from boards of directors and an investment in archival and research support.

Problems of records control and property costs have forced banks, like all businesses, to look at their document resources in a more systematic way. This is not just an issue of real-estate values, it also involves high-cost factors such as security, insurance, copyright, disaster planning and logistics.

Statutory authorities around the world have become increasingly demanding as to the quality and status of information required from banks. Documentation needs to meet high standards and specific formats merely to keep to the rules of national and international authorities. Anyone who has been involved in a major merger or in the foundation of an overseas operation will also be aware of the voracious appetite for key documentation of legal and banking advisers, investments analysts and shareholders' groups. This is an area where banks cannot afford to be casual about the care and safety of their documents. Failure to produce documents and information can quickly be misinterpreted – or worse.

Banks have faced an increasing volume of enquiries from enthusiasts such as numismatists, architectural historians and family historians. This is a postbag which can only be answered from a properly constituted archive. In the past banks (like other businesses) may have been at a loss as to how to answer such enquiries; valuable management time was soon lost in chasing information. More recently banks have recognised that these enquiries often come from their own customers, shareholders, staff and pensioners. They deserve a considered response and bank archivists are ideally placed to take on such a role.

Not least, the banks have seen a huge increase in demand from the academic history community. That demand, originally from monetary historians as a small minority, has grown to take in a wide spectrum of economic and social historians, students of politics and management, biographers and historical geographers. One feature of this work, not universally acknowledged, is that business archivists become much more involved in these research efforts than their counterparts in local or state archives. The nature of the sources means that the archivist cannot simply produce the records and leave the researcher to his or her own devices. The archivist must be translator, interpreter and guide to these rare species of records. Academic supervisors and the banks themselves are perhaps not aware of this role, in which the bank archivist acts as clandestine supervisor and collaborator. In general, however, banks are aware that support for serious research work is valuable to their own companies as well as to the study of banking: the industry learns from the work of historians and other onlookers. As a result, over the last thirty years banks have become increasingly willing to cooperate in new research efforts on all rungs of the academic ladder. A clear signal of this more open approach is their close involvement in initiatives to provide information about their collections, as, for example, in the Business Archives Council's survey of British banking records and in the banking entries for *Deutsche Wirtschaftsarchive* (Pressnell and Orbell, 1985; Orbell and Turton, forthcoming; *Deutsche Wirtschaftsarchive*, 1988).

In perspective, these factors are the *raison d'être* of archives in the setting of modern banking. They have all helped to enlarge the map of bank archives in Europe. The missing ingredient, however, was cooperation and the sharing of expertise. Manfred Pohl was well ahead in recognising this problem, which was discussed at a meeting convened by the Deutsche Bank in 1982. Historians and archivists reviewed the position of bank archives and banking history in Western Europe but, looking back at that meeting, there was a downbeat mood. Delegates were somewhat nervous or even pessimistic about the outlook.

When a similar meeting was held in Frankfurt early in 1989, the atmosphere was quite different. Two developments now made a great difference. First, European aims and ambitions were concentrated on the single market promised for 1992. This was the masthead for our meeting in 1989 and for the foundation of the European Association for Banking History eighteen months later. Although there was an understandable idealism about coming together in this way, there were also practical considerations. Few banks in Europe were not building strategic plans for 1992. Suddenly, from the banks' point of view, the idea that professional archivists and historians should discuss their common experience was comfortable and progressive rather than wildly ambitious.

The second new factor was the significant and sustained increase in provision for archives in the 1980s. In this context, the meeting in 1982 was premature, for it was only in the 1980s that many of the big players in European banking established professional archives units, notably Banco d'España (1982), Banco di Roma (1986), Caisse des Dépots (1987), Banca Commerciale Italiana (1988), Commerzbank (1988), Credito Italiano (1989) and Crédit Lyonnais (1990). These changes in the landscape made it possible to think more seriously about coopera-tion between archivists; they also provided a much broader platform on which to promote links between the banks, their archivists and the history community. This change gave weight to that meeting in 1989 and, after further preparatory meetings, led to the formal launching of the European Association in the autumn of 1990.

Bank archives and the European Association for Banking History

Five years on, we can already begin to assess the Association's achieve-ments. While its contribution to banking history is illustrated elsewhere in this volume, on the archives front there are real practical benefits for the far-flung offices of European bank archivists. These include a number of advantages. First is the widening constituency of bank archives. The Association has already created a new forum for the theory and practice of archives in this sector. There is no comparable body in other sectors of business archives. Looking back to the 1970s and 1980s, there was no shortage of communication between business archivists in existing national and international bodies. Yet bank archivists, few in number, still found themselves whispering in corners. We might meet in small groups to discuss common problems but the foundation of the Associ-ation made it possible to treat banking archives as a more open and – in the long term – a more professional subject.

The Association's activities have played a part in establishing or strengthening the position of archives in individual banks. It would be invidious to mention particular companies but the Association should be especially proud of its link with the Swiss Association for Banking History. This relationship is an example of the real and significant increase in the constituency for bank history and archives.

The Association's conference programme, from a standing start, has provided the opportunity to learn of different traditions in business archives. The imperatives of our work differ from country to country, reflecting the varying patterns of ownership, regulation and resources. We have learned of the fortunes and misfortunes which archivists have inherited in their work. No one who was at the inaugural colloquium in Paris in 1991 will forget Rosanna Benedini, in describing the situation in Italy, quietly mentioning that the Banco di Napoli's archives are housed in 300 rooms in two palazzi in Naples. In contrast we also learned of archivists whose collections were confined to a single room, 'no more than a mere place of deposit for things which are then forgotten' (Benedini, 1992: 45; Teichmann, 1992: 77).

The conferences have also offered practical help to archivists and curators. The list of topics for the five archives colloquia covers a great range of professional concerns, notably:

1. getting started in bank archives;
2. setting priorities for key documentation and finding aids;
3. emergency planning;
4. the consulting and marketing role of banking history and archives;
5. anniversary events and public relations;
6. confidentiality *vis-à-vis* openness; and
7. the challenge of new technologies.

The publication of the proceedings of these meetings has meant that from the outset the Association has been committed to a practical role in the exchange of expertise and experience and in teaching and training for the future (Pohl, 1992, 1993 and 1994).

The Association has also played its part in building links between bank archives and the academic community. Historians have attended the archives colloquia (and vice versa) and this type of integration will be a larger feature in the future meetings of the Association. The Association is unusual in having a deliberate mix of historians and archivists in its committees and working parties. Cooperation at an international level has greatly increased awareness of current research interests, projects and publications. This reduces the danger of overlapping or repetitive work. It has also opened up new lines of communication for the study of broader themes in banking and monetary history. The Association's research grants and the new prize for banking history give a clear message of the Association's willingness to perform a linking role for new initiatives and liaison in banking history.

Perhaps the Association's most obvious and impressive contribution to the business archives scene has been its programme of publications. The publishing output is quite extraordinary for an organisation so recently established. The conference proceedings have already been mentioned. The *Perspectives* magazine brings banking history topics to a wider, non-specialist audience. The *Financial History Review*, only entering its third year of publication, is already a recognised fixture in the international literature of economic and business history. From the archivist's point of view, the journal has the bonus of the comprehensive bibliography and the surveys on collections of individual banks. Following on from the success of *The Evolution of Financial Institutions and Markets*, there are also plans for further monographs published under the Association's auspices (Cassis, Feldman and Olsson, 1995).

Special mention must be made of the Association's *Handbook on the History of European Banking*, published recently (Pohl and Freitag, 1994). This is a colossal achievement in all senses. When it is remembered that this 1300-page volume was produced by an association still in its infancy, we can be sure that many older societies and institutions in the history world would envy this level of output. Its main contribution is the country-by-country introduction to banking history and the short studies of individual banks. It represents a large haul of familiar and new information. A total of 330 banks were contacted in nineteen European countries and the published results have entries for 187 banks. The number of banks described ranges from as few as two or three entries for some nations to as many as 37 in Germany and 21 in Switzerland. As a reference book, it is a remarkable innovation on the banking scene and it will have practical applications for bankers, archivists and historians in Europe and beyond. Above all, it demonstrates that the Association has been diligent and prompt in converting the concept of cooperation into real results.

The opportunities for modern bank archives

Over the next decade it must be hoped that the European Association for Banking History will build on these solid achievements, preferably in a wider international context. When we review the Association's progress over its first ten years, I hope that the focus will have widened beyond Europe to cover the strong and developing traditions of bank archives in North America, Australasia and other financial centres around the world. That change of approach also offers the chance to increase the membership, the readership and the number of active participants in the Association's work.

With so many banks and banking historians already involved in its activities, the Association is also in an unrivalled position to influence the agenda for future research and archives development. This is particularly important on the technology front, which will be discussed elsewhere in this volume. There are also proposals within the Association for a greater emphasis on training and the production of a handbook for bank archivists. Such a programme might also include more examples of multilateral joint projects between banks and centres of banking studies.

In a longer view, the Association can take advantage of its broad constituency by spelling out more clearly, in published or electronic form, the availability of bank archives. This goal can be considered at two levels. First, much can be achieved by survey work (such as the guides to business archives in Germany and the United Kingdom) or by the publication of guides to the collections of individual banks. One difficulty here is to know where to pitch the information about the collection. On one hand there is the handbook option of providing names, addresses and a note on the extent of the archives; essentially the handbook relies on the country histories and bank histories to encourage the interest of the researcher. At the opposite extreme there is the fully equipped catalogue of a collection, series by series and piece by piece. The Banca Commerciale Italiana has produced outstanding works of this kind, which could serve as a model for archivists far beyond the boundaries of banking and business; they are also a lesson for all publishers of this kind of inventory.[4]

At a second level, however, the worry remains that there are hundreds of potential users of banking archives – either as teachers or researchers – who will never or rarely have the chance to visit or to use the collections which have been so carefully built up. It is a brutal fact that few of those who might turn to banking sources can afford the time or money for research visits, particularly if they are interested in the long runs of data which are so characteristic of banking archives. The Association might therefore consider ways of taking banking archives off the shelves and then, in proactive fashion, offering and serving them up in edited form. Such a programme might include key documents from the banks' archives. It should also include data sets based on bank collections, ideally in collaboration with existing users of banking and business records.

This is an objective which would be well matched and well timed with the rapid improvement in computer networks and communications. There is also the opportunity to build up database projects at many different sites, in the same way that the Teaching and Learning Technologies Programme (TLTP) projects are now being developed in the United Kingdom. Historians, archivists and other users could be invited to contribute to these historical databases in a standard, simplified format. Such an approach offers a way forward in increasing the usefulness of the large and often neglected collections of banking archives for a much wider group of users (Moss and Green, 1995: 21–3). Examples of such multi-bank, multinational projects might include databases for:

1. a biographical index of bankers;
2. the classification of bank advances in the long term;
3. interest-rate data on different bank products and services;

4.   the investment portfolios of European banks since *c*. 1880; and
5.   the unpublished archives of bank economics departments.

In each case the objective would be the creation of new resources for the better understanding of the history and significance of the banking industry – resources which would be available to the banks themselves, to their present and future customers, and to the wider community.

Large ambitions of this type would require the active involvement of a cross-section of banks. While this might be achievable in a small number of major companies, a broad spectrum would be more difficult to obtain. This returns us to the question of access to banking archives. The European Association for Banking History would do well to arrange a conference on this issue alone, addressing not only the historians' needs but also the thorny issue of unclaimed balances and dormant accounts. The *Handbook* gives valuable clues here, showing that there is much work still to be done. Of the 187 banks which feature in the *Handbook*, only 50 entries refer to their archives or provide their archivist's address; that is less than one sixth of the number of banks originally approached by the Association. Although the remaining banks were willing participants in the *Handbook* project, and although many of them also gave details of generous cultural and sponsorship activities, it is far from certain that many of them could be persuaded to provide access to their archives.

In this area, the Association's missionary role continues to be needed. Perhaps its most reassuring message to those banks which are uncertain about making their archives more accessible is to turn to the corpus of banking history which has been published or commissioned in recent years. The Association's own output is a case in point. The journal, the conference proceedings and the monographs all rely upon pragmatic cooperation between bank archives and their users, respecting confidentiality where required but enabling researchers to derive meaningful data and examples from these rich sources. In this way, and in only five years, the Association has already made a very strong case. The objective which we agreed to in Frankfurt in February 1989, that 'liberal rules on the use of archives and better cataloguing of the material were still to be desired', is as reasonable and as forward-looking as it was then.

Bankers, quite rightly, should be proud of the quality of their records. Their archives are a record of their own origins and development but they are also a record of the fortunes of their customers, their competitors and their own communities. In many cases the banks' records supply information about firms, companies and individuals which otherwise leave little or no trace. For banks hold privileged information, as George Rae argued in 1885:

A Banker's Opinion of people, in business or out of it, is in daily and universal request throughout the land; and as the reliance placed upon that opinion is well-nigh absolute, it had needs be sound. (Rae, 1885: 17)

The challenge to bankers, archivists and historians in the next phase of the Association's development is to ensure that such valuable evidence is neither lost nor unnecessarily hidden.

Notes

1. London Joint Stock Bank bye-laws, 1870, Midland Bank Archives ref. Q59-61.
2. For example, see Chapter 10 in this book by P. L. Cottrell, 'Aspects of Commercial Banking in Northern and Central Europe, 1880–1931'. I am grateful to Professor Cottrell for this reference.
3. I am grateful to Yolande Hadzi for this information.
4. For example, Banca Commerciale Italiana, *Archivio Storico, Collana Inventori, vol. III, 1, Secretaria Generale (1894–1926) e Fondi Diversi* (Milan, 1994).

References

Banca Commerciale Italiana (1994), *Archivio Storico, Collana Inventori, vol III, 1, Secretaria Generale (1894–1926) e Fondi Diversi*, Milan.

Benedini, R. (1992), 'The situation of the Italian bank archives', in Pohl, M. (ed.), *First European Colloquium on Bank Archives. The Situation of Bank Archives in Western European Countries*, Frankfurt am Main, EABH.

Cameron, A. (1996), 'Confidentiality versus openness: the bank archivist's dilemma', in Pohl, M. (ed.), *Fifth European Colloquium on Bank Archives*, EABH.

Cassis, Y., Feldman G. D. and Olsson, U. (eds) (1995), *The Evolution of Financial Institutions and Markets in Twentieth-Century Europe*, Aldershot, Scolar Press.

Deutsche Wirtschaftsarchive (1988).

Gall, L. et al. (1995), *The Deutsche Bank, 1870–1995*, Frankfurt and London.

Green, E. and Kinsey, S. (1996), 'The archives of the HSBC Group', *Financial History Review*, vol. 3, Cambridge, Cambridge University Press.

King, F. H. H. (1987–91), *The History of the Hongkong and Shanghai Banking Corporation*, 4 vols, Cambridge, Cambridge University Press.

Melis, F. (1954), 'L'archivio di un mercante e banchiere trecentesco, Francesco di Marco Datini da Prato', *Moneta e Credito*.

Moss, M. and Green, E. (1995), 'Reclaiming the history of business communities', in Aldcroft, D. H. and Slaven, A. (eds), *Enterprise and Management. Essays in Honour of Peter L Payne*, Aldershot, Scolar Press.

Nougaret, R. (1995), 'The Crédit Lyonnais historical archives', *Financial History Review*, vol. 2, Cambridge, Cambridge University Press.

Orbell, J. and Turton, A. (forthcoming), *The Banking Industry. A Guide to Historical Records*, Manchester, Manchester University Press.

Origo, I. (1957), *The Merchant of Prato*, London, Penguin.

Pohl, M. (ed.) (1992), *First European Colloquium on Bank Archives. The Situation of Bank Archives in Western European Countries*, Frankfurt am Main, EABH.

Pohl, M. (ed.) (1993), *Second European Colloquium on Bank Archives. The Organization of a Bank Archive*, Frankfurt am Main, EABH.

Pohl, M. (ed.) (1994), *Third European Colloquium on Bank Archives. Priorities in Bank Archives*, Frankfurt am Main, EABH.

Pohl, M. and Freitag, S. (eds) (1994), *Handbook on the History of European Banking*, Aldershot, Edward Elgar Publishing Ltd.

Pressnell, L. S. and Orbell, J. (1985), *A Guide to the Historical Records of British Banking*, Aldershot, Gower.

Rae, George (1885), *The Country Banker*, London, R. Groombridge & Sons.

Sayers, R. S. (1976), *The Bank of England, 1891–1944*, 3 vols, Cambridge, Cambridge University Press.

Teichmann, G. (1992), 'The situation of bank archives in Germany', in Pohl, M. (ed.), *First European Colloquium on Bank Archives. The Situation of Bank Archives in Western European Countries*, Frankfurt am Main, EABH.

Teichmann, G. (1994a), 'Archives and users' in Pohl, M. (ed.), *Third European Colloquium on Bank Archives. Priorities in Bank Archives*, Frankfurt am Main, EABH.

Teichmann, G. (1994b), 'Sal. Oppenheim jr & Cie, Cologne', *Financial History Review*, vol. 1, Cambridge, Cambridge University Press.

CHAPTER THREE

Comment

Youssef Cassis

The first banking documents that I ever had the opportunity to touch were handed to me by Edwin Green, some sixteen years ago, when I was writing my doctoral thesis on City bankers. I was doubly excited. There was the excitement that all historians feel when handling manuscript sources, but these were banking documents, surrounded, especially in the eyes of a young Swiss historian, by a mystique of quasi-inaccessibility.

Inaccessibility was not the preserve of Swiss banks at the time; it still prevailed in many banks and in many countries. The open policy of the Midland Bank was the exception rather than the rule, in Britain as elsewhere. Thus, we must appreciate how much ground has been gained in the last twenty years or so, and Edwin Green has given us an excellent survey of the long-term development of bank archives, of the problems posed by their conservation and by their use, and of the opportunities which could, and should, be seized in the near future. The following commentary will briefly discuss some of the points raised by Edwin Green from the point of view of the historian.

The first point is the long-term perspective adopted by Edwin, to which historians are always sensitive. What is very striking when you take a long-term view is that banks have had a constant need to keep their records. Some of the reasons for the preservation of bank archives might have changed during the centuries but one fundamental reason has persisted over time: the confidentiality of the relationships between a banker and his customers. Paradoxically, it is this confidentiality which has often ensured that documents have been kept in good care. This has been the banking historian's good fortune but it has also been a major problem because access to these documents, given their confidential nature, has not necessarily been a matter of course.

This takes me to the question of accessibility to bank archives, which remains the crucial point for banking historians. Accessibility has undoubtedly improved in the last twenty to thirty years. The reasons given by Edwin Green for this improvement are all convincing; however, another reason should be added. This is the better understanding between the business and academic communities and, more particularly, between bankers and historians. The time is not so remote when the two held each other in suspicion, and those who were students in the late 1960s and early 1970s certainly remember that collaboration with the business world was considered anathema. Today joint projects with the so-called 'private sector' are in demand and becoming a feature of academic life, to the benefit of both parties. The appointment, especially by the major banks, of professional archivists has been an essential part of this better understanding. Most of these professional archivists have been trained as historians and act as intermediaries between bankers and academic historians.

One of the best examples of improved accessibility is Switzerland, where the unthinkable is probably about to happen. Thanks to the efforts of the Swiss Association for Banking History, which was founded at about the same time as the European Association for Banking History and has closely collaborated with it, a few Swiss banks are now prepared to allow, selectively for the moment, the consultation of their records by academic historians. This is only a beginning but it is encouraging, more so as it has been established that historical research is legally compatible with the Swiss banking secrecy.

Accessibility has improved, thanks – and this cannot be over-emphasised – to the work of the European Association for Banking History. However, there is no room for complacency and much remains to be done, regarding both authorisation and organisation. One can reasonably hope that an increasing number of banks will allow historians, and other members of the public, to consult their archives. Yet this must be backed by a proper organisation of their archives. There are many banks which would be prepared to give permission to consult their records, but which are not prepared to devote the necessary resources to their organisation. Yet, as Edwin Green has rightly pointed out, they would clearly benefit from such a move. Thus, this is another case where both parties are likely to gain.

Finally, a word about European, and indeed international, collaborations which are the *raisons d'être* of the European Association for Banking History. Edwin Green made some excellent suggestions concerning this issue, in particular the creation of international statistical databases and the publication of edited selections of key documents from the banks' archives. However, such developments could be taken a step further. The European Association's record in setting up international conferences and publishing reference books is impressive. The success of the *Financial History Review* (jointly edited by Youssef Cassis and Philip Cottrell) has been a source of great satisfaction. However, what is still missing is a proper collective, archive-based research project on a central topic of European banking history. Such a collective project is now possible in practice, due to the huge improvements in the organisation of bank archives in all major European countries. It is now up to historians to coordinate their efforts to take advantage of the opportunities offered by bank archivists.

CHAPTER FOUR

Organisational Structure of Banking Information

Jürgen Rebouillon

Banking historians need not worry about the future: there will be no shortage of the material from which history is written. Even in this age of electronics, banking will remain researchable and an extra course in computer science or information technology will not be necessary to undertake such research. For a long time to come, paper will continue to play its traditional key role in major events, though important documents may be stored and accessed in new ways.

Electronics and the end of paper-based processing are topics of fundamental importance in banking. Our very understanding of money is changing: not money as a measure of value, but rather the need for it to exist in real or tangible form. What is money? It is, in the most basic sense, information on the move. But what vision of the future does that conjure up: banking business consisting solely of electronic impulses or an intangible mass that cannot be penetrated or analysed without the help of technical devices? It might appear that we have nothing to look forward to! However, as the media regularly inform us, technological progress allows true quantum leaps in productivity and quality. The inexpensive availability of appropriate technology will continue to shape the way we work. Nothing has changed business management processes more strongly in the last few decades than integrated information systems.

The first years of postwar reconstruction in the banking industry were largely form-based and highly complex in organisational terms and labour-intensive to an extreme. Technical devices were used sparingly. Work flows depended on the form set. Retail business was not yet part of banking. With the emergence of so-called 'mass processing' from 1957, the traditional banking organisation faced considerable difficulties. The beginning of standardised retail banking saw a sharp rise in the need for staff. Wage costs increased rapidly. Banks came under cost pressure. Their response was data processing based on punch cards. But that was still no solution to the problems in retail and consumer banking, only a step towards the banking and business environment of today. Banks began to look more closely at the possibilities offered by information technology, which is now essential to all banking organisations and is being constantly enhanced. The consequences have been far-reaching. We talk about 'terminalisation' of our working world and banks' back-office structures have changed. In former days entire departments were occupied with obtaining and compiling information. Work flows reflected the standard of technology installed. Efficient use of information technology means concentration on processing, for this is the only way to achieve the critical mass that precipitates greater use of technology. Thus regional computer and processing centres were initially set up and supra-regional facilities were consequently established. The next logical step was the complete automation of work flows. The following phase featured the onset of customer self-service devices, which are not just automated teller machines for cash withdrawals, but also terminals where customers may carry out certain transactions themselves. The next stage was the development of point-of-sales systems, in which the customer can make an electronic payment at the cash desk. This marked the beginning of 'electronic banking', a phrase that is used to describe the automation of payments business. Modern electronic banking products offer package solutions for a wide range of banking problems. Products are networked and information from different locations is combined. What the customers see is an integrated, comprehensive and up-to-date information flow.

The effective use of EDP in consulting, self-service, trading and settlement is only possible thanks to the rapid development of information and communications technology and the availability of increasingly user-friendly software. Efficient mobile hardware, the integration of voice, data and video in a standard environment, the replacement of analogue telephone technology by digital stationary and mobile networks are symbolic of the momentum of this development. Banks must use these new technological possibilities to increase the quality of their services and offer new products to suit market needs. The much greater importance of time in today's system of social values, the high demands on mobility and the ongoing penetration of everyday life by information technology is changing customers' expectations.

As technology changes the complex relationships between customer and bank, it is also turning the traditional bank into an entity that may be called the 'virtual bank'. The personal telephone consultation is being supplemented by electronic interfaces. Bank services are being offered electronically on a broader basis, to high-quality standards and tailored to customer needs. The key elements of this virtual bank are information and communications technology. Rapid data transmission speeds and extensive data networks mean accessible and attractive product offerings. The new interface allows deeper and deeper penetration of household and corporate markets. The 24-hours-a-day, seven-days-a-week service has become reality. Telephone banking and home banking are transcending the constraints of time and space.

In corporate business other aspects are far more important. The phase of data transmission and the execution of back-office and settlement functions are giving banks assignments that are best described as financial management. The combination of information from many sources is leading to a range of financial products that can put companies a step ahead with knowledge, gives a better foundation for decision making and simplifies and accelerates business processes. Banks are becoming service partners who can take on internal work. The client/bank relationship is again changing and there are now more interfaces: to put it in industrial terms, manufacturing depth and service breadth (product range) are increasing.

Banking is in a state of 'electronic evolution' and this will create a new culture among financial service providers and open up new prospects. It is conceivable that in future decades banks in their present form will no longer be needed. Bank services could be supplied by bank brokers. These brokers would have no infrastructure in the sense of premises and staff, and they would be equipped with high-quality electronics, for example information databases, transaction systems and risk systems. A prospective customer will contact his broker electronically and the broker will seek out the suitable product from the many on offer. The product may be a securities transaction handled in the background by Deutsche Bank; it could be a home loan from a specialised institution; or it could be sophisticated project finance from yet another speciality source.

In the future of banking everything will be electronic: money will be digitalised and payment transactions completed by electronic transfer (the buzzwords are e-cash and chip cards). This will apply to purchases from all suppliers, from department store to taxi, travel agent to toilet attendant. In technical terms this is all possible today: the electronic signature exists and safe encryption methods are available. However, people may feel the transition to the new European currency unit to be such a sweeping change that they will be more prepared in the future than they are today to accept the new digital payment methods and thus dispense with paper money and coins. In this environment it sometimes seems that demand does not shape supply, but that supply is what is technically feasible and demand is just the spin-off.

Nevertheless, there is still an interface with paper where, because of legal or corporate regulations, control functions are necessary. The result is that the individual bank service may not be available in paper form, but storage of volumes and unit quantities will still be in paper form. This material is the starting-point for the work done by the auditing teams required by law and for the documentation needed by accounting. It has been shown that EDP or the office of the future does not save paper but tends to consume more of it. Thus, despite the many possibilities offered by today's EDP applications, which also support data analysis and evaluation, a considerable paper input is required, not least for purely legal reasons.

Important agreements and contracts will continue to require paper form for a long time because the legal framework for making them electronic does not exist and in some cases paper is much simpler, quicker and more convenient. An international dimension makes this even more applicable. At the moment it is inconceivable that the completion of important transactions could occur without paper, for example contracts requiring many signatures and sometimes a notary's seal. Here too, of course, there may be other influences at work, such as respect for tradition, old habits and, possibly, standard practice. Yet these transactions are important events for banking historians. They are more than just the securities deal, the remittance, the withdrawal from a teller machine, the restaurant bill, the hired car or the hotel account.

Electronic or microfiche archiving is allowed and customary, though important documents stored in this way have only limited value as evidence in legal proceedings. A judge has considerable discretionary scope when evaluating documents not submitted as originals – in practice this means that all deals which might have legal relevance must remain archived in paper form. For day-to-day work, however, electronic means may be used.

However, despite all these possibilities and prospects, the computer as an organisational tool for general use is today only at the start of its development. At this juncture it is important to distinguish between the external impact of computer systems on relations with customers, with all their diverse demands, and the internal use of computers at every workplace in the bank. These modern technologies, as used inside the bank, are of interest to the historian: just consider scanning and optical character recognition technologies, on-line databases, text retrieval systems, author systems, work group systems and many other new applications. The work of historians will be made easier in future by scanning technology that can photocopy and store electronically (i.e. in digitalised form) and by character recognition systems allowing electronic searches and text editing. In its organisational impact at least, this is a technological quantum leap for the banking historian. Moreover, if properly stored, original documents will be physically handled much less and so retain their original quality for longer. Access to documentation would be possible at any time electronically and a printout looking like a photocopy would be obtainable at the touch of a button.

Scanning technology will allow databases all over the world to be built up by the scanning of relevant documents and their reproduction on paper would always be possible. In addition, documentation where not form but content is important (dissertations, treaties, newspaper articles, annual reports etc.) would be available in electronically processable form. While the originals would be available to only a few users, archiving systems would allow access to a large number of documents by many users at once. This would have positive effects, especially for research work. There are already thousands of databases in use worldwide. It was only possible to create them using scanning technology. Today, many important documents in libraries and museums are available in digital form through database enquiries.

Should the banking historian be alarmed by this? Absolutely not. On the contrary, there will be no need to search through archives or wander from bookshelf to bookshelf to find important documents. Companies, research institutions and governments will supply their data material on a digitalised basis, perhaps even in editable form and will make it accessible to authorised persons. The banking historian may have a different workplace, but not a different career profile. The historian will sit in an office at a personal computer and carry out database searches and will be linked worldwide by the Internet, or other service providers, with databases subject to no time constraint. The historian's partner, a computer system somewhere in the world, is always open for business, always accessible and always in a good mood. The historian will experience a different style of work, but seek and obtain the same result. Original documents may be localised at any time and copied; in addition the miniaturisation of storage media allows immense quantities of data to be concentrated and processed for a single job. The possibilities for historical work in the future will be strongly influenced by modern electronics: not impeded, but enhanced, as historians gain easier access to historical documentation.

It is certainly one of the tasks of our banking historians to see that the relevant documents are properly stored in the bank and that electronic access to them is ensured. The technology is available and its use in banks will make great progress in the next few years. It will be very important to ensure a smooth transition to this technology by big companies which have historical dimensions. In the future there will be, on the one hand, electronic access to documents needed quickly and, on the other, traditional archives containing only those documents that have to be in paper form. The use of archiving technology will save us roughly 80 per cent of the paper volume we use today.

Learning the essentials of this technology may take two weeks at the most. Terminals are becoming increasingly user-friendly. Moreover, nowadays it is difficult not to come across electronic media, with the result that familiarity with them can be reasonably taken for granted and therefore the learning of new systems is likely to be a speedier process.

A look at what modern technology can do reveals a colourful world. Many art collections, for example, are accessible through digital technology. This is how document storage should be pictured: the printout from electronic archives will be a vivid reproduction of the original.

In an electronic world where documents can be accessed by many more people than is possible in our present very paper-based environment, the demand for information will be satisfied more efficiently. The explanation is quite simple: if someone in today's 'old world' has a file in their hands, the documents it contains are accessible to nobody else whereas, in the electronic environment, documents are available anytime, anywhere and people may work when it suits their personal timetable. Furthermore, the well-known problem of urgently requiring from the library a book that is unavailable will possibly become a thing of the past. The conclusion from all this is that the banking historian's job will change dramatically from the point of view of supporting technology but in material terms will become richer and more interesting. Banking historians may look forward to an exciting, fruitful and productive future.

CHAPTER FIVE

Comment

Martin Fase

Rebouillon's paper offers a clear and reassuring picture of life for banking historians and bank archivists. However, it is appropriate to mention four issues for further reflection, mainly for historians but also for archivists.

First, from the perspective of a central banker, it needs to be emphasised that, although perhaps changing the material form of money, computerisation does not affect its function. Indeed, this could be witnessed at the turn of the nineteenth century when notes came to replace coins, or a few decades later, when currency was partly replaced by demand deposits as a means of payment. Essentially, money in whatever form is a bank liability or, to be precise, a liability of the entire banking system with the central bank as lender of last resort. Electronisation *per se* of, for instance, the payment system may mean a shift from coins and notes towards a variety of deposits and payment techniques but this in itself does not affect the money stock as a whole nor the role of a central bank as lender of last resort. A banking historian may observe the changes but nothing fundamental has happened from the monetary point of view, nor will it.

However, and second, it is not necessarily as simple as the above assertion. From the technical point of view, automation of payments has two possible implications that are of crucial importance for both bankers and the banking historian or the bank archivist. The first implication is that automation – information technology (IT) – provides a framework for direct payment, offering a method of payment without the intermediation of a banking system. From the perspective of an economist, this is undesirable because it involves a welfare loss. It implies a return to a pure barter system employing methods of payment which are not issued by a banking system with its accumulated credibility and stability. This is not efficient. The other implication would be a squeeze of central bank profits which should perhaps be compensated for by higher taxation, i.e. an increase in the tax burden. Both elements are of interest to banking historians and deserve careful historical analysis and recording.

A third issue is an extension of Rebouillon's assertion that new technology – IT – will easily be absorbed by archivists and traditional historical research and may be used to improve the productivity of researchers in the field of banking history. From the perspective of one responsible for the human capital embodied in the historical staff, new technology should be used to uncover areas of historical research so far unexplored because the technical tools were unavailable. Indeed, new technology could provide a method of matching historical records, keeping records in different ways, and thus offering new inspiration for historical analysis and storing information. Experience as a manager responsible for, among other things, historical research, has taught me that new techniques and approaches are refreshing for historical research and do sometimes offer new opportunities and knowledge which used to be unavailable and unexplored before the electronisation of banking in the age of information retrieval.

The fourth issue to be raised concerns the implications of automation and the use of sophisticated computer technology for the banking organisation, including archives. On the one hand, computerisation has resulted, and will continue to result, in new banking products, a consideration which should be of interest to the banking historian. Moreover, automation and computer technology have had a tremendous impact on the core of the banking business, namely the management of risks, and on the bank as an organisation. Again, it is to be hoped that future banking historians will note this in their analysis and will use it to deepen the economic content of their story. A crucial concept in this story should be the process of substitution of capital – i.e. computers for labour and paper because of changing price ratios.

As Rebouillon asserts, new electronic technologies are not only advantageous for the banking industry as a whole, but also for banking historians and bank archivists. However, there are probably even better prospects and scope, not just for future historical research, but also for the trade of the banking historian and bank archivist. Therefore, Rebouillon has given us a wonderful contribution on a flourishing future for banking historians, who may have to adjust to the new environment of banking business and society.

CHAPTER SIX

Technology: Future Problems and Opportunities for the Archivist

Piers Cain

Plato said: 'no written discourse, whether in metre or in prose, deserves to be treated very seriously ... but the best of them really serve only to remind us of what we know'. What can be seen in this paradoxical utterance are some important general truths that are helpful when we attempt to make sense of current reality. We are in a period of fundamental transition, just as Plato was over two thousand years ago. Plato was experiencing the shift from the spoken to the written word, and we from the written word to ... what? Like Plato, we cannot know the full implications of what we are experiencing and as Plato belittled the new technology of writing, people today belittle new technology because they find it disturbing.

The subject is huge, and only a few examples can be mentioned in the space allotted, but the implications are profound. Archivists will have to select some electronic records for preservation and others for destruction – as they now do routinely for paper records. The strategies we adopt to preserve electronic records, the choices we make as to what to keep, will shape the evidential base from which historians will construct the history of our generation. The final part of this chapter will give some practical recommendations.

Let us look at some recent developments in the use of voice technology, a technology not normally associated with record keeping. Telephone conversations do not normally generate records unless one or both of the parties to the conversation records the result in a written form, for example as a memorandum to file. But let us imagine that someone telephones you and leaves a message on your voice-mail system. That *is* a record. You now have the possibility of forwarding that voice-mail message to others with a cover voice-note of your own. The voice message is starting to take on a life of its own as a record as it passes through the organisation. Historians often complain that modern records are lacking in information compared to nineteenth-century records because communications which hitherto had been sent as notes are now being made by telephone. As voice-mail systems become more developed, there is the potential for more, not less, information to appear in the records, but these records will have different characteristics. With voice records, not only do we have the words themselves, but we also have other kinds of information, such as accent, tone of voice and background noise – information not provided by paper records.

The voice-mail example may seem trivial, but voice-mail, like other information technologies, is moving on from simply providing the means of improving individual productivity. More and more it is increasing organisational productivity and improving client services. When organisations use such technology to perform routine business operations, then archivists need to pay closer attention. For example, at least one large United States insurance company routinely records telephone calls from its policy holders, conducting its business directly by phone, without sales brokers. A few years ago the company redesigned its business processes to allow customers to make claims by means of a human interview over toll-free telephone lines. The conversations, recorded with the knowledge of the caller, are records, even if they are never transcribed as text. They are subsequently linked to customer data files and maintained for later reference. We can expect other businesses to turn more and more to the use of telephone services to provide more direct 'just-in-time' services to their clients, to reduce costs and to maintain a competitive advantage.

The addition of speech generation and speech recognition capabilities to applications will blur the distinction between the written and the spoken word even more. Speech generation systems simply create computer-generated words and sentences, converting one digital form – text – to another digital form – sound. Speech generation capability has long existed in applications such as those used by the North American telephone Directory Services, when they say 'Please hold for your number'. Speech recognition systems are much more complex because they must convert widely varying sound signals created by individual speech to textual form or other outputs such as computer commands. Such technology can be used to dictate a simple memorandum without using a keyboard. At present the vocabularies are limited to a few thousand words, and the systems have difficulty distinguishing homonyms, making them rather cumbersome to use. It would be easy to emulate Plato's response to the new technology of writing, but if the generations that followed had acted on his statement that 'no written discourse ... deserves to be treated very seriously', the archives upon which most histories are based would never have been created or preserved. We should not make the same mistake. Speech recognition is still an emerging technology, and research is being undertaken to overcome its limitations, but it is to be expected that, by the year 2000, more comprehensive word recognition technology will be widely available.

These capabilities are likely to be incorporated into ordinary office systems. People will be able to choose whether they wish to have their electronic mail converted into voice-mail or vice versa, depending on what is more convenient. For example, the business traveller will be able to access electronic mail messages by dialling into the voice-mail system back home. On the other hand, it is much quicker to skim through text than it is to listen to a voice message, so for searching and retrieval of records it would be more convenient to switch voice messages to text. This ability to switch from voice to text at whim will blur the distinction we make between text on paper (which we now regard as the medium of the formal record) and voice (which generally is not seen as a suitable medium for business records).

The consequences for the researcher of the creation of administrative records in multi-media formats such as using voice technologies, video etc. will be profound. The new media will provide new kinds of evidence that will be richer and more dense in the information they provide but will require new methods of evaluation. There will be a huge increase in the volume of data overall and a much greater volume of raw data suitable for statistical analysis. The research experience of using these new kinds of records will be very different.

Inevitably, the new technologies will challenge current archival practices and have a profound effect on the kinds of records available to future historians. We need to prepare for a world of rapid and sometimes unpredictable change in the realm of record keeping. The novel problem for archivists is how to define more closely what is a record and what is not, before we can even decide which records ought to be kept. In essence the issue boils down to two features of office automation. First, the nature of electronic information is such that it can be very easily overwritten and changed. For obvious reasons, this should be impossible in a records system. Second, some computer applications provide access to 'pure information' rather than access to records. The distinction is an important one: an encyclopaedia is a source of information, but it is not a record. A database of names and addresses that is routinely overwritten so that the user cannot tell when the entry for an address was made or what the previous entry was is an information system, not a record-keeping system. In other words, if one cannot call up a particular entry and prove categorically (for example in a court of law) that one is certain that the information one is seeing now is exactly the same information one saw two years ago, it is not a record.

Archivists have become concerned that the very nature of what constitutes a record is becoming transformed and that the technologists who design systems do not understand the need to record business transactions. These archivists have focused on defining what is a record, primarily to communicate the concept to IT specialists. This is a view that is particularly influential in North America, for example in the writings of David Bearman and Richard Cox, but it is also found elsewhere. Indeed, round the world, teams of archivists have agonised over what can be defined as data or 'information' and what is a record.

There is some point in this effort. All the same, we should not exaggerate the problem. The medium may have changed and become more fluid, but what defines a record remains the same. Records are still documents containing information created or received by an organisation or person for use in the course of business and subsequently kept as evidence of such business. For records to be reliable we still need to be sure that they are authentic, have not been subject to unauthorised alteration and have an unambiguous date. It is true that the data on many automated business systems are routinely overwritten when those data are updated, but this is because the systems were never intended to be record-keeping systems, though indeed they may generate records in hard copy. This is a cardinal point often ignored by archivists, who have become (in my view) over-concerned about recording every aspect of society, whether the originators of the records judge it worthwhile or not. People create systematic records only when they really need them.

We can gain a useful perspective by looking at what happened when societies changed from oral to written communication. We are so used to writing that we find it difficult to consider writing as being as much a technology as printing or a computer. Yet, as the American linguistic theorist Walter Ong observed, writing is a most powerful technology:

> [Writing] initiated what print and computers would only continue, the reduction of dynamic sound to quiescent space, the separation of the word from the living present, where alone spoken words can exist.

Historians and social anthropologists like Ong have understood this point for some time, but the concept of writing as a distinct technology and the implications of this concept have largely been ignored by the archival and information technology professions. We are not experiencing a sudden irruption of 'alien technology' into the archives. We have always been dealing with technology. The new element is the rapid pace of change that is forcing archivists to re-examine long-held assumptions and methods.

Present-day automated systems which are used as record-keeping systems are in an early stage of development. The methods and conventions that will allow the user to rely upon and trust them as records are still being developed. For example, information technologists have developed the concept of 'data warehouses' which, among other things, are designed to prevent data being overwritten and which preserve the contextual information (the 'metadata') necessary to understand the information stored in the data warehouse. There will be a period of trial and error in defining the conventions that will allow a computer to recognise a record, but it is reasonable to assume that the technical problems will be overcome. Where records are less reliable, historians and archivists will work out criteria for evaluating them, as medieval historians have had to do for early parchment records. Already the Science Museum in London has started to work on how to read 'un-readable' computer disks. The most promising strategy is to use the pattern recognition capabilities of neural network procedures to recover the data signal by signal. The age of the e-palaeographer has begun.

As ever with archive management, the biggest problems centre around how to select and preserve. The cost of preserving the new electronic archives will be the prime factor in determining which strategies the archivist will adopt. There has not been any serious independent study of the cost implications of the new technologies on record-keeping systems throughout their entire life cycle. Some have argued that the rapidly declining costs of hardware, data storage and information re-trieval point to reduced costs overall, but I remain sceptical. Informa-tion technology may enhance the productivity of the individual office worker, but experience has shown that it does not reduce costs overall. If keeping archival records electronically is more expensive than keep-ing them on paper, we shall have to be even more selective in what we decide to preserve permanently. We shall need to have clear reasons to justify the cost of migrating data on to new systems when the original technology becomes obsolete. A thorough study of the long-term cost implications of these new systems is urgently needed.

Dealing with the problems of preservation is the most challenging issue at present, not least because potential solutions may also impinge on archival custody – a fundamental concept that ensures the authenti-city and integrity of the archive. Records held in electronic format are much more vulnerable than paper records. Solutions worked out for the earlier generations of databases (essentially to print out the data on to paper or microfiche or to store them in software-independent format) are no longer always appropriate. Now things are much more compli-cated. For example, simply outputting the data from a modern database in the order they are stored in the computer may be of no use to the end user. Relational databases store data in tables and then combine the information in different ways to permit the users different 'views' of the same data, and to service a multiplicity of functions. For the researcher to understand the record, he or she needs information on the relation-ships between the different data elements and in some cases access to the functionality of the system used to present the information to original users.

Similarly, office systems are becoming much more complex. For example, even electronic mail presents problems. Although one can print out the messages themselves, other critical contextual information (the 'metadata'), such as the distribution list for a particular message, who accessed the message and when, and other information, will not be captured. Electronic record keeping means preserving both the records themselves and the context that makes them comprehensible.

The introduction of enterprise-wide systems to allow group work is a major development of the 1990s. These systems are designed to enhance the productivity of the group, to allow teams to share information and work cooperatively, to schedule meetings and control work flow. Typically, they are also looking to increase productivity by allowing ready access to policy records previously kept only on paper. For example, the World Bank is in the process of implementing such a system, called the Electronic Document Management System (EDMS), designed to encompass the full range of information needed by a staff member, including internal records as well as information retrieved from external sources. Again, the system is much more than the sum of its parts. The archivist is faced with the need to preserve both the data and the metadata. In an extreme case, this might mean preserving the applications as well as the information maintained on them. Of course, we are all aware of the difficulties this latter requirement presents, but we should not despair; the situation is likely to get better. The development of 'open systems' based on international standards will ease the problems of archivists dealing with records in electronic form, by allowing the migration of data across different platforms and on to new systems. As businesses increasingly automate their operations, the cost of migrating essential information when systems are upgraded has increased to a point where the old options of discarding the data, rekeying it, or paying for expensive data conversions, are simply too expensive to bear. Already information technology managers are increasingly insisting that new products comply with international standards that allow the easy migration of data when systems become obsolete, because they see big savings from their operational budgets if they do. Archivists will be far better served by relying upon the enlightened self-interest of the in-house IT managers in keeping costs down rather than intervening directly themselves.

Of course it is not sufficient to hope that others will solve all our problems. At the very least we need to cooperate closely with the information technology managers in our organisations. We need to understand their long-term strategy – for example what platforms and standards they intend to adopt – because in the end we shall have a much greater chance of success if we are working 'with the grain' of our organisations' IT strategy.

In the light of these technical problems, who will have custody of future archives? Traditionally, by definition, archival records were held by the archives and were made available to researchers there. In the electronic world it is not only possible but also probably necessary for physical custody to be the responsibility of IT technicians, with the management of the records the responsibility of the archivist.

The technical training of archivists does not serve them well in maintaining electronic archives. Rather than develop the skills within the archives, in many cases it may be more effective and cheaper to hand over custody of electronic records to information technology specialists who do have the skills and who can provide a cost-effective service. Sometimes this may be the in-house information technology department (which performs this function anyway for current electronic records by maintaining an infrastructure of networks, hardware, and system back-ups etc.), or sometimes the work will be outsourced to specialist agencies.

Conservation and custody may not fill the archivist's horizon, but providing access can. The development of the Internet and other large networks means that access to an organisation's electronic archives can be provided easily and cheaply from remote sites. Thus the physical location of the records away from the archives would not be an impediment to this policy. None the less, many archivists are uncomfortable with this development. What we are seeing is a trend towards greater specialisation and a major break from the archival tradition that the archivist has physical control over the archives.

Does this mean that we don't need archivists and archives any more? I don't think so, although many archivists have expressed concerns that it might. We shall continue to manage all records of permanent value, whatever their physical form. We shall be the people with the 'big picture' who can see how all the pieces fit together. Archivists will exercise responsibility, on behalf of their institution, to identify records of permanent value that are no longer used for operational purposes and to take the necessary action to ensure these records' long-term management and preservation. Our input will be in providing the finding aids that will provide the context, allowing researchers, both from within the company and from the historical profession, to evaluate the records as evidence and to understand why the records were created and how they relate to the history of the organisation. We shall become archive managers rather than archive keepers.

Another important issue is the selection of records for permanent preservation. We are in a transitional phase: for the moment some kinds of records will remain on paper (these are mainly policy records), while others are increasingly stored electronically (typically high-volume, low-value transactional records, such as payroll). Policy records are likely to continue to be kept on paper until such time as electronic media establish a reputation for stability and robustness at least equal to paper. At present that seems a long way off. However, the superior cost advantages of electronic searching and retrieval are likely to encourage dual record-keeping systems which we shall have to appraise in their totality. In other words, policy documents will be searched and retrieved electronically but, to ensure their long-term survival, a paper original will also be stored in the archive.

A radically different future is to be envisaged for transactional records, which typically are generated by large databases. In the past, operational records in paper form have usually been discarded as bulky and expensive to store. Also, because it was impossible to manipulate the information without inputting it on to a database (itself a very expensive operation), the information itself was of little use. Now, records in electronic format can be easily aggregated and analysed for statistical purposes. Moreover, the paper records generated by transactional databases are usually only a small fragment of the information available electronically. Thus the value of the electronic record is much greater than that of the rather limited paper output. For example, credit card companies have enormous amounts of information about individuals' purchasing transactions for goods and services that will be invaluable to future historians interested in purchasing patterns of different social groups, different regions, etc. Of course, this information will not only be of value to historians, but it is also a unique and valuable asset of the particular credit card company, either to be used for internal purposes or perhaps, when stripped of information identifying individuals, sold to other businesses. And this is the key to one of the issues raised above: how is the cost of migrating these data on to new systems to be justified when the original technology becomes obsolete? The answer: because it will be more costly for the company not to find the money.

In the past, paper records were initially preserved because they were of value to their originators. The same will be true of electronic records. It is true that some records of value to historians are likely to escape the nets, but late twentieth-century society is awash with multiple sources of information. The archives of the future will be the most 'information-rich' in history. Businesses are recording more information than ever before and archivists are keeping more. Historians of our century will have an unprecedented breadth of primary and secondary sources. There is no serious risk that any major aspect of our society will be unrecorded because data from a particular transactional database are not migrated to a new system. Archivists should keep a sense of proportion and take quite a robust view about discarding records that are not of unique cultural or historical value.

This point reduces the pressure on the archivist to adopt a strategy advocated by some archival theoreticians such as David Bearman, namely to become involved in the definition of systems requirements and the design of new systems in order to ensure the long-term preservation of records. In fact the 'Bearman school' goes much further. It argues that on occasion archivists should be telling the line managers what records they ought to be creating to ensure that the evidence of transactions is available to managers for purposes of accountability. The danger of this strategy is that archivists and records managers are typically too remote from the daily operations of a business to be able to exercise such influence, or to judge whether the costs of creating and preserving the information outweigh the benefits of recording it in the first place. The operational line manager is in a better position to do this. It is the role of the archivist, in conjunction with other stakeholders, to decide what records that already exist are to be preserved permanently. Archives simply do not have the resources to be involved in the design of all their organisations' applications. We have to take a more strategic approach.

Let us now turn to the recommendations promised in the introduction. First of all, we need to understand the business objectives of our organisation. We need to know whether it needs highly developed record systems or whether a cost analysis would point to cheaper but less efficient systems.

Second, archivists must become 'technologically aware': we need to keep up to date with developments in the information technology field in so far as they have an impact on records. Inevitably our knowledge of any one technology will be at a relatively superficial level, but this need not be disastrous. We need to know enough to be able to communicate our concerns as record keepers to the technologists in a way they can understand and, equally, to comprehend the advice they give us. We do not need to become technologists ourselves.

Third, we need to match our costs more closely to our likely resources, as far as practicable. Traditionally we have reckoned that only about 5 per cent of an organisation's records are of archival value. There is no reason to suppose that a greater range of formats will change that proportion radically. But with the continuing trend towards ever-dropping costs for computer memory, the concern will be not so much the sheer volume of data but rather the increasing diversity and multiplicity of systems. We need to survey our organisations regularly to keep up to date with what databases and other electronic records are being created and using what software. We can then anticipate which systems will become obsolete, determine which are creating records of archival value, and consider how they may be best preserved once they cease to be of daily use to their originators.

Fourth, we need to forge alliances with our organisations' information managers, or become information managers ourselves. Increasingly archives management will mean working as part of a team of information specialists. At present few organisations manage their information resources effectively. This situation is likely to change as organisations recognise the size of their investment in information and the high cost of failing to manage information sensibly. In any case, the roles of archivist, records manager and information manager are likely to move closer to each other and even overlap as the proportion of an organisation's records in electronic format increases.

We shall have to put a higher priority on selecting for permanent preservation classes of records that earlier generations regarded as of lesser importance. The user manuals and operations manuals for office record systems and databases will provide future historians with invaluable contextual information about how archives were created and used even after the original application has long been superseded and the data transferred to more modern systems.

Finally, we need to listen more to historians. We must beware of slavishly following the latest academic fashion, but radically new kinds of records offer opportunities for new kinds of research. Plato's remark that 'no written discourse ... deserves to be taken very seriously' is paradoxical because it was the new technology of writing, regarded by him as frivolous, that ensured his immortality. In looking at the implications of the new technology for the archives of the future, we should be open to entirely new ways of thinking about records. What may seem trivial now may turn out to be very important. Archivists, historians, technologists and bankers all need to be talking to each other. This chapter is offered as a contribution to that dialogue.

CHAPTER SEVEN

Comment

Wilfried Feldenkirchen

Cain sees the present period of information technologies as a period of transition, comparable to the phase of transition from spoken to written language. The development and application of new information technologies in companies and administrative bodies also requires modern methods of assessing and passing on information, thus confronting the archivist with new tasks and challenges.

Using his selected examples, Cain shows the extent to which multimedia information technologies have already been incorporated in the business procedures of large organisations and how they affect or transform administrative processes. The use of 'voice technologies' (i.e. speech generation systems and speech recognition systems), for instance, enables other kinds of information to be conveyed (emphasis, background noise, accents) than that strictly confined to the written word. The volume of transmitted information is becoming larger, richer and more differentiated.

The archives of the future must adapt to these new realities. These developments are confronting archivists with new tasks, forcing them to meet new requirements. They must rethink outmoded methods and adapt to new administrative and organisational techniques, since the increasing use of information technologies requires corresponding methods of passing on and archiving information; a new approach to the archivists' main tasks of appraisal and conservation is necessitated by the increase in electronically stored data. At the same time, the archivists of the future must familiarise themselves with the latest information technologies so as to be able, if necessary, to design new systems with archive requirements in mind.

The occupational profile of archivists, and the way they see their own role, will change in the future. According to Cain, the main task of the archivist of the future will continue to be: 'to decide which existing records are to be preserved permanently'. The future will see a shift, Cain contends, in the archivist's remit in the direction of strategic functions: 'We will become archive managers rather than archive keepers'.

Cain's vision of the future stimulates many questions which archivists need to address. First, what form will the archive of the future assume?

Will it be more than a collection of databases? These databases will need to have protection for the data they contain, and this will necessitate back-up copies. However, these copies could be electronic copies, microfilm copies or paper copies and therefore the archives may contain a variety of formats. Second, how are we to control access to electronic records? Will the databases be linked to others and how will we decide who has access entitlements to the necessary systems? This question is linked to that of the physical location of the archives – Cain suggests that electronic records may well be located with information technologists but access to them managed from the archives. Third, the archives of the future will be influenced by the knowledge and skills that the archivist brings to these contemporary problems. In addition to addressing the question of the archives of the future, we also need to address the training needs of the archivists of the future.

CHAPTER EIGHT

Comment

Victor Gray

Although Cain's contribution has covered many of the issues that beset the subject, especially on the technical front, I would like to consider or reaffirm a few down-to-earth practicalities. These are worth restating lest, by staring too hard into the darkness of the techno-jungle, we overlook the broader, more familiar landscape.

The issues relating to archives and electronic records have been debated for a number of years. During this time the technology and the jargon have changed and so have some of the concepts. But the tone has remained remarkably consistent. As archivists, we look at a brave new world about to open before us. We speculate on the kinds of steps we shall have to take to convert the digitised information of the late twentieth century into the accessible archive of the twenty-first. We map the future, see the pitfalls, take avoiding action and construct a programme to bring us to the promised land. But always during these debates the tense has remained the same – and it is the future tense. This is always something we *shall* do – when the time is ripe.

Meanwhile, computer tapes have been with us for nearly forty years, longer than the lifespan of some of us here today. We have had floppy disks for perhaps fifteen years. These are the media not of the future, but of today. Many of the tapes and disks filled in the last decades are older than some of the paper archives in our stores. Indeed, many have long gone, unloved, unattended, recycled, destroyed. But how many of the archivists among us can truly say we have done justice to the task of seriously considering their historical potential before they were recycled into oblivion? Many of us have bold programmes for action. When are they going to be turned into a firm date in our diaries?

And why have so few of us come to grips with this? Is it because it is too complex or too expensive a matter to contemplate or spend time on? Is it because we are frankly inefficient? Have we somehow failed? Or is it because it doesn't really matter?

The latter view has been expressed many times, even at the Association's Edinburgh symposium in 1995. The really important matters, it is argued, will continue to be kept on paper anyway. Paper self-selects itself as a medium because of its long history and the deep-rooted conventions which surround it. For a thousand years we have accepted that what is on paper is more trustworthy than what is spoken. Laws have been built around it, conventions of signature, sealing and registration have grown up around it. For the foreseeable future – often qualified, revealingly, as 'or at least until I retire' – we can therefore rely upon the organisation itself deciding what is worth retaining, and expressing it by keeping it on paper. It follows logically that what is not retained on paper is not worth having anyway.

This is worrying. It may be true, but I am influenced by a very vivid memory of one organisation I advised which was genuinely surprised when I questioned the wisdom of their archiving policy. They had selected their archives for preservation on the basis that anything which was in a book between covers was likely to be valuable and should be kept; any loose papers were certain to be worthless and could be thrown away. There is, perhaps, little substantial difference between the criteria they were using and the belief that nothing held electronically can be of long-term interest.

In the case of electronic information it is even more dangerous to turn our backs, since there is so often a gap between those who create or use electronic records and those who manage the systems and the data on a daily basis and make the decisions about what should be kept and what should not. Frequently these decisions are being made out of sight and out of mind – and in some cases out of control – by system managers who are more concerned with the storage capacity of the computer system than with any information held on it. And there is, moreover, a real difference in terms of what you can judge by the cover between a file of papers and a disk or tape. A computer tape is far more anonymous than a file, far more likely to conceal from the casual view the secrets of what it holds, and so far more easily disposed of without proper caution.

Despite the complexities of access associated with electronically held data, the process of analysing and assessing long-term historical value and retention should be fundamentally no different from the methods which records managers have been using for years. There is no substitute for an informed involvement in this process, and that informed involvement has to be that of the archivist. However diffident he or she may be, however many mistakes may be made, there is no one else within the structure who can fulfil the role as effectively. No one else has the breadth of vision of historical potential or need. No one else can tap the views and preoccupations of the historical community.

Equally, if this issue is to be addressed, it cannot be done by what I would call the reactive archivist, that is the archivist whose role in the organisational structure is confined to that of receiving only such material as is offered after its current life is complete. To make a successful inroad into the issue the archivist must be in a position to observe the kinds of electronic data which are being generated and to influence to some degree decisions about their longer-term life. That cannot be done from a base of reactivity in the basement.

There is, then, a fundamental structural issue that may need addressing in some companies even before we reach the core issue of selection and retention. If the archivist's job description does not include a responsibility in this area, if he or she is not ready to get his/her hands dirty in dealing with this messy electronic stuff, then there is no way that a sensible historical judgement will be made.

Alongside this, there is another prerequisite: an archiving policy in place within the bank which predefines the level and type of information which triggers long-term or permanent retention. There are, for example, banks where the decision may have been taken that it is enough to retain documents which indicate managerial and board decisions and reflect changes of policy. Beneath this the minutiae of activity are of little worth. It may equally be the case that there are organisations where the decision is to retain records of client involvements – contracts, agreements etc. – but not the details of individual transactions within a relationship. Or again, in a High Street bank, it may be that a record of customer names is kept but not of account details.

All these and more are individual choices which may and should be exercised within the organisation. What is important, regardless of whether the medium is electronic or not, is for the decision to have been thought through, agreed at the highest level and signed, sealed and delivered. With such a policy in place, the question of medium – paper or electronic – becomes a secondary issue. Decisions about what electronic data to keep then fall within the overall policy framework agreed for the organisation. They are decisions not about medium, but about relevance – a far more useful criterion in the long term. Of course, none of the technical difficulties has gone away, and none of the problems of costs which may flow from them. But the context is now correct. The focus is properly on the end rather than the means, and decisions on cost and methodology can be taken in the context of a clear objective – the retention of a satisfactory legacy of historical record.

There is nothing new in what has been said in this commentary. Indeed, that is the point. I believe much of our inactivity in this area has been induced by confusion touched with panic. There is no need to overturn the principles on which we have previously acted. Let us keep cool. Let us stick to the procedures long since established for effective assessment and selection of materials for historical purposes and let us apply them. Then and only then, armed with the knowledge of what the true impact of change is going to be, are we in a position to argue the case wherever we need to for the resources to tackle the undoubted complexities which arise from electronic records. Above all we cannot, or should not, stand back and wait or wash our hands of responsibility. We must get them dirty and there is no excuse for not getting them dirty now.

PART II
Concentration and Internationalisation in Banking

English Banking Concentration and Internationalisation: Contemporary Debate, 1880–1920[1]

Lucy Newton

Any bank merger or amalgamation, past or present, provokes much debate in the public domain, and by the banking community in particular. Similar responses are generated by international developments in the financial sector. The tendencies towards concentration and internationalisation in English banking from the late nineteenth century onwards are not new topics of discussion but the reaction of the banking profession to these developments has not been widely considered. This chapter will examine the contemporary debate surrounding these changes in English domestic commercial banking from 1880 to 1920, particularly views expressed by bankers, and thus examine developments from an alternative, somewhat neglected, perspective.[2]

The public discourse of contemporary English bankers concerning their professional environment is predominantly found in the *Bankers Magazine*, the 'trade journal' of the banking profession. The monthly journal *Bankers Magazine* was first published in 1844 as part of an attempt to spread sound banking practices (Collins, 1988: 85). The *Magazine* published a variety of opinions, often printing conflicting views, and in using this source over forty years of changing responses to developments in banking may be examined. Another professional journal was that of the Institute of Bankers, a body established in 1879 with 2000 members at a time when professional bankers were pressing for reform and reorganisation of the domestic banking system after the crisis induced by the failure of the City of Glasgow Bank in 1878 (Green, 1979: 51). The *Journal of the Institute of Bankers* was distributed to its membership, which increased rapidly to nearly 4000 by 1900 and reached 10 542 by 1914 (Green, 1979: appendix). Bankers also expressed their opinions regarding concentration to the Colwyn Committee and in the debate surrounding its findings. This Treasury committee was established in 1918 in order to examine amalgamations and provide recommendations as to possible future legislation concerning banking concentration. Appointed by the Chancellor of the Exchequer, it comprised Lord Colwyn and a number of leading bankers and industrialists.[3] In compiling its report, the Committee examined a body of witnesses mainly made up of bankers but also including an academic, a member of the Board of Trade and representatives from other financial institutions.[4]

By focusing upon such sources, the following discussion necessarily reflects the rather partial world of the English, and particularly the London, banker. However, the amalgamation movement in England and Wales in the late nineteenth and early twentieth century was at the forefront of the European movement towards concentration in banking. Moreover, London was the financial centre of Europe during the period and provided a focus for the internationalisation of banking in Britain. These two factors offer a justification for considering events from the perspective of bankers on this small island.

The first section of the chapter will examine the general trends in amalgamations and concentration in the banking sector in order to provide some background to the developments under consideration. There follows a detailed examination of contemporary bankers' opinions concerning concentration as expressed in the *Bankers Magazine*, the *Journal of the Institute of Bankers* and in connection with the Colwyn Committee. The extent and nature of concentration will be considered, in addition to its impact on the banking sector as a whole; the banks themselves (their shareholders, customers and staff); local business communities; and the domestic economy in general. An examination of bankers' reactions to the internationalisation of banking is undertaken in the penultimate section, and the final section provides a summary.

General trends in amalgamations and concentration

The amalgamation of banks in England and Wales occurred throughout the nineteenth century but towards the end of the century there was an increase in concentration in the banking sector. Amalgamations accelerated from the 1860s onwards, with the peak of merger activity occurring in the late 1880s and early 1890s – between 1880 and 1894 a total of 69 mergers took place (Collins, 1988: 78–9). Another surge of merger activity occurred in the decade leading up to the First World War. The result was that the number of joint stock banks fell from a peak of 128 in 1880 to only 65 by 1905 and the total number of banks fell from 600 in 1825 to 70 by 1913 (Nishimura, 1971: 6; Collins, 1988: 78). Amalgamations did not stop during the First World War and the emergence of the 'Big Five' – Barclays, Lloyds, the National Provincial, the Midland

and the Westminster – in 1918 was the culmination of concentration in banking in England and Wales which established the structure of domestic banking for the next fifty years.

Amalgamations led to the concentration of banking into fewer and fewer hands, the exact relationship of the two phenomena having been examined in detail by Capie and Rodrik-Bali. They argue that the initial amalgamation movement did not immediately lead to concentration in the banking sector of England and Wales due to internal growth, but rather concentration occurred after 1890 and increased dramatically after 1910 (Capie and Rodrik-Bali, 1982: 287–8). Furthermore, Cottrell maintains that the effect of early mergers was initially offset by the growth of smaller banks (Cottrell, 1992: 48). However, by examining the merger movement between 1870 and 1920, Capie and Rodrik-Bali conclude that 'the main force behind the growth in concentration in British banking was mergers' (Capie and Rodrik-Bali, 1982: 287–8).

The most common form of amalgamation was the absorption of a private bank by a joint stock bank (Sykes, 1926). As a result, private banking was all but extinguished by 1918. However, the nature of amalgamations did change throughout the period. Initially small, usually private, institutions were absorbed by larger, usually joint stock, banks. After 1900, as the number of small private institutions available for absorption diminished and competition between the large banks increased, both parties to the merger were usually large joint stock concerns. As a result, the joint stock limited concern which possessed a branch network in both London and in the provinces emerged as the dominant form in the banking system.

The concentration in banking that produced the 'Big Five' banks by 1918 caused much contemporary debate and often concern. Indeed, such was the concern voiced in public and in Parliament that the Colwyn Committee was established in 1918 to examine the bank amalgamations and to recommend legislation or supervision.[5] Despite the preparation of a parliamentary bill as a result of the Committee's recommendation for anti-trust legislation, the bill was dropped and a private agreement was made between the Treasury and the bankers. Thus the British banks were allowed, unimpeded, to concentrate business into the 'Big Five' banks but agreement was reached that amalgamations, without special clearance from the Treasury, should then cease.

The extent and nature of amalgamations

The *Bankers Magazine* recorded the progress of absorptions in detail and provided a flow of comments and essays on the phenomenon which provide an illuminating insight into the process of concentration. The amount of material and debate stimulated by developments illustrates that their importance was obviously felt by late nineteenth- and early twentieth-century bankers.

Lloyds Bank and the London & Midland Bank led the field in the merger movement of the late nineteenth and early twentieth century. Both had originated in Birmingham and were therefore part of the movement of country banks from the provinces into London. In 1895 the *Bankers Magazine* commented that 'the London and Midland Bank still continues to absorb any banks which come in its path' and that '11 banks had been absorbed by the Midland since 1883'.[6] Concerning Lloyds, the journal commented that the bank 'has shown over its somewhat brief career as a joint stock concern, the most astonishing power of absorption'.[7] In the rapidly changing banking world of the early 1890s, the *Magazine* commented that 'rumours of amalgamations fill the air. One hears of them on all sides.'[8] Such a climate no doubt stimulated further absorptions as banks competed in their race for size (Cassis, 1994: 21). In 1889, in an article about amalgamations, an author wrote that 'it is clear that the tendency of the time is certainly towards the construction of large and powerful banks, either by growth or by amalgamation'.[9]

The *Magazine* was keen to measure changes in the incidence of amalgamations. An article in 1901 surveyed the extent of changes in the structure of banking, concluding that in England and Wales the incidence of amalgamations had slowed towards the end of the nineteenth century. Comments in the 1880s and 1890s had referred to the rapid pace of amalgamations, whereas by 1901 the article asserted that the reduction in the number of banks 'has been gradual'.[10]

The *Magazine* also provided figures to illustrate the degree of concentration in provincial banking, as shown in Table 9.1. The reduction in the numbers of private provincial banks is particularly striking – an 80 per

Table 9.1   The number of provincial banks in England and Wales, 1850–1900

Year	Private provincial banks	Joint stock provincial banks
1850	272	93
1888	156	98
1893	106	88
1900	54	47

Source: *Bankers Magazine*, 1901, vol. 72, pp. 1–3.

cent decrease between 1850 and 1900. This shows the combined effect of the amalgamation movement, which led to the decline of private banking and to the rise of joint stock banks. The decrease in the numbers of provincial joint stock banks is not as great as that among the private provincial banks (approximately a 50 per cent decrease) but the overall decrease in numbers is, none the less, quite considerable – a 72 per cent decrease in the number of provincial banks between 1850 and 1900.

Table 9.1 shows the dramatic decrease in the number of private banks by 1900. As the decline of private banking and the growing dominance of joint stock banks progressed, the *Magazine* viewed the changes with some regret. In 1888, following the failure of Eland's Bank in Northamptonshire (the last of the private banks in the county) and the resulting merger of two private banks to form a joint stock concern, the *Magazine* bemoaned the decline of

> the pleasing relation of confidence between banker and customer which was brought to perfection under the private banking system. Joint-stock banks do not extend to their customers quite the same privacy and personal interest that the partners of a private bank can bestow and have been in the habit of bestowing for generations past. These relations are what make private banking a profession, as distinguished from mere trading in money.[11]

These comments formed part of the ongoing debate in banking circles concerning the merits of private banks over joint stock banks, especially regarding privacy, which had taken place since the introduction of joint stock banking in 1826. Similar sentiments were repeatedly expressed. In 1891, when four private banks in Bath and Bristol merged and adopted joint stock form,[12] the *Magazine* declared that 'there is a ring of sadness in the announcement of four large private houses ... sinking their identity as private firms and joining the ranks of joint stock companies'.[13] However, the private banks were unable to compete successfully with joint stock institutions due to their lack of branches and deposits (Kynaston, 1995: 284). Moreover, as provincial banks extended into London, they no longer required the services of London agents, a task previously performed by the private banks (Cassis, 1994: 21).

Even by 1915, when the amalgamation movement had progressed considerably and successfully, the *Magazine* commented that 'we are by no means enamoured of an excessive number of bank amalgamations and are among those who often regret the disappearance of the old private banker'.[14] Bankers realised, however, that the decline of private banking and the growing dominance of the 'new upstarts', the joint stock banks, was inevitable.

> Step by step, surely and yet steadily, the trade of banking is becoming concentrated in a few large companies. Year by year, we shall

> see the process of amalgamation, or absorption, continues until,
> may-be in twenty or thirty years time, a dozen big banking compa-
> nies will conduct the financial operations of the nation.[15]

The initial phase of amalgamations had witnessed joint stock banks
absorbing smaller, private institutions. However, a common type of
merger during the late nineteenth century was that of the provincial
joint stock bank with a London bank. The move to London provided
an ideal opportunity for expansion when further growth in the provinces was limited and enabled provincial banks to diversify their customer bases, both in terms of lending and deposits. Moreover, there
was the attraction of the London money markets and membership of
the London Clearing House, together with the need to compete with
other banks which had established themselves in both the country and
the City (Holmes and Green, 1986: 79–82).

The merger in 1884 of Lloyds Bank Limited with the London-based
private bank, Messrs Barnets Hoares & Bosanquets Bank, provided Lloyds
(a Birmingham joint stock bank) with a London office.[16] The *Bankers
Magazine* described the absorption by Lloyds of its London agent as
'entirely natural' and the move to London as being motivated by the
desire for prestige and membership of the London Clearing House. In the
merger mania of the early 1890s, the movement of provincial banks into
London was the cause of further, more circumspect, comment.

> Liverpool, and indeed, Lancashire generally, are watched with curi-
> osity, since several well-known and very important banks there,
> with splendid business connections, are known to be anxious to
> make their *debut* in London. A London office and a seat in the
> clearing house, form wonderful attractions to provincial banks.[17]

By the late 1890s the *Magazine* appeared to be expressing some concern
about the movement of provincial banks into the City. When, in 1899,
the Lancashire & Yorkshire Bank acquired the Adelphi Bank (Liverpool), it was viewed as a natural step for a bank already well established in Lancashire to take, but the following commentary from the
London-based journal was telling.

> We have got so accustomed to our friends in the North capturing
> the Metropolis, that an aggressive policy in Lancashire to-day means
> a head office in London to-morrow. The supply of available con-
> cerns in town is running rather short, however; and country cous-
> ins not desirous of losing their identity must be in time.[18]

By 1902 a clearer resentment at this phenomenon was being expressed.

> The pushy country banker, in fact, came to London, and using that
> centre as a fulcrum, increased his influence often to the detriment
> of the banker with a strictly London business.[19]

The difference between banking in the provinces and in London is implied or stated directly by the *Bankers Magazine* throughout this period, as the journal expressed the views and perspectives of the London banker. In 1902 an author comments that it was well known that 'country banking business differs widely from that in London'.[20] From the provincial perspective, however, Holmes and Green assert that:

> As far as English country banks were concerned, the National Provincial's introduction of banking services in London in 1866 pushed the traditional separation of London and country banking towards obsolescence. (Holmes and Green, 1986: 82)

Thus, differing attitudes existed in London and the provinces towards the movement of country banks into the metropolis. It appears that provincial banks seized the opportunity to expand their business and capital whereas the London banker watched the invasion with some trepidation. Yet provincial banks often did not immediately embrace an *outright* move to London. Many were unwilling to lose their identity to the metropolis: when the Birmingham and Midland Bank merged with the London-based Central Bank in 1890, and first established a presence in the capital, 'there was no question of the wholesale transfer of headquarters functions to London'. Board meetings alternated between Birmingham and London, in a similar system to that adopted earlier by Lloyds. It was not until the late 1890s that the Midland converted from a provincial to a metropolitan bank, when the bank's headquarters and management transferred fully to London (Holmes and Green, 1986: 87).

Contemporary perceptions – the advantages of concentration

The amalgamation movement was not only inspired by the desire of country banks to infiltrate the London market. Expansion by merger also had the advantage that banks could extend their branch network relatively quickly and cheaply – avoiding the costly investment involved in establishing new premises and organisations.[21] The Midland Bank realised in the 1880s 'that the opening of new branches demanded hard work and increased expenses for relatively little return', whereas branch acquisition through amalgamation 'produced immediate results' (Holmes and Green, 1986: 74 and 103). The *Bankers Magazine* of 1900 noted that amalgamation had the advantage of a bank being able to acquire, 'in one stroke', 'ready-made' branches in 'working order'.[22]

Concentration via amalgamations also had the benefit of economies of scale, as costs for a large combine were reduced upon introducing more efficient, centralised management and operating systems. In 1889 the *Magazine* commented that, as a result of amalgamation, 'the resources of banks will be in future, if possible, better disciplined than before'.[23] Furthermore, when commenting on two absorptions by Lloyds Bank in the same year, the journal stated that 'There will, or should be, less working expenses, while the same supervising power should not be diluted by being spread over the concentrated business of 3 banks instead of 1.'[24] Indeed, banks actively reformed their management systems following amalgamation rather than allow separate constituent banks to continue operating autonomously (Holmes and Green, 1986: 109–12; Carnevali, 1995). Following the merger of the City Bank with the Midland, the *Bankers Magazine* asserted that 'the combined general management, which will be a feature of the London City and Midland Bank, will be a good guarantee for the continued success of the joint undertakings'.[25]

Thus, amalgamations enabled banks to expand by a cost-efficient method. What of the further advantages, as perceived by contemporary banking practitioners, of a fast-developing new system in which large, joint stock banking institutions dominated? It has already been noted that regret had been expressed at the demise of private institutions, but joint stock banks also had their supporters. Between 1880 and 1920 the contributors to the *Bankers Magazine* pointed to the virtues of the new joint stock banks and the inherent advantages of the new system. However, it is interesting to note that, although the supporters of joint stock banks became more vocal as the period progressed, some bankers still expressed their preference for the 'old' system of banking. The *Magazine* not only reflected changing opinion over time but also different responses by bankers to developments in their profession.

The merger of Lloyds with the Birmingham Joint Stock Bank in 1889 prompted the *Magazine* into a general discussion of the merits of what it described as a 'new phase' in banking, concluding that the 'new amalgamations will, no doubt, be of great advantage to all the banks concerned'.[26] Furthermore, banking concentration was also perceived to have provided advantages for the financial system as a whole. An increase in the strength and stability of resultant institutions was seen by some to promote greater strength in the English and Welsh banking sector:

> the understanding amongst the great banks will tend to be closer; and that altogether the banking industry will be, in course of time, so strongly knot together that attacks from without will be better resisted.[27]

A contemporary publication for the banking profession entitled *Bank Notes*[28] emphasised that the most important impact of bank amalgamations was 'increased stability afforded to the banking fabric generally'. The article goes on to comment that 'To promote solidity is an axiom of modern banking' and that in the modern system of large joint stock banks 'the risks of failure are well spread'.[29] A more stable banking system would enable financial institutions to better withstand shocks such as the City of Glasgow Bank induced crisis of 1878 and the Baring crisis of 1890. Furthermore, the development of a stronger banking structure meant that such bank failures were less likely to occur. Holden (Chairman of the Midland), in his evidence to the Colwyn Committee of 1918 in defence of banking concentration, stressed that there had been 'no bank failures of importance' between 1900 and 1913, a contrast to the nineteenth century (Holmes and Green, 1986: 130).

Even as early as 1901, the *Bankers Magazine* was extolling the virtues of the large, centralised bank with a branch network. It acclaimed the branch banking system, stating that the 'branch of a strong bank has all the vigour of the strong bank at its back'.[30] An article from the *Manchester Guardian* was reprinted in the *Magazine* which asserted that 'an amalgamation adds real strength to the capital resources of a bank and commands superior ability in its management'.[31]

The result of concentration meant that a smaller number of banks were in business but these banks operated a large branch network which provided them with a greater geographical scope to their business. Many in favour of concentration argued that nationally operated and efficient branch networks allowed the redistribution of deposits to those areas, especially industrial districts, which were in need of advances.[32] Thus a more even distribution of both business and risk and a greater mobilisation of capital were achieved. Such a redistribution of funds was perceived to be in the interests of the domestic economy. Moreover, such a bank acquired, through amalgamation, a larger capital and thus had greater financial resources at its disposal. A geographically dispersed institution with a large capital enabled the potential reduction of risk, or rather a perceived increase in a bank's 'strength' and stability.[33] The *Bankers Magazine* observed in 1898 that 'the economy of well spread risk means ... relative freedom from bad debts'.[34] The risks inherent in small, unit banks were commented on in the following year. 'There are many risks when the business is conducted on too small a scale, for a loss, comparatively trifling in its extent, may cripple a feeble bank permanently.'[35] Indeed, the growth in the size of banks provided an important break from the previous system whereby small unit banks often became dangerously 'locked into' a small number of relatively large, local industrial accounts. *Bank Notes* commented that:

> The suspension of payment by a large business house ... will not work so disastrously for the amalgamated institution as it would have done for the smaller bank relying only on its local and often precarious resources.[36]

Geographical diversification allowed diversification of a bank's business and thus, combined with the greater financial resources of a large joint stock bank, reduced the danger of bank failure as a consequence of a depression in local industry or through the failure of an individual account (Cottrell, 1979: 223–8; Newton, 1996). The benefits of release from the dependence upon, and dangers inherent in, such large-scale lending were recognised by the Chairman of the Midland in the 1880s (Goodman). After a series of Yorkshire amalgamations he declared that 'Our policy of late has been to spread our risks as much as we possibly can, avoiding all large and unwieldy accounts' (Holmes and Green, 1986: 82).

The small, independent banks could not compete with the large banks which possessed branch networks in London and the provinces, and some of these smaller banks acknowledged their weaknesses. When the Oldham Joint Stock Bank was amalgamated with the Midland Bank in 1898, its Chairman admitted that his provincial bank could not compete 'with the large institutions which have offices in different parts of the country' and that

> large banks with large resources are able to transact a great deal of business which is both safe and profitable and which is altogether out of the reach of such a small bank as ours. (Holmes and Green, 1986: 98)

The branch banking system was frequently compared to the previous system of unit banking. In 1901 the *Bankers Magazine* argued that the branch of a large bank would be less likely to extend 'dangerous' advances or to support 'weak' businesses 'at an undue risk'.[37] The essential difference was accounted for by the different management of the two systems, with the individual banker in a small town possibly finding 'it difficult to refuse to make advances which his better judgement would lead him to decline', whereas the branch manager 'must put the case before his "board", which will go into the matter dispassionately and from the point of view of business suitability alone'.[38] The author concluded that 'bad local business is less likely to be undertaken by a large bank with a good system of management than by a separate individual concern'.[39]

Thus the advantages of a system of large, centralised banks was highlighted over the previous unit banking system. This is an interesting contrast to the regret frequently expressed elsewhere in the journal concerning the demise of the personal, *local* service provided by the private banker. The *Magazine* reflected changes in contemporary opinion and a variety of conflicting views, as expressed by bankers. In general, from the late nineteenth-century 'sadness' at the decline in private banking, there developed an early twentieth-century enthusiasm for the new, larger joint stock form of banking institution and its ability to meet the changing needs of the domestic economy.

The perception of banks operating for a broader economic and public interest recurred in contemporary discourse. The advantage of adopting joint stock form and subsequent concentration in banking was seen to be in the public interest by the Deputy Chairman of Lloyds at the Bank's Annual General Meeting in 1915. The *Magazine* reported his comments regarding the First World War:

> if in last August our banking system had consisted of isolated banking units scattered up and down through the country with no general policy to guide them, the situation would have been still more difficult to handle.[40]

Indeed, Holmes and Green argue that the turn of the century witnessed a change in attitude of both bankers and government as banks were acknowledged to have a role in both economic and foreign policy (Holmes and Green, 1986: 122).

The potential role of banks in the domestic economy was highlighted by Holden in his evidence to the Colwyn Committee in 1918. He argued in favour of amalgamation and concentration in the banking sector as larger banks were, he believed, best able to meet the needs of postwar industrial recovery, as opposed to the limited ability of small banks to aid such regeneration.

> There is no doubt in my mind that those Banks which have become large and powerful by amalgamation will be in a much better position to aid the industries than they would have been had they preserved their individuality. It is a fallacy to assume that the small Banks will be able to do very much.[41]

An article in the *Bankers Magazine* of 1919 went a step further, asserting that 'reconstruction in the industrial world called for something approaching to reconstruction in the machinery designed to finance such industry'.[42]

The demands of large-scale industry were an important consideration for the banking community. Manufacturing concerns were also expanding and undertaking mergers. Industry was inexorably increasing in size, especially in the first two decades of the twentieth century, with consolidation accelerating to meet the escalating demands of the First World War. Thus, the bankers argued, their institutions necessarily had to increase in size in order safely to meet the requirements of their ever-increasing customers. This was emphasised by Cecil F. Parr, Chairman of Parr's Bank, in a report in the *Magazine* in 1914.

> He mentioned that in these days of large industrial combines a small bank, however ably conducted, cannot in the nature of things undertake the financing of the big concerns which constitute an ever-increasing proportion of the commercial and manufacturing enterprises of the country, and therefore much of modern good business goes past it.[43]

The journal itself wrote that the amalgamations taking place in the banking sector were largely attributable to 'the demands made upon it by the corresponding movement in commerce'.[44] However, despite the assertion by bankers that amalgamation occurred to meet the needs of industry, some argue that mergers in the banking sector preceded those in manufacturing (Capie and Rodrik-Bali, 1982: 291).

The smaller banks which were absorbed by larger concerns often realised the necessity of concentration in the banking sector in order to meet the demands of industry and to compete with other banks. In 1898 the Oldham Joint Stock Bank quickly agreed to amalgamation with the Midland better to cope with demand from the local cotton industry, an especially difficult sector for banks to deal with due to the huge seasonal demands of the industry. The scale and scope of the cotton industry in Lancashire also required Oldham manufacturers and their bankers to have connections throughout the region. With regard to the Oldham Joint Stock Bank, it was 'impossible for mill-owning customers to contemplate a future for the bank without proper representation in Manchester and Liverpool'. Likewise, the Leicestershire Banking Company merged with the Midland in 1900 as its lending to local boot, shoe and hosiery manufacturers was in danger of outstripping the growth of its deposits. The Chairman of the Leicester Bank admitted that 'We have now arrived at the position that we must either refuse new business, however good, or increase our resources.' In 1890 the Leeds and County Bank's Chairman conceded that 'large and powerful combinations' were 'a necessity to meet the calls now made upon them by mercantile and manufacturing firms' (Holmes and Green, 1986: 96, 98, 105–6). Indeed, the eagerness which some small banks showed for amalgamation was noted by the *Magazine*, with some humour, when reporting the comments of the Lloyds Bank Chairman at the annual meeting of shareholders in 1901. 'In the matter of amalgamations, it would appear that Lloyds are simply embarrassed with offers from smaller concerns which wish to be taken over.'[45]

Banking opinion tended to agree that, from the perspective of large-scale customers, a bank with a large capital and widely spread connections was able to deal with the demands of such clients. Moreover, in

1919 one enthusiastic banker summarised the benefits for all commercial and industrial customers as a result of amalgamations:

> In short, since the concentration of banking business in the hands of a few large and well-managed institutions, with wider ramifications, the small borrower had found a willing lender nearer to his door, and the big borrower had found in his banker an equally ready lender with ampler resources.[46]

In addition to business customers, bankers emphasised the benefits of amalgamation to their private clients and their depositors. Private customers of large banks with branch networks benefited from a more accessible and convenient form of banking as branches spread throughout the country and payment systems were streamlined. When considering the issue of bank deposits, the advantages of amalgamation were also conveyed. From the depositors' point of view, the advantage of amalgamations was that they could trust their money to a more sound and solvent bank with the resources to withstand external pressures due to a large bank's capital resources and ability of its management.[47]

The strength of local opposition from shareholders and customers to a merger could, however, prevent amalgamation. The proposed absorption of the Manchester and Liverpool District Banking Company by Lloyds Bank did not go ahead in 1904, despite lengthy negotiations. Local opposition in Manchester was the main reason for the abortive attempt at amalgamation (Sayers, 1957: 262). The *Magazine* claimed that provincial pride was 'deeply wounded' by the proposal. The potential loss of independence of what was viewed as 'the most important bank in the County Palatine' in order to become 'a mere appanage [*sic*] of a great London institution' produced 'loud and emphatic' opposition from shareholders and customers of the Manchester and Liverpool Bank and a 'hostile' reaction from local commercial interests and thus negotiations were halted.[48] This is an important but rare example of effective opposition to the seemingly inexorable movement towards large joint stock banks with a centralised system based in London.

Shareholders and staff in bank amalgamations

Shareholders of banks involved in amalgamations were generally in favour of such a course of action. From a shareholder's perspective, those with stock in joint stock banks usually benefited from the merger movement, as is verified in the *Magazine*. When the Midland absorbed the City Bank in 1898, commentary in the journal noted that shareholders of the City Bank had 'scored considerably' and, furthermore, when the Midland took over the Central Bank in 1891 'the shares of the latter bank improved some four points on the announcement being made public'.[49] In addition to raising share prices, amalgamations could result in shareholders obtaining 'a wider and freer market for their shares';[50] moreover, 'the economy of well spread risk means greater uniformity of dividend'.[51] A commentator in the *Magazine* in 1900 summarised the financial benefits of amalgamations to bank shareholders thus:

> The shareholder of the smaller bank gains in pocket; the share-holder of the larger concern in fresh business and greater prestige. The advantage is mutual. When these considerations are borne in mind, one ceases to wonder that amalgamations ... go through with so little friction.[52]

Circulars issued by banks upon amalgamation, unsurprisingly, emphasised the benefit to shareholders of the banks concerned. On the merger of Lloyds with the Birmingham Joint Stock Bank in 1889, a circular from Lloyds claimed that 'It is believed that the fusion of these two banks will be mutually advantageous.'[53] A circular issued by the directors of the Bank of Liverpool on its absorption by the Liverpool Commercial Banking Company stated that 'The result it is believed will be advantageous to the shareholders of both banks.'[54] The price paid for amalgamations and concentration in banking was the loss of control and identity: the larger the organisation, the weaker the direct control of the shareholders and customers over the conduct of a bank. However, there were few examples of widespread objections from shareholders and customers of banks that were absorbed, apart from the one in Lancashire cited above. Holmes and Green argue that this was due to generous bids from absorbing banks and the strength of contemporary public arguments in favour of amalgamations (Holmes and Green, 1986: 98).

Banking concentration and mergers also had an important impact upon the banks' staff. Unlike the almost unanimous approval to mergers extended by bank shareholders, staff frequently complained about the amalgamation process. The most common complaints of staff involved in absorptions appeared to be the change in the systems of book-keeping and returns necessary to provide a uniform system throughout the new bank, and the amount of extra bureaucracy involved in the amalgamation itself. The latter meant that staff had to work overtime during the initial process of amalgamation.

Bank employees had further cause to worry on a bank's amalgamation. Staff who worked for smaller institutions which were absorbed were likely to feel more insecure in their new positions due to their lack of familiarity with the 'new regime'. When overlapping branches were closed, managers and staff could be relocated but could also lose their jobs (a later example is provided in Greene, 1969: 9). Favourable pension schemes may also have been lost in a merger.[55] Holden was aware of the dislocation and difficulties faced by staff in newly acquired branches, especially those remote from the bank's head office, and was keen to provide support. In 1904 he told the junior manager of a new branch 'Write to me personally every two days ... report how you are getting on and what progress you are making' (Holmes and Green, 1986: 112).

However, objections to mergers by bank staff in 1899 were treated with little patience by the *Bankers Magazine* in its informal 'Notes and Comments' section where the views of contributors were expressed freely. Little credence was given to complaints about extra work.

> We do know that, as you cannot have omelettes without the break-
> ing of eggs, so you cannot take over another bank without entail-
> ing a large amount of extra work upon your staff – work which is
> generally cheerfully borne, because so frequently recognised in a
> practical form by directors, in the shape of a bonus.[56]

Moreover, the journal contested:

> The staff of a bank which has been taken over by another bank is
> never satisfied with its lot. You may give the men a bonus, and
> assure them that their status in the service will be unaffected by the
> change, but it is of no use. They have a grievance, and prefer to
> hug it.[57]

An article the following year commented further upon the effect of mergers on staff, noting that the subject was 'a matter of personal interest, though not of intrinsic importance'. The same article maintained that staff 'apprehensions' concerning amalgamation 'are generally groundless, and, when not groundless, exaggerated'.[58] Such observations demonstrate the relative lack of importance placed upon the impact on staff by some in more elevated banking positions who expressed their opinion in the journal.

However, in 1909, quite the opposite view was expressed by a contributor to the *Magazine* who objected to the impact of amalgamations upon bank staff. 'A bank clerk is becoming a cross between a typewriter and an automatic machine ... The natural result has been a reduction in the salaries paid.'[59] By 1914 a more moderate and optimistic tone was taken. The advantages of bank amalgamations were highlighted to staff who might have complaints.

> Banking amalgamations are brought about mainly to improve the
> status and business prospects of the institutions concerned, and the
> extra growth and prosperity of the banks should be reflected in
> better conditions and greater opportunities for the staff.[60]

By this date, concentration in the banking sector had brought about greater stability and greater security of employment. Moreover, the *Magazine* argued, opportunities for promotion had increased as a result of rapid branch expansion and the new, large-scale joint stock institutions were less conservative, had a more progressive attitude towards their staff and were more likely to reward ability with promotion.[61] Thus amalgamations were viewed by the *Magazine* as having positive repercussions for the career progress of bank staff (Holmes and Green, 1986: 112).

The attitudes of bank staff could be detrimental to the process of banking concentration if they did not adapt fully to the new bank's identity or systems. The *Magazine* declared that staff often

> identify themselves very closely indeed with their particular institution, and so much is this the case that even when two banks have been amalgamated for some years the different staffs may not yet have become assimilated, and are often still divided into two camps.[62]

Such staffing difficulties would have caused the banks problems but, given the continuing policy of bank amalgamations, it appears that such difficulties were overcome and did not deter the process of banking concentration.

Contemporary perceptions – the disadvantages of concentration

Reservations about the concentration in English banking and the new financial system that was developing were debated in the *Bankers Magazine*. Objections to a merger in Lancashire and regret expressed with regard to the decline of private banking have already been considered. There was also much contemporary debate about the loss of local connections with the concentration of banking during this period. Concern was expressed about the implications for the lending activity of banks as a result of the change from the local, unit banking of the mid-nineteenth century to the centralised system of the 'Big Five' reached by 1918. Focus was placed upon the adverse impact on small customers, especially small-scale businesses in the provinces, and the issue was also considered by the Colwyn Committee in 1918.[63] One contributor to the *Magazine* in 1909 voiced his objections to concentration thus:

> with the gradual absorption of country banks by great joint stock institutions, the most important part of the business of banking – the lending of the bank's funds – has become centralised in the advance department at the head office of each bank, so that the managers and chief officials at the branches have been relieved of much of their responsibility.[64]

The *Manchester Guardian* was also not entirely convinced by the arguments for increased concentration. An article from the newspaper, reprinted in the *Magazine* of 1904, commented on the detrimental effects of large banks operating a centralised system, noting that the strength of a bank did not necessarily go on increasing in proportion to the increase of its capital, nor would the ability of its directors and managers necessarily improve in proportion to the extent of its business.[65] Moreover, the disadvantages that arose from a loss of local control to a head office in London were also discussed.

> The moment a chief director loses a firm grasp of every part of the organisation an element of weakness and danger is admitted. In this respect a local combination may be superior to one which has its centre of control in London.[66]

This opinion was reiterated in 1914 when the new, large-scale banks were considered. The need for strong central control of the 'great' banks was noted but the view was expressed that it was necessary for banks not to 'over-centralise' and that if 'the human factor is allowed full and proper play, all will be well'.[67]

Holden argued strenuously against such claims when giving evidence to the Colwyn Committee. He argued that, in the case of the Midland, the system that arose out of amalgamations and concentration actually favoured small businesses and private customers (Holmes and Green, 1986: 129–30). In 1919, another banker, F. E. Steele (from the London & County Bank) also maintained that the new branches opened by amalgamated banks resulted in 'bringing credit facilities within easier reach of the small customer in general and the small trader in particular'.[68]

There was a general acknowledgement that the former provincial banks had been more flexible in their industrial lending, as opposed to the London and provincial branch banks of the early twentieth century (Sayers, 1957: 271). Such flexibility was particularly relevant to the provision of collateral security on industrial credit. In 1900, an article in the *Bankers Magazine* contended that 'purely provincial banks pay less rigid attention to the proper completion of securities than the big London banks with ramifications in the provinces'.[69] However, the same article asserted that although a new, London head office may 'rectify' such flexible practices regarding security, 'it does not start calling in advances right and left' but rather makes arrangements 'that borrowers feel the change of management as little as may be'.[70] More recent historical debate has also considered the lending policies adopted by the large, London-based joint stock banks in the twentieth century (Carnevali, 1995; Cassis, 1985, 1991; Cottrell, 1979: 237–9; 1992: 52–9; Holmes and Green, 1986: 115–17).

More general disadvantages of banking concentration were also discussed in the *Magazine*. The spectre of power becoming concentrated into the hands of a few 'great' banks frequently worried contributors to the journal. In 1889, an author rather alarmingly declared that 'the dangers of the rise of great banks will, in course of time, be comparable to those political dangers which arose from the baronial or feudal system of the middle ages'.[71] Furthermore, in 1904 the *Magazine* warned that 'unlimited amalgamation is fraught with danger'.[72] However, in general, the publication took a pragmatic view of concentration, emphasising that 'In the last result banking must depend on the personal qualities of the men who control it'[73] and that the supervision of the system by the Bank of England should ensure its safety for both a bank and its customers.

> There are risks, too, when the scale becomes over extended, as then the business may be too large to admit of proper supervision; but ... we trust that for many years to come banks in England will continue, as in the past, to extend their operations skilfully and securely.[74]

Therefore, throughout much of the amalgamation movement, the *Bankers Magazine* presented the arguments for and against amalgamation, in terms of the local versus national and the small versus large, but repeatedly placed the emphasis on the professional banker practising sound business. 'It has to be remembered that, however great the bank may be, fundamentally it is the "Banker" who counts.'[75]

The Colwyn Committee

With the upsurge in amalgamations witnessed during the First World War, reservations about excessive banking concentration were repeatedly expressed, both by bankers and in the public domain. The most obvious result of such misgivings was the appointment of the Colwyn Committee, whose report summarised the main areas of public unease with regard to banking concentration. Two of the main issues discussed were the potential reduction of competition resulting from amalgamations and the danger of the concentration of the entire banking facilities of the country into one powerful institution.[76] Such a banking combine was referred to as a 'money trust' and the Committee was vocal in its opposition to this outcome due to the power it placed in the hands of a few individuals who would work in the interests of their shareholders rather than the interests of depositors or commercial and industrial customers.

The banking community repeatedly countered criticisms of a 'money trust' and a banking system stifled by competition. In 1919 the *Bankers*

Magazine maintained that amalgamations had led to increased competition by the opening of numerous new branches and that banking competition was more intense at that time among the remaining banks, not least amongst the 'Big Five'.[77] Holden, in addressing the shareholders of his bank with regard to the proposed amalgamation between the London Joint Stock Bank and the London City & Midland Bank in 1918, dismissed the idea of any reduction in competition as a result of banking concentration and the idea of a 'money trust' as 'absolute nonsense'.[78] The *Magazine* also reported the address of F. E. Steele to the Birmingham Institute of Bankers in November 1919:

> We had not, and we were not in the least danger of having, a 'money trust'. Never was legitimate banking competition in this country more keen than it was now between the 'big five', and never were the requirements of the deserving borrower more readily or fully met.[79]

The *Bankers Magazine*, despite expressing reservations about bank amalgamations and the decline of private banking from 1880 onwards, repeatedly and strenuously denied any notion of a money trust developing or a reduction of banking competition in the contemporary public debate surrounding concentration. Rather, criticism from the *Magazine* during this period centred on the *speed* of banking concentration. In August 1918 it maintained that 'while we do not endorse much of the criticism of banking amalgamation along the line of banking monopoly or a money trust, we do regret the rapidity and feverishness of the movement'.[80] The same author added that arguments in favour of the undoubted and many advantages of greater concentration 'are somewhat weakened by the rush' to amalgamate 'so that there shall be no question of being left behind in the competition for attaining a certain position as regards size'.[81] A further article the following year professed that the *Magazine* had 'more than once expressed regret that the movements should have been quite so rapid and so extensive'[82] and decried the speed of recent amalgamations as being 'rather out of harmony with the general spirit of the recommendations' of the Colwyn Committee.[83] Indeed, the *Magazine* asserted that 'it can scarcely be a matter for surprise that the movement should have occasioned criticism in many quarters' given that the 'Government has never raised a finger in the direction of a Banking Bill', absorptions continued and a 'complete disregard of the spirit of the recommendations' of the Committee had been shown.[84] Therefore, despite countering the criticisms levelled at their sector by the Colwyn Committee's report and in public debate, bankers expressed reservations about the speed of concentration and about public perceptions of a profession which was seen to be ignoring government recommendations. They recognised that the fears of the general public and of the City were 'natural' and did their best to provide reassurance in their arguments for greater banking concentration.

Another argument frequently used by bankers in favour of greater banking concentration was the ability it afforded to meet the increasing competition from foreign banks and, more generally, foreign economies. Holden, in his evidence to the Colwyn Committee, emphasised the need to consider foreign competition. He drew particular comparisons with Germany, where concentration in the banking sector was also taking place, and emphasised that amalgamations in England and Wales meant that domestic banks were larger than their German counterparts.

> It would be a very great mistake if we entered the financial struggle, which will assuredly take place after the War, without being provided with proper means for meeting our competitors. There can be no doubt that there is a grave danger of our losing the financial supremacy which this country enjoyed before the War. Germany will certainly do everything she can to wrest from us our International business.[85]

Holden also recognised the threat from American banking competition, with their aim to 'make New York the Financial centre'.[86] He concluded that:

> First competition from Germany, and second from US, so that it is quite evident to me that unless we pursue a policy similar to that being pursued by those countries and make our Banks as large as and powerful as possible, we shall not be able to retain the high financial position we have held hitherto.[87]

Herbert Hambling, Chairman of the London Provincial and South Western Bank, also commented on foreign competition when his banks merged with Barclays in 1918. He asserted that a prominent reason for his support of this particular merger, and amalgamation in general, was the threat 'of the German banking and industrial machine, and ... its enormous power'.[88] Thus bankers voiced their concern at the growing competition from foreign banks and industry during this period and many expressed the opinion that the only way to compete was with large-scale, strong British joint stock banks.

By the time of the Colwyn Committee, the banking environment and the opinions of bankers had both changed. From the support for small-scale private banking, and the regret at its demise, there was a gradual, if not universal, acceptance of bank amalgamations and subsequent concentration. Indeed, the supporters of the new form of banking organisation became more vocal as the period under examination progressed to the point when, in 1918, the merger movement was challenged, and they persuaded the government to leave the system that had developed intact. Moreover, the *Magazine* reflected changes in the attitudes of British bankers, especially from those of the First World War, as they increasingly looked outwards from domestic commercial banking to the international stage. The next section will examine more closely the internationalisation of English/British banking between 1880 and 1920.

The internationalisation of English banking, 1880 to 1920

British commerce had long operated in an international environment due to Britain's standing in world trade and in its colonies. London was the financial centre of Europe from the 1870s (Cottrell, 1992: 40) and, moreover, had a long history of international merchant banking. Thus London itself, or rather 'The City', was international in terms of its financial operations during the period under examination. This section examines the internationalisation of English/British banking in the late nineteenth and early twentieth century, and considers the response of bankers to such developments.

Cottrell discusses the internationalisation of banking in London and Europe during this period in some detail (Chapter 10). In the late nineteenth and early twentieth century, banking in London was international in the sense that business conducted by English banks (usually private institutions) was international in nature, providing finance for world trade, and that foreign banks and bankers established offices in the capital during this period. Furthermore, from the 1830s London possessed corporate overseas banks and by 1914 such banks possessed more than 1000 overseas branches, many in the British Empire (Jones, 1993: 1). However, in relation to domestic English commercial banking, international developments did not get under way until the early twentieth century. Before 1880 the English banking system comprised two almost separate financial sectors: the City, which was primarily concerned with international trade, and provincial banking, the focus of which was domestic regional economic development (Cottrell, 1992: 39). The amalgamation movement from 1880 onwards saw the development of large-scale clearing banks which consequently expanded into foreign business, most notably from the turn of the century. London joint stock banks had been involved in international acceptance business since the late 1860s (Cottrell, 1992: 51) but the provincial banks only entered this field on their amalgamation with London banks. For example, the Midland undertook such business in 1898 as a consequence of its absorption of the City Bank. In 1902 the accounts of overseas 'correspondent' banks inherited from the City Bank were consolidated with the Midland's foreign agencies into the 'Foreign Banks Department' (Holmes and Green, 1986: 32).

A relative lack of discussion concerning English international banking by the *Bankers Magazine* in the late nineteenth century may be seen as indicating a certain lack of activity in this area. Whilst numerous articles and opinions were presented with regard to concentration in English and Welsh commercial banking, little such specific material was generated concerning the international business conducted by banks in London. Regular reports were printed about colonial trade and banking, but a flow of commentary similar to the one sparked by the amalgamation movement was largely absent until the turn of the century. Foreign business by British overseas banks, possibly through its long-established nature, appears to have been somewhat taken for granted. However, the successful establishment and development of branches by foreign banks in London and the development of foreign business by British banks in the early twentieth century produced much comment. It is to such observations, and those few on the internationalisation of banking in Britain and Europe in general, that we now turn.

In one of the infrequent articles concerning the international nature of English banking before 1900, Professor Leone Levi noted in his 1891 Gilbart Lecture on banking:

> We have banking institutions specially organised for the better and more economical management of international payments. At this moment there are a large number of foreign and British colonial joint-stock banks having offices in London, and of British colonial and foreign banks having agents in London, with branches in all the seaports and centres of commerce in the world.[89]

He concluded that:

> International banking is, I imagine, as yet in its infancy, but it may render enormous services to international trading and intercourse ... It is fitting that with the extended communication with, and more intimate knowledge of, foreign countries, our bankers should step somewhat beyond the limits of national wants, and enter with caution, yet with a firm purpose, into operations of a more international character alike in their investments and their discounts.[90]

This early commentary provides a positive view as to the future of British international banking, recognising its value to the domestic economy and trade.

The international nature of banking in the City was emphasised by contributors to the professional banking journals. The reproduction of a speech to the Institute of Bankers in its own journal commented that 'the London money market is the money market of the world' and an 'international clearing house'.[91] Responses to the same speech reiterated that 'the importance of our Metropolis as the world's clearing house still remains unchallenged', although the *potential* challenge from

America was also noted: 'they propose to oust us from our position as the world's financiers'.[92]

The *Bankers Magazine* and the *Journal of the Institute of Bankers* provided further comment upon the internationalisation of banking after the turn of the century. Developments which prompted debate were the successful progress of foreign banks in London and the establishment of foreign branches by domestic commercial banks. Encroachment into London by European banks began in the 1870s – offices in the capital were initially opened by Crédit Lyonnais in 1871 and the Deutsche Bank in 1873, and the Dresdner Bank and the Comptoir National d'Escompte followed in 1879 (Holmes and Green, 1986: 82; Jones, 1982: 186). These banks were attracted to London by its 'preeminent position in world finance' and 'by the dominant role of sterling in the financing of international commerce' (Jones, 1982: 186). A paper entitled 'Foreign competition in its relation to banking', presented to the Institute of Bankers in London in 1900, and reprinted in its journal, is one of the first to provide a detailed examination of the development of foreign banking in the City. The authors (Fuller and Rowan) comment that much had been written concerning the effects of foreign competition in the industrial sector but that:

> Hitherto ... the effect of foreign competition in the banking world does not appear to have attracted the active interest which we think it deserves. No doubt, all British banks feel sore about it, but with the exception of occasional newspaper paragraphs there is not much literature on the subject.[93]

In the same year, the *Bankers Magazine* emphasised the importance of the development of foreign banking in London.

> Few changes among the constitution of the English money market which have taken place of recent years have been more marked than the vast increase which has taken place in the numbers and the vigour of the colonial and foreign banks which have offices or agents in London.[94]

In order to attempt to measure these developments, the *Magazine* provided some figures on this type of banking in Britain (Table 9.2). It also emphasised the changing international nature of banking in London, recognising that 'a very large part of the banks, foreign and colonial, existed, more than twenty years since', but that 'their connection with the English money market has become more distinctly marked of recent years, and the opening of offices in London has also become a much more usual thing'.[95]

The development of foreign bank branches in London stimulated criticism of domestic British banks. Following the paper given to the

Table 9.2   British, colonial and foreign banks in London, 1880–1900

	1880	1890	1900
Number of banks in the United Kingdom	385	372	259
Number of British, colonial and foreign banks mainly having offices or agencies in London	102	237	988
Total number of banks	487	609	1,247

Source: Bankers Magazine, 1900, vol. 69, p. 355

Institute of Bankers in 1900, the 'Notes and Comments' section of the *Bankers Magazine* condemned the parochial attitude of London bankers towards foreign business, as compared to their European counterparts.

> It does not appear to have struck anyone who listened to the paper, that the large business now transacted by the London offices of the Crédit Lyonnais and Deutsche Bank was, in a measure, a reflection upon the insular policy adopted by London bankers.[96]

The same author continues to find fault with domestic banks, 'strong and powerful as regards to internal business' but 'their relations with the outer world are singularly weak for an international trading country like Great Britain'.[97] Unfavourable comparison was drawn with continental banks which, 'with their branches and alliances all over the world, keep their fingers upon the pulse of international trade'.[98] This commentator reasoned that 'in the matter of international fiscal economy, the British nation may be losing something in limiting the scope of its branch establishments to the United Kingdom'.[99] The following year another commentator asserted that 'If London is not to become a mere rendezvous for foreign bankers doing cosmopolitan business, its own branches must take a leaf out of the foreigner's book and become as cosmopolitan as he.'[100] Such bankers appeared to realise the need to rise to the challenge of foreign competition.

In 1901 the *Magazine* printed comments under the titles 'Lombard Street Under Foreign Control' and 'The Encroachment of Foreign Banks' and thus illustrated their readers' concern about direct foreign competition in London.[101] The threat felt by such developments was expressed by the writer of the former article who declared, somewhat excessively, that the foreign banks in London were 'now so strong as to be practically in control' and that the City was 'assuming a distinctly foreign aspect'.[102] By this date, French banks had successfully established branches in Britain: the Comptoir National d'Escompte de Paris had branches in London, Liverpool and Manchester, and the Crédit Lyonnais had two branches in London – one in the City and one in the West End.

However, not all bankers reacted unfavourably to foreign competition in London; indeed some welcomed such changes. The two bankers addressing the Institute of Bankers in 1900 asserted that such developments were beneficial to the maintenance and protection of London as the financial capital of Europe.

> The more strongly the financial interests of other nations centred in London, the more firmly would they restrain each other from any action likely to endanger the credit of that market where so large a share of their own capital was deposited ... Common interests, and common dangers, are more likely to draw men and nations together.[103]

The presence of foreign bank branches also, the speakers argued, generated business for domestic clearing banks, brought information to London and stimulated British trade.[104] Elsewhere, the encroachment of foreign banks into the capital has been viewed as a stimulant to British banks and as a result 'appreciably broadened the range and depth of facilities offered by London' (Kynaston, 1995).

The same speakers noted that, while foreign banks had been successfully establishing and developing branches in London since the 1870s, 'the benefits to be gained by our banks abroad seem to have been overlooked'.[105] One of their respondents also questioned: 'why should not our leading joint stock banks here open branches in Berlin and Paris?'[106] Subsequently, in the early twentieth century, British domestic commercial banks followed their overseas competitors and ventured into foreign branch banking. The *Bankers Magazine* turned its attention to these new developments, and was prompted in 1913 to issue the following comments in its 'Educational Section':

> Owing to the fact that several of our clearing banks have now taken an extensive participation in the foreign field, this branch of banking business is of more general interest, and, owing to the varied nature of the transactions, deserves special attention.[107]

One of the first areas of expansion for the British domestic banks was France. In 1911 Lloyds Bank purchased Armstrong & Co. of Paris and changed its title to Lloyds Banks (France) (Jones, 1982: 187). In 1913 the *Bankers Magazine* recorded the expansion of the London County and Westminster Bank into Paris through the acquisition of the premises and approved accounts of the Banque Franco-Americaine. Such a move, the journal asserted, had 'probably been prompted by the success of Lloyds Bank in the same sphere' and other banks were likely to follow.

Indeed, the author believed that 'there is little question that business in the French capital offers considerable inducement for an English bank'.[108] The First World War also stimulated the establishment of overseas branches as domestic commercial banks provided branch banking for British troops and filled the gaps in the market left by the expulsion of German banks from Allied cities (Jones, 1982: 187).

Such foreign expansion was commented upon favourably in the *Journal of the Institute of Bankers* in 1914. A contributor (Hubert V. Burrell) argued that the opening of foreign branches by British banks saved the necessity of dealing with a foreign agent, thereby reducing costs and ensuring 'keener' and 'personal representation'.[109] Furthermore, foreign expansion 'provided fresh fields in which to expand their business' and the 'opportunity of obtaining accurate and early information on financial movements and possible developments in the monetary centre in which the branch is opened'.[110] The *Bankers Magazine* in 1919 also provided positive commentary:

> Most people have welcomed the way in which the joint stock banks have thrown off that mantle of insularity with which they have enshrouded themselves for so many years; the zest with which they are now entering into foreign business is entirely creditable.[111]

Yet, as with other developments, the need for such rapid development was questioned and concern expressed at the cost of such ventures, in terms of both staff and premises.

> Also it is natural that there should be anxiety as to whether this sudden entry by our deposit banks into connections with foreign and semi-foreign institutions should lead to banking of a too venturesome character.[112]

This opinion demonstrated the rather cautious tendency of contemporary bankers. Burrell, in arguing against the fears that foreign branches of British banks would be tempted to change their 'safe and sound' banking methods, described the cautious nature of the British banking community 'whose leaning towards conservatism is ... strongly marked'.[113]

Such caution, however, could be well founded. Jones asserts that 'these Continental investments met with little success' (Jones, 1982: 186). In 1919 the Westminster realised that its overseas expansion had been undertaken with too much haste, too little planning, and at too great an expense. From the early 1920s, all the clearing banks began to close a number of their overseas branches (Cottrell, 1992: 52). Jones concludes that the British banks' expansion into Europe had been too rapid and ill planned (Jones, 1982: 189–90). Such failures did not, however, deter the 'Big Five' domestic commercial banks from future expansion into overseas business. In the 1920s they sought such objectives through the purchase of controlling stakes in British overseas banks (Cottrell, 1992: 52).

The Midland had undertaken a different strategy, preferring to act as a London correspondent for foreign banks. Such a course of action proved to be more sound and more profitable. Holden was not in favour of extending British bank branches into foreign areas. In giving evidence to the Colwyn Committee in 1918, he highlighted the different opinions of bankers concerning foreign expansion.

> One class of banker believes that the proper course is to open abroad branches of their own bank, in which case they will compete with foreign banks in their own country. Another class believes that the better policy is to work from London in conjunction with the foreign banker, and not to go into direct competition with him.[114]

Expressing his reservations about foreign expansion (except in France), Holden advocated the latter view – the cultivation of connection with foreign bankers themselves. He argued that opening foreign branches could mean that the money of English depositors might be used to help commerce and industry abroad which were in direct competition with their British counterparts. Furthermore, Holden argued that such foreign branches might be 'called upon to assist in the reconstruction of the countries in which they are situated' at a time when resources were required 'at home to reconstruct our own industries and manufactures'.[115] He also argued that going into direct competition with foreign bankers in their own country could lead to antagonism and 'that we may drive their business to Germany or New York' rather than encourage them to retain London as the financial centre of the world.[116] Thus, the Midland Chairman once again expressed his concern that British banks should do their utmost to assist domestic industry and commerce against international competition and to ensure that London remained Europe's financial centre.

The extension of foreign business by the other British clearing banks necessitated the establishment of 'Intelligence Departments' to obtain information and monitor the economies of the countries in which the branches or agencies were situated, their customers and other banking firms with which they came into contact.[117] The flow of information from the overseas branches to the headquarters in London was important to their success and the lack of it could undermine a branch's business. Further minor obstacles could also arise from undertaking banking business abroad. The *Magazine* noted in 1913 that a 'knowledge of French, German and Spanish is very desirable, and it is here that we find Englishmen at a great disadvantage compared with men of continental nationality'. However, this problem was not viewed as insurmountable, as the Institute of Bankers promptly arranged for language tuition for its members, albeit 'at a nominal fee'.[118]

Despite the difficulties that the British domestic commercial banks had in establishing branches abroad, it was inevitable that these banks would continue to undergo a process of internationalisation due to their cosmopolitan environment (the City); the impact of foreign competition in Britain; the development of communications; and the ever-expanding global markets of the twentieth century. As early as 1891, the *Bankers Magazine* commented that:

> As every additional link in communication between one country and another is added to the already existing and extensive chain – as the telegraph takes the place of the ordinary post, and the telephone of the ordinary telegraph – it is more and more the case that the markets of the world become one.[119]

Conclusion

Contemporary sources demonstrate the differing responses of bankers to developments in their profession around the turn of the century. Opinions expressed not only differed but changed considerably over time, and the *Bankers Magazine* in particular reflected this variety of debate. With regard to concentration in banking, regret at the decline of private banking and the upsurge of joint stock banks tended to be replaced by a positive attitude towards larger joint stock institutions, especially as the First World War progressed. Bankers came to accept, despite their fondness for the 'old' methods of private, personal banking, that large banks with extensive resources were required to meet the growing demands of the twentieth century. However, such enthusiasm for growth was not always shared by all, as demonstrated by the reservations expressed concerning the speed of the amalgamation movement and the establishment of the Colwyn Committee. Bankers were consequently required to justify the changes in their profession and defend the growth in size of their institutions.

The increasing internationalisation of the City of London and the expansion of the domestic clearing banks abroad also evoked mixed responses. The insular attitude of the English commercial banks was called into question and the spectre of foreign banks on 'home soil' produced a realisation that British banks would have to compete on a new and different level. The consequent expansion of British banks on to the Continent, however, was not a success. Those who had expressed reservation about the speed of foreign excursions by British banks were therefore justified.

Overall, the banking profession demonstrated a willingness to change and develop the financial system in England and Wales, especially those at the forefront of their field, such as Holden. The public reaction to such change, from bankers and elsewhere, displayed a gradual acceptance of and adaptation to developments – these voices were usually responding to rather than leading change. The innate caution of British bankers may be discerned in many of the views discussed in this chapter. British bankers are frequently criticised for such conservatism but in the case of expansion abroad, more reticence was required by the clearing banks. Moreover, it is likely that displays of caution would have been welcomed by depositors in British banks, if not their borrowing customers!

An attempt has been made here not to measure concentration or internationalisation in monetary or performance terms but rather to measure these developments in terms of the perceptions of contemporary bankers. These perceptions were (and are) just as important to opinion makers and governments as actual business outcomes.

Notes

1. Many thanks to Phillip Cottrell; to Sara Kinsey and Edwin Green of the Midland Bank Archives; and to the staff at the Guildhall Library, London.
2. The most comprehensive coverage of London responses in the *City* of London to changes during this period are provided by Kynaston (1995).
3. For a complete list of members see the *Bankers Magazine* (hereafter *BM*), 1918, vol. 106, p. 46.
4. Ibid.
5. 'The Report of the Treasury Committee on Bank Amalgamations', *BM*, 1918, vol. 106, pp. 46–50.
6. *BM*, 1895, vol. 59, part 1.
7. *BM*, 1889, p. 385.
8. *BM*, 1893, vol. 55, part 1, p. 566.
9. *BM*, 1889, p. 529.
10. *BM*, 1901, vol. 72, p. 2.
11. Ibid.
12. Messrs Prescott, Cave, Buxton, Loder and Co., Messrs Dimsdale, Fowler, Barnard and Dimsdales, Messrs Tugwell, Brymer and Co. (of Bath), and Messrs Miles, Cave and Co. (of Bristol).
13. *BM*, 1891, vol. 11, part 1, p. 96.
14. *BM*, 1915, vol. 99, p. 404.
15. *BM*, 1891, vol. 11, part 1, p. 96.
16. *BM*, 1884, pp. 374–8.
17. *BM*, 1893, vol. 55, part 1, p. 566.
18. *BM*, 1899, vol. 68, pp. 219–20.
19. *BM*, 1902, vol. 74, p. 28.

20. Ibid.
21. *BM*, 1889, p. 385. Amalgamations provided 'a means of business expansion which, without a large expenditure in the institution of branches, is not otherwise possible'.
22. *BM*, 1900, vol. 70, p. 325.
23. *BM*, 1889, p. 389.
24. Ibid., p. 387.
25. *BM*, 1898, vol. 66, p. 588.
26. *BM*, 1889, pp. 387–8.
27. Ibid., p. 389.
28. The journal was established as a rival to the *BM* but only one compendium volume for 1905 has been found in the Midland Bank Archives (hereafter MBA).
29. *Bank Notes*, Jan. 1905, p. 10.
30. *BM*, 1901, vol. 72, p. 4.
31. *BM*, 1904, vol. 78, p. 160.
32. MBA: Sir Edward Holden's Statement to the Standing Committee on Bank Amalgamations, 12 June 1918, p. 13.
33. *BM*, 1889, p. 385.
34. *BM*, 1898, vol. 66, p. 588.
35. *BM*, 1889, p. 530.
36. *Bank Notes*, Jan. 1905, p. 10.
37. *BM*, 1901, vol. 72, p. 4.
38. Ibid.
39. Ibid.
40. *BM*, 1915, vol. 99, p. 404.
41. MBA: Sir Edward Holden's Statement to the Standing Committee on Bank Amalgamations, 12 June 1918, p. 11.
42. 'Banking Fusions', *BM*, 1919, vol. 108, p. 618.
43. *BM*, 1914, vol. 97, p. 393.
44. *BM*, 1904, vol. 78, p. 4.
45. *BM*, 1901, vol. 71, p. 391.
46. *BM*, 1919, vol. 108, p. 693.
47. *BM*, 1904, vol. 78, p. 160.
48. Ibid., p. 59.
49. *BM*, 1898, vol. 66, p. 588.
50. *BM*, 1914, vol. 97, p. 393.
51. *BM*, 1898, vol. 66, p. 588.
52. *BM*, 1900, vol. 70, p. 327.
53. *BM*, 1889, p. 385.
54. *BM*, 1888, p. 1301.
55. *BM*, 1914, vol. 98, p. 164.
56. *BM*, 1899, vol. 68, p. 320.
57. Ibid., p. 216.
58. *BM*, 1900, vol. 70, p. 328.
59. *BM*, 1909, p. 736.
60. *BM*, 1914, vol. 98, p. 163.
61. Ibid.
62. Ibid.
63. 'The Report of the Treasury Committee on Bank Amalgamations', *BM*, 1918, p. 48.

64. *BM*, 1909, p. 736.
65. *BM*, 1904, vol. 78, p. 160.
66. Ibid.
67. *BM*, 1914, vol. 98, p. 138.
68. *BM*, 1919, vol. 108, p. 693.
69. *BM*, 1900, vol. 70, p. 330.
70. Ibid.
71. *BM*, 1889, p. 389.
72. *BM*, 1904, vol. 78, p. 160.
73. Ibid.
74. *BM*, 1889, p. 530.
75. *BM*, 1914, vol. 98, p. 138.
76. 'The Report of the Treasury Committee on Bank Amalgamations', *BM*, 1918, pp. 49–50.
77. *BM*, 1919, vol. 108, p. 618.
78. *BM*, 1918, vol. 106, p. 396.
79. *BM*, 1919, vol. 108, p. 693.
80. *BM*, 1918, vol. 106, p. 78.
81. Ibid.
82. *BM*, 1919, vol. 108, p. 616.
83. Ibid.
84. Ibid., p. 617.
85. MBA: Sir Edward Holden's Statement to the Standing Committee on Bank Amalgamations, 12 June 1918, pp. 1–2.
86. Ibid., p. 8.
87. Ibid., p. 9.
88. *BM*, 1918, vol. 106, p. 401.
89. *BM*, 1881, p. 191.
90. Ibid., pp. 193–4.
91. *Journal of the Institute of Bankers* (hereafter *JIB*), 1900, vol. 21, pp. 51 and 61.
92. Ibid., pp. 74 and 66.
93. Ibid., p. 49.
94. *BM*, 1900, vol. 69, p. 354.
95. Ibid., p. 355.
96. Ibid., p. 403.
97. Ibid.
98. Ibid.
99. Ibid., p. 404.
100. *BM.*, 1901, vol. 71, p. 376.
101. Ibid., pp. 376 and 754.
102. Ibid., p. 376.
103. *JIB*, 1900, vol. 21, pp. 66–7.
104. Ibid., pp. 66 and 76.
105. Ibid., p. 68.
106. Ibid., p. 76.
107. *BM*, 1913, vol. 96, p. 165.
108. Ibid., pp. 53–6.
109. *JIB*, 1914, Jan., p. 42.
110. Ibid., pp. 42–3.
111. *BM*, 1919, vol. 107, p. 417.

112. *BM*, 1918, vol. 106, p. 79.
113. *JIB*, 1914, Jan., p. 41.
114. MBA: Sir Edward Holden's Statement to the Standing Committee on Bank Amalgamations, 12 June 1918, p. 10.
115. Ibid.
116. Ibid.
117. *BM*, 1913, vol. 96, p. 167.
118. Ibid., p. 166.
119. *BM*, 1891, vol. 52, p. 159.

References

Capie, Forrest and Rodrik-Bali, Ghila (1982), 'Concentration in British banking 1870–1920', *Business History*, 24.

Carnevali, Francesca (1995), 'Finance in the regions: the case of England after 1945' in Cassis, Y., Feldman, G. D. and Olsson, V. (eds), *The Evolution of Financial Institutions and Markets in Twentieth-Century Europe*, Aldershot, Scolar Press.

Cassis, Youssef (1985), 'Management and strategy in the English joint-stock banks, 1890–1914', *Business History*, 27.

Cassis, Youssef (1991), 'Financial elites in three European centres: London, Paris, Berlin, 1880s–1930s', *Business History*, 33.

Cassis, Youssef (1994), *City Bankers, 1890–1914*, Cambridge, Cambridge University Press.

Collins, Michael (1988), *Money and Banking in the UK: A History*, London.

Cottrell, P. L. (1979), *Industrial Finance 1830–1914: The Finance and Organisation of Manufacturing Industry*, London, Methuen.

Cottrell, P. L. (1992), 'The domestic commercial banks and the City of London, 1870–1939' in Cassis, Youssef (ed.), *Finance and Financiers in European History, 1880–1960*, Cambridge, Cambridge University Press.

Crick, W. and Wadsworth, J. (1936), *A Hundred Years of Joint Stock Banking*, London, Hodder and Stoughton.

Green, Edwin (1979), *Debtors to the Profession. A History of the Institute of Bankers, 1879–1979*, London, Methuen.

Greene, Graham (1969), *Travels With My Aunt*, London, Penguin.

Holmes, A. R. and Green, Edwin (1986), *Midland. 150 Years of Banking Business*, London, B. T. Batsford.

Jones, Geoffrey (1982), 'Lombard Street on the Riviera: the British clearing banks and Europe 1900–1960', *Business History*, 24.

Jones, Geoffrey (1993), *British Multinational Banking 1830–1990*, Oxford, Oxford University Press.

Kynaston, David (1995), *The City of London Vol. 2: Golden Years, 1890–1914*, London, Pimlico.

Newton, Lucy (1996), 'Regional bank–industry relations during the mid-nineteenth century: links between bankers and manufacturing in Sheffield c.1850 to c. 1885', *Business History*, 38.

Nishimura, S. (1971), *The Decline of Inland Bills of Exchange in the London Money Market 1855–1913*, Cambridge, Cambridge University Press.

Sayers, R. S. (1957), *Lloyds Bank in the History of English Banking*, Oxford, Clarendon Press.

Sykes, Joseph (1926),*The Amalgamation Movement in English Banking, 1825–1924*, London, King.

CHAPTER TEN

Aspects of Commercial Banking in Northern and Central Europe, 1880–1931[1]

Philip L. Cottrell

> As banking develops and becomes concentrated in a small number of establishments, the banks grow from humble middlemen into powerful monopolies having at their command almost the whole of the money capital of all the capitalists and small businessmen and also the larger part of the means of production and of the sources of raw materials of the given country and in a number of countries. This transformation of numerous humble middlemen into a handful of monopolists represents one of the fundamental processes in the growth of capitalism into capitalist imperialism; for this reason we must first of all deal with the concentration of banking. (V. I. Lenin, 1916)

Lenin was not the only commentator at the beginning of the twentieth century who called attention to the rapidly altering configuration of Europe's financial sector, and to its possible causes and consequences. In his pamphlet, Lenin drew upon and responded to both Hobson (Hobson, 1902)[2] and Hilferding (Hilferding, 1910),[3] and utilised Riesser's work (Riesser, 1905) in developing his arguments and counter-arguments. Riesser was a director of the Darmstädter, a German 'great' bank, and his monumental volume derived from an attempt to defend these institutions against the possibility of government regulation. Contrary to Lenin, he maintained that banking concentration had not diminished the extent of competition within and across the financial sector (Tilly, 1992: 93).

The impact of changes in the structure of banking within Northern and Central Europe during the opening decades of the twentieth century produced reactions not only from political philosophers and defenders of vested interests. The creation of the 'Big Five' in 1918 – the climax of the amalgamation process within English banking – resulted in public fears of a 'money trust'. This anxiety was so deeply felt that the Chancellor of the Exchequer established the Colwyn Committee to investigate the issue. The arising report recommended controls to sustain spatial banking competition, and called for the creation of a small committee to monitor further mergers. Although the government allowed the arising legislation to lapse in May 1919, none the less at the close of that year the Treasury required each of the 'Big Five' to abstain from further major merger activity and, moreover, Walter Leaf, Chairman of the Committee of the London Clearing Banks, was required to give additional assurances. However, the Governor of the Bank of England found this informal understanding increasingly unsatisfactory, to the extent of drawing up a code of practice in 1923, which was subsequently agreed with the Chancellor. This barred the 'Big Five' from mergers either among themselves or with other banks (Sayers, 1976: 235–43).

Montagu Norman, Governor of the Bank of England, was anxious to sustain banking competition, and during the 1920s tried to use the difficulties of provincial banks in Lancashire to create a 'Big Sixth'. Despite the burdens of their illiquid engagements to the cotton industry, independence none the less remained an ingrained trait of northwestern banking. As a result, the only success of the Governor's competition policy was the merger in December 1927 between the Bank of Liverpool & Martins and the Lancashire & Yorkshire (Chandler, 1964: 443–7). At the same time, Norman campaigned to prevent the 'Big Five' from becoming international banks, maintaining this obdurate stance until he retired from the Bank.

These few, illustrative instances indicate the importance of changes in banking structures – concentration and internationalisation – for early twentieth-century European society. However, their discussion requires us to consider the period from the late nineteenth century until the early 1930s. Although the First World War is often taken as a demarcation point, the resulting historical periodisation can be artificial, since in many respects the Great War, through its various, varying demands and effects, acted as a catalyst in accelerating the pace of processes already under way. The war's impact upon banking was substantial but it was the global economic events of 1931, especially the international liquidity panic, that finally brought to a close the changes in banking that had set in during the late nineteenth century. The half century taken for examination will be largely viewed from a mid-way vantage point in 1914. It allows a survey of the inception of the major waves of banking concentration and internationalisation that had got under way during the late nineteenth century, and a review of the culmination of these processes during the 1920s.

Support for this perspective comes from recent scholarly examinations of the development of European banking and finance over the period 1880 to 1960. These led Harold James to point to the parallel inception from the 1880s of significant structural changes in banking within Belgium, Britain, France, Germany and Switzerland, which 'also coincided with the growth and development of overseas financing'. Furthermore, he found that the world depression of the early 1930s brought about 'a quite dramatic shift *within* the financial sector', so that 'the years between the 1880s and the 1930s thus emerge as a sort of golden age, the "era of the great banks", within the broader framework of financial innovation and modernization' (James, 1992: 114–15).

The following discussion will necessarily have a broad-brush nature but, to give at least some depth and perspective, it will be restricted to a consideration of the banking experience within Northern and Central Europe. As already indicated, this region was the cradle of late nineteenth-century changes in banking. The context for the rise of concentration and further internationalisation within the area, in terms of variations in the medium-term development of the national economies that comprise it, was broadly neutral. Any national differences in banking experience therefore cannot be attributed simply to either very marked disparities in economic development or sharply diverging trends in economic performance. Table 10.1 indicates that the economies of Northern and Central Europe were the richest, materially, while France, Germany and the United Kingdom, the leading industrial and trading states, collectively accounted for 47.3 per cent of European total GNP in 1913.[4] Some caveats, none the less, do have to be entered.

Whereas the economy of Austria–Hungary, like that of France, had experienced slow but sustained industrialisation over the nineteenth century, its fabric was shattered by the geopolitical results of the First World War, which had effects on its banking system. The economic modernisation of Scandinavia became marked during the decades before 1914 and, although affected by the war and its consequences, was not impeded. The German economy came under the greatest strain over the 1910s and 1920s. None the less, whereas the impact of the First World War fragmented, in some important respects, the economic homogeneity of Northern and Central Europe, it did not halt concentration and internationalisation within this region's banking systems.

Concentration and internationalisation will be considered initially – in Section I – by reviewing some of the relevant work concerned with comparative banking undertaken by a group of applied economists. Their studies, carried out during the 1950s, commented upon banking structures in which there had been little significant change since the mid-1930s. This section also considers, albeit briefly, the extent to which banking historians have undertaken generic studies of internationalisation and concentration. In Section II, this chapter returns to the quotation with which it opened, through trying to discern how a (hypo-

Table 10.1   Real GNP per capita, in 1960 US dollars and prices, for Europe and selected European countries in 1880, 1913 and 1929

	1880	1913	1929
United Kingdom	680	965	1038
Belgium	589	894	1098
Denmark	396	862	945
The Netherlands	542	754	1008
Norway	464	749	1033
Germany	443	743	770
France	464	689	982
Sweden	303	680	897
Austria	(315)	(498)	720
		(600)	
Europe	388	543	571

Note: With the exception of Austria, data for 1880 and 1913 are with respect to national boundaries pertaining in 1913, while data for 1929 relate to post-1918 national boundaries. In the case of Austria, the data for 1880 are for Austria–Hungary and have a higher margin of error – significantly greater than 4 per cent – than elsewhere within the table; with respect to 1913 the first figure is for Austria–Hungary, while the second is a 'guess-estimate' for Cisleithania (i.e. the Austrian 'half' of the Dual Monarchy) and the data have higher margins of error; and for 1929 the data are for Austria alone.

Source: P. Bairoch, 1976

thetical) English banker in 1914 might have tried to confront the arguments of Lenin and others. Data abstracted from the *Banking Almanac* for 1914 are deployed (Inglis Palgrave, 1914, hereafter *Banking Almanac*) and, following a review of their nature, they are then utilised to explore the extent of competition within Northern and Central European banking, with attention paid to the size of banks and the nature of banking markets. The focus of Section III is an examination of Northern and Central Europe's largest 25 banks in *c.* 1914 through surveying the various strategies employed by their managements to secure expansion. An attempt is made to place the position of these 25 banks in perspective by estimating the extent of concentration in 1914 within the nine national banking systems under review, which also reveals the shortcomings of the data source. Section III concludes with a discussion of how concentration developed during the 1920s. Internationalisation is considered in Section IV but in terms of a process that had been well established during the eighteenth century and, furthermore, which took on a wide variety of forms, being not simply confined to the conduct of business overseas. Section V is in lieu of a general conclusion.

I.   Review of studies[5]

'Comparative banking' flourished at the London School of Economics as a result of one of the interests of Professor Richard S. Sayers. An outcome of these scholarly endeavours, which had involved close contact with bankers and financial institutions, was the publication in 1962 of *Banking in Western Europe*. The central concern of this volume's contributors was an 'analysis of the process of credit and the control of monetary flows' (Johnson and Sayers, 1962: 237), but the starting-point for each country study was a careful description and review of the respective banking system, often largely unchanged since the mid-1930s.[6] As the fieldwork for the various essays was undertaken during the 1950s – a decade of domestic recovery and inconvertible currencies – it is understandable that the process of internationalisation was not addressed. However, Sayers was aware of the new directions that were becoming apparent during the late 1950s and pointed out in the preface that the volume had been conceived before the development of the Eurodollar market (Sayers, 1962: vi).

Perhaps more surprising, especially with the historical perspective provided in many of the country studies, is the lack of any particular attention paid to the development of concentration. Instead, this process was accepted by all the contributors as being almost a natural occurrence with, for instance, Wilson regarding the French banking system as having undergone a 'gradual process of evolution' with the consequence that the 'tendency towards concentration and integration will be maintained' (Wilson, 1962: 1). Clayton, in his commentary on Sweden, took a comparable stance, if not putting it in stronger terms, by maintaining that there has been 'since the beginning of the century the slow but *inevitable* [my stress] concentration of resources in the hands of fewer and fewer banks' (Clayton, 1962b: 260). All in all, this group of academic commentators found concentration unremarkable, although they addressed its consequences.[7] Instead, it was the exceptions to concentration that they felt required an explanation.

Wilson went to great lengths to try to account for the survival in the mid-1950s of regional, but especially local, banks within the French system (Wilson, 1962: 6–7). Opie pointed to both the still-flourishing condition of private banking in West Germany (BRD) and the sustained independence of local banks in Southern Germany (Opie, 1962: 55, 58). The persistence of unit banking in Norway was ascribed to geo-

graphical causes, particularly the country's terrain with its costly consequences for the development of transport and communication (Sayers,
1962b: 300). Lastly, with regard to the perceived need to account for
countervailing forces to concentration, Clayton emphasised that Denmark still lacked a banking system since, in his view, banking in this
country during the 1950s was marked by 'diversity' and the 'absence of
strong connecting links'. Furthermore, he not only stressed the competitive tensions present between branches of the four major Danish banks
and local, unit institutions, but also pointed to the important role
performed by savings banks, arising from their highly developed and
strongly rooted nature (Clayton, 1962a: 318, 320–21).

A substantial review of the fruits of this approach to the study of
banking has recently been produced by Wilson, a member of the group
that had collaborated with Sayers (Wilson, 1986). Whereas, once more,
Wilson omitted to consider internationalisation,[8] he attempted to determine the factors responsible for differences between banking structures
and concluded that they were 'environmental'. Wilson argued that an
economy's industrial character, coupled with the historical tradition
and political outlook of its society, accounts for any particularities
displayed by its banking system in the late twentieth century. However,
this is substantially qualified by the insistence that such intra-country
differences have greatly diminished, due to the growth of global communication in various and manifold forms. Arising from this perspective, Wilson put forward a general rule that there has occurred over
time a 'gradual reduction in the number of banking units', 'a growth in
their average size', and 'a more widespread resort to branch banking'
(Wilson, 1986: 1–4).

Whereas those who undertook the country studies during the 1950s
had accepted concentration in banking as natural, in retrospect Wilson
argued that economic growth has played a central role in its rise. He
maintained that the prime cause of concentration has been economic
structural change – in terms of the conjunction of rising population and
the emergence of urban industrialism, with an important feature of the
latter being the increasing size of the business unit. The growth of an
adequate communication system was seen by Wilson as being related to
these two developments, while, for banking, it facilitated the transmission of remittances, the spread of information and the spatial expansion
of branch networks. Furthermore, improved communication enabled
the establishment of wider banking areas, implicitly considered by Wilson
as bank hinterlands, or financial catchment basins. The spatial expansion of a bank's sphere of business led to both 'a better spread of risks
in the distribution [of] loans and advances', and the greater gathering of
'resources for expanding loan business' (Wilson, 1986: 12–15).

With an approach that linked concentration to structural economic change, Wilson was forced, as in the earlier country banking studies, to give considerable attention to the persistence of what he termed 'hybrid' banking systems. These arise from the coexistence of large banks, possessing nationwide branch networks, with regional or local institutions, as in Belgium, Denmark, France, Germany (BRD) and the Netherlands.[9] Yet, it was only in the cases of Denmark and France, and largely with respect to the latter's banking system, that Wilson provided an explanation for these exceptions to his posited 'general rule'. He maintained that it was contravened in these particular countries' banking systems due to certain social, almost psychological, attitudes. They consist of deeply rooted individualism; personal and/or family loyalties over generations within certain social groups to particular banks; a demand for personal service; and particularism as in local patriotisms or ties (Wilson, 1986: 134–7, 217).

Banking historians have generally paid almost as little attention to the development of concentration as have scholars interested in comparative banking. Although concentration features as a shaping force in the histories of particular banks, it is somewhat remarkable that until very recently there have been few generic studies of the process, as an examination of the historiography of either England or Germany demonstrates. In the case of England, Sykes's monograph, written immediately following the creation of the 'Big Five', remained the sole authoritative commentary for 58 years (Sykes, 1926). In their reconsideration of the effects of the English banking amalgamation movement, Capie and Rodrik-Bali (1982) pointed out that the mergers by themselves did not automatically bring about concentration – certainly during the initial phases of the decline in the number of banks. They used the share of total deposits as an indicator and found that the proportion held collectively by the largest five banks only increased substantially after 1910. Previously, the position of the five largest banks had been counterbalanced by the continuing expansion of smaller banks whose collective share of deposits – in the case of the sixth to the tenth largest banks – increased from 7.8 per cent to 21.7 per cent between 1870 and 1910. Likewise, in terms of historians' interest, Riesser's vast contemporary study of German banking concentration (Riesser, 1905) stood the test of time until 1982,[10] when Pohl's monograph was published (Pohl, 1982).[11]

During the second half of the twentieth century, the study of the historical development of European banking has largely focused upon what functions and roles banks performed and discharged as financial intermediaries within industrialisation. This built upon Gerschenkron's hypothesis (Gerschenkron, 1952), together with theoretical develop-

ments, such as the work of Gurley and Shaw. Some of the most significant work, utilising a comparative context, has been undertaken by a
group of scholars established by Cameron since the mid-1960s. They
took the onset of concentration as an end-point for their respective
country studies since, in their view, it marked 'financially' the conclusion of the first phase of modern economic growth (Cameron et al.,
1967; Cameron, 1972). More recently, scholarly effort has been substantially directed to reviewing the role of banks within Europe's smaller
economies during the interwar period. This has been led by Alice
Teichova, Håkan Lindgren and their senior associates (Cottrell et al.,
1992; Teichova et al., 1994). These investigators have also largely employed concentration to establish the framework for their approach,
since they have to a very great degree been concerned with the industrial relationships of the largest banks – those that were the products of
amalgamations and mergers.

However, there has not been the same comparable neglect by banking
historians of the development of internationalisation. The most recent
product of the collaborative work of the 'Cameron group' is a consideration of international banking during the fifty years before the First
World War (Cameron and Bovykin, 1991). In the case of Britain, the
centre of international banking during the nineteenth century, the long-
standing surveys of Baster, published during the 1920s and 1930s (Baster,
1929, 1935), have recently been replaced by Jones's wide-ranging, mag-
isterial analysis (Jones, 1993). Given the current position of the scholarly literature, the central and major parts of this chapter will be
concerned with concentration, whereas aspects of internationalisation
will be considered in the concluding section.

II.   The structure of banking in Northern and Central Europe c. 1914

An English banker during the 1910s, provoked by the arguments of
Hobson, Hilferding or Lenin, may well have turned in his parlour to a
copy of *The Banking Almanac* to seek foundations for his reactions.
This English yearbook, first published in 1844, will also be used here to
gain some impression of the extent of the processes of concentration
and internationalisation. Compiled in London, its coverage is substantially complete for the United Kingdom. Furthermore, it included a 'List
of the principal foreign and colonial banks and bankers' which, in the
1914 edition, formed a section of 337 pages covering 1368 institutions.
However, this began with the cautionary note that 'The great increase
in the number of Banks and Bank Offices included renders economy of
space essential, but every care is taken to supply the information needed

by Bankers.' As a result, any set of European banks abstracted from the *Almanac* is likely to be biased. On the one hand, United Kingdom institutions will be fully represented but, on the other, banks of other countries will be under-represented. It is very evident that, in particular, smaller, non-United Kingdom banks are not included in the *Almanac* and it would appear that the main criterion applied by its compilers for giving a foreign financial institution an entry was that it had London agents and therefore might be of interest to a British banker.[12]

Yet, it is also doubtful whether any positive improvement upon the data provided in the *Almanac* is feasible. This is very evident from the recent, exhaustive work of Nishimura on the business of French provincial banks during the *fin-de-siècle* period (Nishimura, 1995). He concludes that 'there were thousands of provincial banks in France before 1914', but the precise number of these institutions remains difficult to establish. Estimates indicate 1318 in 1891, between 1000 and 1200 in 1908 and, in terms of the best-based 'census', 2418 banks in the provinces and 740 in Paris (besides the four major joint stock banks) in 1910. Moreover, there are substantial implications for any attempt to measure concentration in the French banking system immediately before 1914. An extrapolation, based on the geometrical average provincial bank by balance sheet size, amongst those for which Nishimura was able to find evidence in the files of the Bank of France (65 in all), results in these provincial institutions having in 1910 a possible aggregate balance sheet total of FF 24 180m, as against FF 6453m for the four joint stock deposit banks. His data allow no further incautious development to the whole domestic banking system, since they do not provide any indications for Parisian banks. None the less, this cautionary outcome has continually to be borne in mind in what follows, because, with the nature of the source deployed – the *Almanac* – all that can be provided are indications and tendencies. They may well be sufficient for present purposes, but no greater weight can be placed upon them.

The entries in the *Almanac* for both United Kingdom and 'foreign' banks vary considerably in terms of the amount of detail they provide. The minimum given is the name of the bank, the location of its head office and its London agents. The maximum is extensive, including date of formation, the composition of its board, if corporate, its balance sheet and the location of its branches. The following discussion is based upon, when possible, abstracting from the *Almanac* for 1914 for Northern and Central Europe the following information: the name of a bank, the location of its head office(s), the number, if any, of branches within its network and its balance sheet total. However, some of these details are in themselves problematic.

One difficulty arises from what constituted a branch – as opposed to a sub-branch or agency – which is directly emphasised by the *Almanac*'s own commentary. The 'Preliminary notice to readers' in the 1914 edition included a list of new United Kingdom branches, but many, especially outside London, also have noted against them that they were only open on certain days of the working week. This practice is amplified in the 'Introductory remarks', where it is pointed out that:

> The proportion of offices not open daily has increased in England and Wales. From being about one-twelfth in the years 1886–1888 it is now nearly one-quarter of the whole number [6709]. The proportion is only 2 per cent of the whole number in Scotland [1235], it has increased distinctly in Ireland, where it is now 37 per cent of the total [841].

These cautionary remarks have resulted in the adoption here of what might be called 'a global approach to counting bank branches'. All subsidiary offices, whether branch, sub-branch or agency, have been aggregated to produce the total number of 'branches' for an institution. Any attempt to differentiate further appeared to be undercut by the United Kingdom evidence of there being, particularly in Ireland and England, often little difference between a branch, sub-branch, or agency in terms of hours opened and therefore business conducted during the years before 1914. As a result, derived quantitative pointers to the prevalence of branching, or the extent of branch networks, are probably over- rather than underestimates. The problem arising from the use of balance sheets (where available) need not be laboured to the same extent. Hansemann of the Disconto-Gesellschaft may have had a point when he maintained that the rise of the Deutsche Bank to surpass his own institution was due to 'nothing but entry cancellations' (Gall, 1995: 22).

All the bankers and banks listed in the *Almanac* for Austria (Cisleithania), Belgium, Denmark, France, Germany, the Netherlands, Norway, Sweden and the United Kingdom have been abstracted to form the basic data set, which is provided in the Appendix.[13] In the case of the United Kingdom, not only have all domestic banks been itemised, but details have also been taken for British international bankers and banks – but only when either the head office was located in London and/or the house's, or institution's, balance sheet was denominated in sterling, showing that they were British-based concerns. This approach is necessary in order to place the United Kingdom data on a par with those abstracted for banks in other countries. It arises from, for instance, French banks, such as the Crédit Lyonnais or the Société Générale, having sizeable overseas branch networks; Belgian, French and German overseas banks having European headquarters in the same manner as

many of their British peers; and the continuing presence of a significant
private/merchant banking community throughout Northern and Central Europe. The result is a data set consisting of 598 bankers and
banks. It contains balance sheets for 334 bankers and banks but, in
general, omits such information for private banks and what would
seem, from other information provided in the *Almanac*, smaller institutions. There are many ways of deploying this data set.[14] Initially its
general characteristics will be considered.

One striking feature is the age profile of the bankers and banks that
comprise it, with some 396 entries providing the date of the establishment of the house, or the institution, concerned; this is portrayed in
Figure 10.1. Within the data set, 50 banks had been established before
1820, with the earliest dating from before 1700, namely De Neuflize et
Cie (1667), Child & Co. (1673) and the Bank of Scotland (1695). By
1837, 100 banks and banking houses had been established, the numbers being augmented in particular by the first major pan-European
wave of joint stock bank formation which occurred during the first half
of the 1830s. The 200 mark is reached by 1866 and the 300 by 1892,

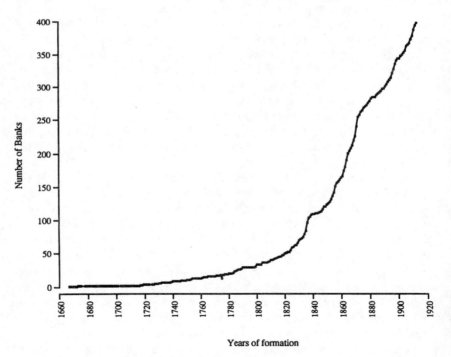

10.1   Longevity of banks within the sample
       Source: *Banking Alamanac*, 1914

following the mid-century liberalisation of company law. From all this, the longevity of many banks is clearly evident, with over half the banks and banking houses in the set having been in business in 1913 for over 47 years. Equally, as Figure 10.1 also shows, the data set also contains a sizeable number of more recent formations, 90 having been founded between 1894 and 1913 during the *fin-de-siècle* upswing of European economic growth.

This age profile does give confidence in the general validity of the data set. It comprises, in something like the appropriate proportions, whole ranges of age cohorts of banks and bankers. These mark out particularly those waves of formation that occurred, first, during the 1830s, second, over the liberal 'golden age' of the mid-century (1850–73), and lastly during the further acceleration of economic growth experienced by Europe from the 1890s.

The composition of the age structure of the data set points, generally, to a service industry within Northern and Central Europe characterised by freedom of entry. The sustained rise in the numbers of banks displayed by the age profile of the data set indicates freedom of entry, since, overall, there are no significant periods when the gradient of the curve eases to any appreciable degree. Indeed, short pauses in the profile are only noticeable on close inspection during the 1840s and early 1880s. The continually rising number of banks and banking houses provides one indication of the persistence of a competitive banking market. Moreover, banking generally did not involve sizeable sunk costs, although they may have become more significant as banks came to house themselves in increasingly specialised buildings.

These bald generalisations, however, necessarily require some further comment and qualification. In France, on the one hand, branches of the three national deposit banks were opened from the mid-century along provincial towns' main thoroughfares, while, on the other, local banks' premises were located in the side streets and were far less grand establishments. This indicates a bifurcated national market and, indeed generally, Northern and Central Europe was not one, all-embracing banking market. It was further segmented by political boundaries, of which one consequence was differing legal jurisdictions and codes, and, due to differing organic economic processes, by the varying degree of specialisation of banking functions within national economies. Moreover, the development of the various constituent national economies within Northern and Central Europe (and, within them, at a regional level) had led to the emergence of a spectrum of banking habits. One example is sufficient to underscore this. Whereas bank deposits comprised about 85 per cent of the money stock in England and Wales in 1913, in France the comparable proportion in 1910 was about 44 per cent (Cameron et al., 1967: 42,

116). In addition, there were different national institutional structures and relationships. The continuing prevalence of independent provincial banking within France and Germany in 1914 was broadly facilitated by the readiness of the respective proto-central banks, through sizeable branch networks, to provide immediate access to discounting and remittance facilities. In some contrast, and with respect to other forms of national institutional structures, newly established English banks from the last quarter of the nineteenth century appear to have made little headway in gaining significant national market shares. This was due to the inability of their managements to obtain access, directly or indirectly, to the clearing system. The only exceptions were specialised overseas trade banks, such as the British Bank of Northern Commerce (formed in 1912), whose managements had little need in their activities for the domestic cheque-clearing system (Capie, 1988: 93–100).

The functional stratification of the banking market, national and local habits, and national institutional practices, all tempered the extent of general competition within Northern and Central Europe. But what was of concern to contemporaries by the opening years of the twentieth century was the growing size of banks. Figure 10.2 indicates the size of banks within the data set but also shows some of the problems in deploying the *Almanac* as a source.

The tall column to the left of 0 on the x axis arises from the number of banks and bankers – some 264 – where no balance sheet information is provided in the *Almanac*. It dominates the figure to the extent of minimising the value of the rest of the graphic display. It might be argued that to go any further in utilising the *Almanac* as a source would be comparable to mounting a production of *Hamlet* without the ghost. However, there are indications that the omission of these 264 institutions, when considering banks' sizes by balance sheet total, is not totally distorting. One portion of that dominating, but uninformative and disrupting, column in Figure 10.2 consists of a number of London merchant banks. Chapman's painstaking work (Chapman, 1984: 62) indicates that the total capital for 41 such houses in *c.*1900 amounted to £32.2m, from which he estimated an aggregate capital of £48.5m for this group's total known population of 106 houses. In terms of capitalisation, most were small – between £0.1m and £0.5m – while their intrinsic assets – reputation and connections – would never have properly featured in a balance sheet, even if it were available. All in all, the most that the inclusion here, if it were possible, of this group of London merchant banks would bring about is a heightening, to a degree, of the first eight columns to the right of 0 on the x axis in Figure 10.2.

If the institutions and houses for which balance sheets are not available in the *Almanac* are removed, then far more detail can be observed

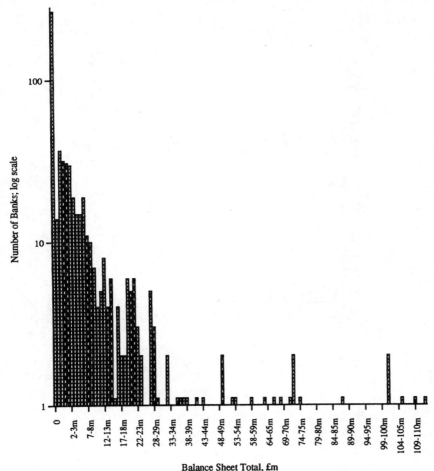

Note: y axis = log scale and where 1 arithmetic = 1.1 in order to give a log greater than 0

10.2   Size of banks in Northern and Central Europe by balance sheet total, c.1914
Source: *Banking Almanac*, 1914

for the remaining 334, as shown in Figure 10.3. This bar chart can be described simply because it reveals the presence of a few, very large banks and a multitude of much smaller institutions. One per cent of the number of houses and institutions that feature in Figure 10.3 have individual balance sheet totals in excess of £105m, whereas 50 per cent have balance sheets of less than £5m. It displays a polarised community

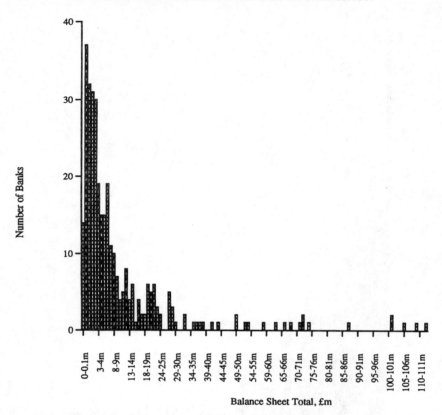

10.3   Size of banks in Northern and Central Europe by balance sheet total, *c.*
1914 (omitting institutions whose balance sheet total is not given in the
Banking Almanac)
Source: Banking Almanac, 1914

of a few giants but very many dwarfs, so that even amongst the largest
25 institutions balance sheet totals range from £112.9m to £29.7m. It is
clear why contemporaries were struck by the presence of a few, very
large banks in Northern and Central Europe immediately before 1914.

Equally evident from Figure 10.3, but perhaps less clear in its fullest
extent to observers in 1914, is the pyramidal nature of the banking
community due to the presence of numerous lesser institutions. Furthermore, there are some indications of banding within the size distribution
of the data set. This is a subjective observation, simply arising from
inspection of Figure 10.3, and, consequently, not too much weight must
be placed upon it. One band possibly lies between £75m and £49m
(balance sheet total) and contains 12 banks and another, although even

less clearly demarcated, lies between £30m and £20m and comprises 26 banks. Differentiation cannot be taken further as, in the case of banks with balance sheet totals of less than £20m, any attempt to do so encounters the broad base of the pyramid of size distribution. Contemporaries were concerned about the emergence of a few large banking concerns and this anxiety must be addressed. Yet, there are other aspects of concentration which call for at least some attention and which may cast some further light on national differences, upon which comment has already been made.

As well as the position of particular institutions in the marketplace, there is also the question of markets, aspects of which can be reviewed through examining geographical concentration. Table 10.2 provides some indications, but once more it must be emphasised that no great weight can be placed on the individual numbers contained within it – more important are relativities and ranking. This table lists in its upper portion the 'top ten' banking centres by three criteria, whereas the lower portion consists of the largest centres for other Northern and Central European countries which are not featured elsewhere. The order and position of London, Paris and Berlin will not cause surprise, but rather, perhaps, give further confidence in what else is portrayed. However, amongst these three centres there is one difference in that Berlin was not a major centre of branch banking, at least in its strictest sense. London ranks highest by any of the criteria applied and, given all that is known about the City's development as a banking centre over the nineteenth century, this requires no further comment. The positions of both Paris and Berlin have equally a substantial volume of contemporary and other literature documenting their growth and importance. Instead, what may cause some remark is that by 'aggregate balance sheet total', Vienna and Edinburgh are placed on a par, although this may be simply due to the paucity of the coverage of Austria (Cisleithania) within the relevant section of the *Almanac* for 1914. Perhaps the greatest interest might be aroused not so much by the 'league leaders' in Table 10.2 as by the other banking centres that feature there.

Some general points can be made about Table 10.2. Firstly, the inclusion of both Brussels and Antwerp under 'aggregate balance sheet total' is indicative of the nature of the economy and society of Belgium. Second, this particular criterion brings out the continuing importance of provincial centres, such as Dresden and Manchester, while also indicating the approximate parity of Amsterdam, Copenhagen and Stockholm. Column two, 'number of head offices', adds a little more detail, especially as it is based upon the whole data set and therefore includes those banks for which balance sheet totals were not available in the *Almanac*. As a result, with London or Hamburg or Frankfurt, smaller

Table 10.2 Ranking of banking centres in Northern and Central Europe, *c.* 1914

Banks with head office in:	Aggregate balance sheet total in £m	Banks with head office in:	Number of head offices	Banks with head offices in:	Number of branches
London	1069.7	London	141	London	6173
Paris	404.2	Paris	57	Paris	1875
Berlin	304.3	Berlin	21	Edinburgh	781
Vienna	197.5	Amsterdam	20	Manchester	658
Edinburgh	195.5	Hamburg	19	Belfast	378
Brussels	138.5	Frankfurt	15	Glasgow	323
Munich	126.9	Antwerp	14	Birmingham	206
Dresden	82.2	Brussels	14	Vienna	197
Manchester	81.7	Stockholm	9	Dublin	193
Antwerp	68.9	Vienna	9	Salisbury	181
Amsterdam (11th)	46.3	Copenhagen (11th)	7	Berlin (11th)	152
Copenhagen (12th)	42.8	Oslo (20th)	5	Amsterdam (17th)	78
Stockholm (13th)	41.3			Gothenburg (20th)	72
Oslo (29th)	15.1			Copenhagen (31st)	37
				Brussels (71st)	8
				Oslo (78th)	5

Source: Banking Almanac, 1914

106

and private institutions have something of a presence in this column of the table – to augment London's leading position and emphasise the importance of other German cities, besides Berlin and Dresden, as banking centres. Column three, 'number of branches', signifies clearly the importance of branching for general English, Irish and Scottish banking development through the presence of Salisbury, a Wiltshire cathedral city and agricultural marketing centre, but equally indicates the part it played in the growth of Paris and Vienna as metropolitan banking centres.

It may overstrain the strength of the data set but at least a cursory examination of the 'average institution' will bring the discussion back to individual banks, albeit, to begin with, anonymously, and may generate some shading to the commentary already made. Table 10.3 provides the detail, where column four, 'average number of branches', re-

Table 10.3   Ranking of banking centres in Northern and Central Europe by average balance sheet total and size of branch network

Banks with head offices in:	Average balance sheet total in £m	Banks with head offices in:	Average number of branches
Belfast	92.2	Birmingham	206.0
Munich	42.3	Salisbury	181.0
Dresden	41.1	Edinburgh	156.2
Edinburgh	39.1	Aberdeen	149.0
Cologne	35.5	Belfast	126.0
Berlin	27.7	Glasgow	107.6
Leipzig	23.6	Newcastle	99.0
Nyköping	23.2	Manchester	94.0
Vienna	21.9	Cork	91.0
Liverpool	21.7	Leeds	75.0
Paris (11th)	18.4	Helsingborgs (16th)	38.0
Brussels (12th)	17.3	Paris (19th)	32.9
Copenhagen (34th)	7.1	Dresden (21st)	29.0
Oslo (46th)	5.0	Vienna (27th)	21.0
		Amsterdam (57th)	8.6
		Copenhagen (65th)	5.3
		Liege (72nd)	3.5
		Skien (82nd)	2.0

Source: *Banking Almanac*, 1914

emphasises the importance of branch banking within the United Kingdom. This is underscored by, in the cases of Birmingham, Salisbury, Aberdeen, Newcastle and Cork, the 'average' branch network being for one bank only – the United Counties, the Wilts & Dorset Banking Co., the North of Scotland Bank, the North Eastern Banking Company and the Munster & Leinster Bank, respectively. In turn, this points to the continuing resilience of provincial banks in certain circumstances.

Similarly, but in a different way, column two, 'average balance sheet total', underlines that even during the 1910s, *pace* the presence of Berlin, geographical concentration had not yet diminished totally the importance of the provincial banking centre, or rather the provincial bank, and in the case of Nyköping, Sweden, this is again related to one institution – the Sodermanlands Enskilda Bank.

III. Expansion of Northern and Central European banks: strategies and implications

Table 10.4 lists in rank order the largest, in terms of balance sheet total, 25 banks in Northern and Central Europe, *c.* 1914. With regard to the overall distribution of the data set, this 'élite' group also includes banks within that stratification band, discerned subjectively above, as lying between £75m and £29.7m. In terms of their age in 1914, half of this élite group were founded during the mid-nineteenth century or later, but the remainder had enjoyed even greater longevity.

Lloyds has some claim to be the oldest institution amongst this cohort, but which bank had greatest longevity in *c.* 1914 is a moot point. Although a progenitor of Lloyds – the private bank of Taylors & Lloyds – had been established in Birmingham in 1765, Lloyds did not begin to assume its modern – i.e. 1914 form – until 1865 with the incorporation of Lloyds Banking Company, which was eight years after the bank's association with the Taylor family had ceased. The changing legal and financial constitution of banks over their historical development was commonplace, the origins of Barclays having been traced back to 1690, but, again, the amalgamation and incorporation to form the kernel of the 1914 bank only took place in 1896. The longevity of banks within this élite group is not simply an antiquarian interest, as it may have a bearing upon concentration.

It has been suggested that concentration within industries composed of incorporated companies – undertakings whose mortality is not directly linked to that of their proprietors – increases over time due to what has been termed 'spontaneous drift'. With undertakings having long lifespans through incorporation, concentration may arise from 'as

Table 10.4   The largest 25 banks in Northern and Central Europe, *c.* 1913, ranked by balance sheet total

Bank	(i)	(ii)	(iii)	(iv)	(v)
Deutsche Bank	1870	Berlin	d	14	112 998 222
Crédit Lyonnais	1863	Paris	f	373	110 332 716
London, City & Midland Bank	1870	London	gb	845	105 951 247
Lloyds Bank	1765	London	gb	651	101 846 765
London County & Westminster Bank	1836	London	gb	358	101 079 034
Société Générale	1864	Paris	f	1031	87 062 868
Comptoir National d'Escompte de Paris	1848	Paris	f	331	74 555 737
National Provincial Bank of England	1833	London	gb	418	72 310 905
Dresdner	1872	Dresden	d	50	72 275 403
Société Générale de Belgique	1822	Brussels	b	0	71 884 257
Bayerische Hypotheken und Wechsel Bank	1835	Munich	d	0	66 852 603
Barclay & Co. Ltd	1896	London	gb	598	62 960 616
Direction Der Disconto-Gesellschaft	1851	Berlin	d	13	58 013 331
Parr's Bank	1865	London	gb	276	52 409 246
Österreichische Credit-Anstalt für Handel und Gewerbe	1855	Vienna	a	20	49 796 143
Union of London & Smiths Bank	1839	London	gb	214	49 284 778
Bank für Handel und Industrie	1853	Berlin/ Darmstadt	d	48	44 726 489
Capital & Counties Bank	1834	London	gb	480	43 671 404
London Joint Stock Bank	1836	London	gb	301	41 395 548
London & River Plate Bank	1862	London	gbf	30	38 193 519
Allgemeine Österreichische Boden-Credit-Anstalt	1864	Vienna	a	1	36 542 210
Schaaffhaus-en'scher Bankverein	1848	Cologne	d	30	35 474 833
Österreichische Länderbank	1880	Vienna	a	33	32 698 478
Bayerische Vereinsbank	1869	Munich	d	12	32 598 990
Standard Bank of South Africa	1862	London	gbf	216	29 724 123

Key: column (i) date of foundation; (ii) location of head office; (iii) national-ity: d = German; f = French; gb = British; b = Belgian; a = Austrian; gbf = British foreign bank; (iv) number of branches; (v) balance sheet total (in sterling)[15]

Source: *Banking Almanac,* 1914

simple and apparently innocuous a process as unconstrained variability in the growth rates of firms'. Drift will lead to concentration taking place in three distinct phases: initially at a slow rate; then marked acceleration; and finally a more gradual rise (Prais, 1976: 25–40). Spontaneous drift has not been accepted by all scholars of the development of business enterprise, with some placing considerably greater stress on the role of mergers in the emergence of large companies and thereby rising concentration (Hannah and Kay, 1977; Hart, 1979). The reasons for the size of some of these élite 25 banks will be considered below, but in general those of considerable longevity only began to expand once they had adopted a corporate form.

Northern and Central Europe's largest banks on the eve of the First World War were to be found in five countries. That they were located in the capitals of Austria (Cisleithania), France, Germany and the United Kingdom, given either the physical size of these countries or the nature of their economies, is not remarkable.

However, Table 10.4 indicates that some of the most important European banks in 1914 were located beyond Europe's metropolises. Four had their head offices situated in major provincial centres, but the way that the Bank für Handel und Industrie – the Darmstädter – is described in the *Almanac* is none the less telling, as it points to both this bank's provincial roots and the increasing centripetal power of the Berlin financial market from the 1880s. Lastly, the table indicates that a sizeable branch network was not a necessary concomitant of being a major European bank in 1914, and so appears to confront the Wilson rule. Three out of the top 25 banks had no branches whatsoever, while a further eight had apparently no more than 50 branches each. However, there was no simple relationship between the size and importance of a bank measured by its balance sheet total and by its branch network. Furthermore, information provided within the *Almanac* is not complete as it generally omits, with somewhat English myopia, to indicate subsidiary relationships and the presence of *Interessengemeinschaften*, or pooling agreements.

Any discussion of bank growth through the development of a branch network, thus bringing about *pari passu* greater banking concentration (the Wilson general rule), requires some differentiation. Broadly, three strategies for developing networks, or greater banking hinterlands, were pursued by the managements of the banks currently under discussion. These were: direct branch expansion not involving the acquisition of the offices of existing banks (and therefore not by merger), so perhaps pointing to 'spontaneous drift'; the acquisition of branches through amalgamation; and the establishment of subsidiaries, or other arrangements such as pooling, to form banking groups. Yet these approaches were not alternatives and the late nineteenth-century expansion of many of the 25 banks arose from combinations of all three strategies.

Amongst this élite group, the clearest case of growth through self-generated direct branch expansion is that of French institutions. Both the Crédit Lyonnais and the Société Générale rapidly developed networks of branches, following a pattern already established by the managements of the Comptoir National d'Escompte de Paris and the Crédit Industriel et Commercial. As a consequence, in 1881 the Crédit Lyonnais had offices in all major French towns and in 1889 the Société Générale had 148 branches. Moreover, the total domestic branch networks of all three large French banks continued to be expanded – from 195 offices in 1880 to 1519 by 1912 (Gueslin, 1992: 63). This drive into the domestic market was accompanied by direct canvassing for deposits, through the activities of door-to-door salesmen and the advertising by the banks of their services. Given the experience of their English peers, which generally indicates that the creation of branches *de novo* during the late nineteenth century was an expensive development, the question immediately arises as to why the managements of these French institutions did not expand their catchment areas by acquiring the offices of the numerous regional and local banks. Indeed, only the Crédit Industriel et Commercial followed something of a variant of the English approach through limiting spatially its direct branch expansion to the Paris area while acting as the metropolitan correspondent for the bigger provincial banks.

That comparative question simply does not apply to the way that the major national French corporate banks also rapidly established branch networks abroad. English domestic banks did not begin to open overseas offices until the years immediately before 1914, whereas the English overseas banks such as the London & River Plate Bank and the Standard Bank of South Africa directly created their respective branch networks in the southern hemisphere from their foundations in the 1860s. By 1860 the Comptoir National d'Escompte de Paris had offices in Bombay, Brussels, Calcutta, Hong Kong, London and Saigon. The Crédit Lyonnais opened in London in 1870, the Société Générale the following year and thereafter both these banks established considerable overseas presences (Nougaret, 1995: 71). Such was the extent of this foreign expansion that during the early 1910s the Crédit Lyonnais had 24 branches outside the domestic economy, excluding its offices in Algeria – a country regarded in many respects as a constituent of metropolitan France. Although the direct internationalisation of the Société Générale would appear to have been smaller – the bank had only two London offices and eight overseas agencies by the early twentieth century – its foreign presence was actually much greater, having been developed through interests in affiliated banks. These provided links to outlets in Alsace, Bulgaria, Belgium, Hungary, the Ottoman Empire, Russia, South America and Switzerland.[16] In terms of its arising 'banking group', by *c*. 1914 the Société Générale had 1463 subsidiary offices and a combined balance sheet of £164m.

Acquiring interests in other banks was one way of establishing a group; another consisted of converting a geographically related set of branches into a subsidiary bank, a procedure which the Comptoir National d'Escompte de Paris followed in the case of some of its oriental offices to form the Banque de l'Indo-Chine.

In general, the major English banks arose from amalgamations, so leading to concentration coming about through merger activity as opposed to spontaneous drift. The National Provincial was the exception as it had been conceived as a bank with a branch network during the 1830s, and this difference in approach continued to distinguish this bank until the mid-nineteenth century. Nationwide growth through amalgamations in English banking from the 1880s was led by Lloyds and Midland, two Birmingham-based banks. These institutions, in 1884 and 1890 respectively, acquired London clearing banks in order to gain direct access to the clearing, while in parallel their managements began applying strategies of competition through size. This became very evident in the case of Midland from 1898. Under Holden's leadership, Midland developed an expansionary policy which drew upon previous experience that had clearly indicated the considerable expense involved in directly opening new branches. Consequently, Holden turned to acquiring undercapitalised multi-branch regional banks in areas of England and Wales where the Midland's representation was slight (Holmes and Green, 1986). The initiatives taken by the managements of Lloyds and Midland caused a group of private country and London banks to coalesce to form a federation – Barclay & Co. Ltd – and, in turn, provoked comparable countermoves by other major joint stock banks. For instance, in 1909 the London & Westminster merged with the London & County (Cottrell, 1992: 48–9). Although outwardly monolithic, these major Edwardian banks had varying managerial structures which reflected differing degrees of retained provincial autonomy. Midland, with Holden, was the most centralised, whereas the federated nature of Barclays was displayed in a high degree of constituent autonomy, increasingly institutionalised as banking districts overseen by local directors, some of whom were also members of the bank's main board. Lying half between these approaches to managing a major bank was Lloyds's use of regional boards.

Table 10.4 indicates a very different banking scene in Germany, with large, important banks still managed from provincial centres and most

banks having apparently limited branch networks. The political structure of the *Kaiserreich* might be very evident in this spatial pattern,
arising from the continuing importance of provincialism within the
economy and society which, in turn, provided the support for non-
metropolitan large banks, so giving rise to a 'hybrid' structure. The
developmental paths of the Deutsche and the Bayerische Vereinsbank
are indicative of the varying and diverging forces at work.

As with the London & River Plate Bank, the Deutsche was initially
established as an overseas bank, or at least as a bank to support
German overseas trade. Richard Tilly has already explained that the
Deutsche was 'organised by a group of private bankers in 1870 for the
purpose of capturing a greater share of the foreign short-term credit
and payments business ... "needlessly flowing into British hands"'(Tilly,
1991: 93; Seizenzahl, 1970). It was designed by its founders and major
shareholders to be a financial institution to complement their domestic
private banking businesses. To these ends, branches in the major ports
of Bremen and Hamburg, and in Shanghai and Yokohama, were opened,
followed by the successful establishment of a London agency in 1873
after a false start in 1871. Furthermore, the management of the Deutsche
also cooperated in the foundation of the Deutsche–Belgische Laplata
Bank. However, the growth of German overseas trade eased cyclically
after the *Krach* of 1873, with the consequence that the finance of
international transactions proved not to be a reliable major source of
either profits or expansion. As a result the bank's management turned
inward, a move not entirely welcomed by its founders. None the less,
the bank's configuration was changed, particularly with the acquisitions
in 1876 of the Deutsche-Union Bank and Berliner Bank-Verein Bank
(Gall, 1995: 21). However, further domestic branch extension by the
Deutsche's management only began again from 1886 and then cau-
tiously with the acquisition of the Frankfurter Bankverein.[17]

This domestic strategy[18] had other parallel aspects, one of which
consisted of the Deutsche's management purchasing interests in key
regional provincial banks to gain customer contact within industrial
areas. It became institutionalised from 1897 through the inception of
Interessengemeinschaft arrangements – communities of interests or pooling arrangements (Gall, 1995: 22).[19] Such relationships preserved outward independence, thereby sustaining any local particularism, but
supplied the local institutions involved with greater resources – from
Berlin – to meet the growing demands for accommodation from especially sizeable industrial customers. The resulting disguised provincial
branches of the Deutsche, and of its seven Berlin peers, were also used
to gain resources so that the great bank began to compete for small
deposits which previously had been the preserve of savings banks and

credit cooperatives, thus initiating what Pohl has called 'the competition of systems'.

The Deutsche built up, from the inception of its inward turn during the late 1870s, a significant domestic banking ensemble. Just before the formal acquisition of the Bergische Märkische Bank in 1914, it consisted of a network within Germany of over 138 offices and had a combined balance sheet in excess of £192m.[20] Yet, from 1886 the Deutsche's management also returned to the original conception of the bank through the formation of the Deutsche Uebersee-Bank, an overseas extension later buttressed in 1889 by a participation in the Deutsch–Asiatische Bank. When these further interests are taken into account, the extent of the 'Deutsche group' at home and abroad by 1914 amounted to over 176 branches, with combined assets in excess of £216m.

However, not all German banks of the *Kaiserreich* followed the path of growth and development clearly adopted by the management of the Deutsche from 1886. The Bayerische Vereinsbank resolutely remained a provincial institution and, like many others, its management thought that a bank required only one front door. This attitude, still common at the turn of the century, was challenged in the case of the management of the Vereinsbank by the competitive threat posed by branches opened, or acquired, within its catchment area by banks with head offices outside Bavaria. As a result the Vereinsbank bought the Bankhaus Adolf Böhm in 1899 and then gradually established a provincial network as it became possible to acquire other private Bavarian banks. However, this conservative policy, which capitalised on local loyalties and regional particularism, enabled the bank to develop to be the twenty-fourth largest in Northern and Central Europe by 1914.

Further discussion of these varying policies which led to the growth of major European financial institutions must, necessarily, be curtailed. However, it should be noted that the boards of Austrian banks also pursued strategies of directly establishing branches, albeit precociously in the case of the Credit-Anstalt during its early years. With the greater and more extensive growth of commercial branch banking from the 1890s within Cisleithania, Vienna-based banks also established affiliates and augmented their groups through equity interests in provincial institutions. The management of the Société Générale de Belgique equally developed a policy of establishing a banking group both within Belgium and overseas.

The presence of very sizeable commercial banks does not automatically bring about high levels of concentration. Table 10.5 provides, it must be stressed, a somewhat distorted view of the degree of banking concentration *c.* 1914 within the national financial systems of the nine countries under discussion. The degree of misrepresentation in the table

Table 10.5 An estimate of banking concentration in Northern and Central Europe, *c.* 1914, by share of aggregate balance sheet total (per cent)

Share of:	France	Germany	United Kingdom
largest bank	24	12	7
3 largest banks	59	27	20
5 largest banks	70	39	29
10 largest banks	83	55	44

Share of:	Belgium	The Netherlands	Norway	Sweden
largest bank	35	32	18	15
3 largest banks	59	59	43	30
5 largest banks	70	78	62	42

Share of:	Austria	Denmark
largest bank	19	44
3 largest banks	47	80

Source: Banking Almanac, 1914

becomes clear when examining concentration in Denmark, which apparently had the most concentrated banking system within Northern and Central Europe. However, excluded from the underlying calculations that produced Table 10.5 are 510 Danish savings banks which in 1914 held in aggregate more deposits than the commercial banks. The data in the table are only for the commercial banks, yet, being drawn from the *Almanac*, do not even relate to all 140 such Danish institutions. As a result, even the position of the three major Copenhagen institutions within Danish commercial banking is overestimated in the table. Other, more exhaustive sources point to these three particular banks holding in excess of 50 per cent, *c.* 1914 (as opposed to 80 per cent in Table 10.5), with all twelve banks domiciled in Copenhagen accounting for 68 per cent of total Danish commercial bank assets. The balance – 32 per cent – was held by 128 country unit banks and 87 commercial banks based in 73 provincial towns (Johansen, 1991: 171–3). The Danish example is instructive in many ways. At first sight, the data confirm Lenin's conclusions, but a focus solely on major banks (through the lens of the *Almanac*) leads to the significant omission of Danish commercial banking beyond Copenhagen, which remained important until the 1950s. An equal impediment arises from considering only commercial banking, thereby excluding what might be termed the tertiary financial sector, comprising savings banks and cooperatives. These institutions, as with provincial banks, continued to be a vital force over the course of the twentieth century, provoking Clayton's comments on the Danish banking scene in the 1950s.

The Netherlands had a multi-tiered banking structure in 1914, like that of Denmark, but the Dutch data in Table 10.5 have some value in being indicative of the rapid changes that occurred in the topmost tier from 1910. In 1911 the Rotterdamsche Bank under W. Westerman, to be nicknamed 'William the Conqueror', took over the Deposito-en Adminstratie Bank, a move which initiated a phase of mergers so that by 1920 five big banks dominated the Dutch money market – in sharp contrast to the structure of banking within the Netherlands of the turn of the century (Jonker, 1995: 187–8).

As already shown in Section II, through an extrapolation from the Nishimura study of provincial banking, the estimates of concentration in French banking displayed in Table 10.5 are not representative since a considerable number of local banks are excluded from the data set deployed. Consequently concentration for French banking is overestimated. The opposite is the case for Germany, where the data do not take into account the consequences of *Interessengemeinschaften*, banking subsidiaries and deposit offices. Furthermore, as with the Danish case, yet another and very different picture of concentration in German banking would come into focus if savings banks were also included.[21] Most confidence can be had in the data for the United Kingdom, although many commentators might consider the estimated levels of concentration to be too low. The outcome in Table 10.5 is due to the data set embracing all United Kingdom financial institutions – both domestic and overseas. As a result, the concentration effects arising from greater coalescence within domestic, primarily English, commercial banking from the 1890s are masked to a considerable degree by the maintenance of independence among London-based international banks.

There was no single reason accounting for the development of concentration within banking in Northern and Central Europe from the 1880s. The managerial aspiration to build 'empires' played its part, whereas the rise to dominance of the group centred on the Société Générale de Belgique was assisted by the effects of the financial crises of 1876 and 1885 on the Banque de Belgique, its old rival (Kurgan van Hentenryk, 1992: 317). The English experience of financial crisis in 1878, and again in 1890, also led to an acceleration of the process of banking amalgamation, but not directly to concentration. Banking mergers precipitated the development of concentration in Sweden from 1910, when the two largest banks combined, but almost immediately the legal environment changed, with new legislation enacted in 1911, which also had consequences for the Swedish banking structure.

Continental investment banks, in the processes of fusion and of concentration, diversified to become universal banks through their managements giving greater emphasis to the development of a deposit base, a policy which was instituted by the Société Générale de Belgique from 1871. Two decades later, managements of provincial English banks, such as the Midland, wanted to widen the spectrum of risks within their banks' assets by acquiring business, through mergers, in non-industrial areas. Conversely, the directors and managers of the Berlin banks perceived an increasing need to gain greater industrial customer contact and so sought a presence, through pooling agreements, in areas such as the Ruhr. In terms of timing, the period of exceptional low interest rates during the mid-1890s appears to have had some importance and certainly witnessed competition for depositors between the commercial banks and the savings banks in England and Germany. Lastly, once large banks began to emerge, they became a fashion or sparked competitive/defensive reactions. In many respects, and especially as the overall structure of interest rates was largely given by the operation of the international gold standard before 1914, size became one of the few ways for commercial banks to compete. This was very evident in England, where there were widespread agreements linking deposit and advance rates to Bank rate and the payments system centred on the clearing, a 'privileged club'.

The effects of some of these factors were augmented by the First World War, while the operation of others, especially the international structure of interest rates, was broken by the consequences of the hostilities. One particular force that arose from the war was greater centralisation within the private sector in reaction to the emergence of the state as the major, all-powerful customer in every market. This also had secondary effects, as in England, where the military demand for labour resulted ultimately in a reduction of banking staffs, the closure of branches and a ban on the opening of new branches. With these restrictions, the only way that banking managements could achieve strategic aims, involving a greater national presence, during the hostilities or immediately after the peace, was by merger which produced the 'Big Five' of 1918.

During the 1920s the path of banking concentration in Northern and Central Europe was affected and directed by the severe fluctuations in the price level. In Britain, the Netherlands and Scandinavia, the banking system was placed under severe stress by the widespread and manifold effects of the collapse of the postwar boom in 1920. Within Britain the most affected were the few remaining independent banks of any size, whose managements had to shoulder the burden of salvaging bad and doubtful debts. Although long and drawn out in its execution, the solution to these difficulties was found in amalgamation, with the necessary discussions mediated and financially assisted by the Bank of England. In the Netherlands, the 1920 crisis resulted in the five major banks retreating from the new issue market and developing instead a branch-generated deposit business so that they became collectively known as *algemene banken* (general banks) (Jonker, 1995: 188). The sharp break between inflation and deflation in 1920 had even greater consequences in Scandinavia, although in Sweden the development of concentration also stemmed from the requirements of the Banking Law of 1911. This introduced provisions covering the capitalisation of financial institutions, deposit regulation, the opening of new branches and the founding of new banks. Such legislation may have established the necessary context, but it was declining asset values from 1919/20 that propelled Swedish banking concentration (Larrson, 1992). Swedish banks during the mid-1920s were relieved by state assistance; in Norway the central bank played that role. The severity of the Norwegian crisis was to call into question the integrity of the banking system during the mid-1920s, as three of the largest banks were forced to close. This gave rise to greater concentration within commercial banking, but, equally, to a greater role being played by savings banks (Knutsen, 1995). The outcome in Sweden of the crisis of the early 1920s was a fall in the number of independent commercial banks from 80 in 1910 to 32 by 1925, whereas in Norway the number of commercial banks almost halved, from 195 in 1919 to 104 by 1939.

Hyperinflation made the experience of extreme volatility in asset prices considerably harsher in Central Europe. In both Austria and Germany, the inflation of the immediate postwar years resulted in the creation of new banks (as also occurred in Norway). These were the *Winkelbanken,* the butterflies of the rising price level, but these new, minor institutions had little impact on the increased extent of competition confronting the great German banks. This arose primarily from the Reichsbank itself, albeit only at the height of the inflation, but also, over the whole decade, from savings banks. The ravages of inflation on the balance sheets of the great banks only became evident with stabilisation, which led to a further round of mergers, now of a comparable nature to those which had produced the 'Big Five' in England half a decade before. In Austria the post-stabilisation implosion of the commercial banking system went almost as far as reducing it to a monobank, when in 1933 the Credit-Anstalt took over the current banking businesses of both the Wiener Bank-Verein and the Niederösterreichische

Escompte-Gesellschaft. Previously the Credit-Anstalt had acquired the Austrian business of the Anglo-Austrian Bank in 1926 and the Boden-Credit-Anstalt in 1929; the latter had already acquired other major banks *in extremis* during the second half of the 1920s.

France and Belgium experienced persistent inflation until 1926 which, in turn, engendered banking expansion, although not to the mushroom extent that took place in Austria between 1920 and 1922, and in Germany from 1921 until 1923. The further consolidation of the Belgian system during the 1920s was shaped by 'industrial banking' and the competition for the limited retail market characterised by 'over-banking'. Furthermore, the decade saw a competitive struggle between the Société Générale de Belgique and the Banque de Bruxelles, which had got under way in 1916. The outcome of this was that the Banque de Bruxelles was forced to reconfigure its business in 1931, involving amalgamation with its subsidiaries to form a deposit bank and the establishment of a holding company, Brufina, to nurture its industrial assets. The crisis of 1930 and 1931 within the French system reduced the number of banks by a quarter over the previous decade, after the national deposit banks had faced competition from *banques populaires* and agricultural savings banks when trying to increase their deposit bases.

The bitter decade of the 1930s allowed little respite from the liquidity crisis with which it had opened. Many of the banking systems of Northern and Central Europe were almost put into cold storage as the managements of the banks that had survived attempted to liquidate the acute problems which had come starkly to the fore in 1931. Their strivings were often shaped by new legislation which tried to confront the problems of 'universal banking' that had been highlighted by the recent crisis. But this was not the universal experience because, in marked contrast, the banking systems of the United Kingdom and Sweden became increasingly liquid over the mid-1930s. This bewildered senior commercial bankers and their advisers in London and Stockholm, who saw, in particular, industrial customers finding other sources of finance and so leaving bank deposits unmobilised. Banking concentration had not necessarily resulted in major banks enjoying a monopoly in the financial sector.

IV. Internationalisation

The year 1931 equally marked the end, for what proved to be a quarter of a century, of a period of sustained internationalisation within the banking systems of Northern and Central Europe. This process had become marked from the 1880s but it built upon a well-established foundation, with some of the first footings laid in the mid-eighteenth century, if not earlier. Indeed, whereas internationalisation is often taken as a modern feature of the development of banking, perhaps even a characteristic of its most mature phase, a strong case can equally be made that internationalisation was one of its earliest features.

The focus of the current forum is the nineteenth and twentieth centuries and, consequently, this is neither the place nor the time to introduce considerations of the nature of banking in late medieval or early modern Europe. However, to appreciate the origins of post-1880 internationalisation, it is necessary to consider developments from 1700 in outline.

During the eighteenth century banking and merchanting in Northwestern Europe were not entirely separated, while a considerable proportion of houses had a cosmopolitan nature. London was the new, developing financial market and a recent estimate indicates that during the 1760s three-quarters of its merchants were possibly 'of recent foreign extraction'. Moreover, they were not transient, but rather formed settled communities within the City, each with their own church or synagogue. The largest consisted of Huguenots, drawn to London to deal in Indian textiles but then becoming merchant bankers. They conducted their highly heterogeneous business affairs through networks arising from personal relationships which brought the City into contact with Amsterdam, Basle, Frankfurt, Geneva and Neuchâtel. The next biggest group was composed of Sephardi Jews, who specialised to a degree in the Iberian, Latin American and Anglo-Italian trades, together with dealings in oriental diamonds. The Dutch were the smallest segment numerically, but generally they were the wealthiest of London's settled foreign merchants and the most involved not just in mercantile banking but also finance (Chapman, 1992; Luthy, 1961; Carter, 1959; Cottrell, 1985; Yogev, 1978; Wilson, 1941).

Many of these houses in London, or in Amsterdam, Antwerp, Frankfurt and Paris, failed to survive until 1914 so as to be registered in the data set abstracted from the *Almanac*. There was a continuing high turnover in Europe's cosmopolitan private banking community. Structural changes within it came about as a result of the impact of the Revolutionary and Napoleonic Wars and subsequently arose from differential rates (and forms) of industrialisation. Furthermore, formalised private banking developed in different ways within Northwestern Europe's primary and secondary banking centres. There were no clear, general patterns in the paths that led to the greater institutionalisation of international banking and, with those that can be faintly discerned, trends in London almost always appear to have been an exception, or at least different to a significant degree.

London continued to be the most cosmopolitan of Northern Europe's financial markets. As Chapman has argued, trade in British manufactured cottons from the 1780s acted as a magnet to attract, successively, Germans, Greeks and Americans, whereas the consequences of the quarter of a century of European warfare from 1793 pushed merchant proto-bankers to London, such as Frederick Huth from Spain. This community, which increasingly came to have global interests, further developed from the 1830s.

London's cosmopolitan bankers also stood apart from domestic developments to the extent that the City had two almost distinct groups of private bankers, one looking inward to the domestic economy for its business, the other outward to Europe and further afield. The extent of this differentiation is difficult to judge, as the nineteenth-century growth of London's domestic private bankers – in Lombard Street and along the Strand – remains to be considered by banking historians. Some houses, such as Glyn Mills, straddled both worlds through being involved in domestic and international business. The major link that the cosmopolitan community of increasingly merchant bankers (although many continued to style themselves as merchants) had with the domestic economy was through the finance of imports and exports by providing acceptance credits. But this business equally became international – the provision of finance to support a large part of world trade. A common pattern between London and other European centres existed in that London cosmopolitan bankers institutionalised some of their expanding and developing business through the establishment of corporate overseas banks. However, this came earlier in London – from the 1830s, with the foundation of chartered overseas banks – and further developed another of London's particular characteristics: specialisation of financial function. As a result, over the nineteenth century, the City came to comprise a series of highly developed parallel financial markets, each made by its own particular group of financial intermediaries with the consequence that universal banking found little soil in which to establish a root – to be shown clearly by abortive attempts during the 1860s.

The development of banking within Europe from the 1830s was marked by the transfer of expertise and capital. London gained primarily through the continuing growth of its private merchant and foreign banking community arising from immigration. Banking oriented to the home economy in the City and elsewhere in England and Wales was little affected, although Scottish practice was introduced with the foundation of the London & Westminster Bank, and foreign subscriptions, often via the cosmopolitan network, to the shares of corporate domestic and international banks formed over the mid-century, played some part. The internationalisation of continental European corporate banks before 1870 took place to a greater extent than was the case in London, or England. Unlike in London, the development of corporate commercial banking on the Continent, at least in the major financial centres, was primarily due to the institutionalisation of private banking, which in the process drew upon cosmopolitan relationships linking a number of markets. The Société Générale de Belgique obtained French capital during the 1830s; the European role played by the Crédit Mobilier, as with the Darmstädter, is well known; whereas the successful establishment of the commercial banks in Copenhagen was often due to capital participations from Bremen and Hamburg.

The internationalisation of banking therefore took on many forms and had, as its seed bed, the long-standing cosmopolitan nature of the major financial centres. Internationalisation, in terms of European banks undertaking further business beyond the continent and its offshore islands, came with the greater growth of international trade over the nineteenth century and its geographical diversification. Here, again, there are differences between Britain and continental Europe. Compared with other European economies, Britain's overseas trade grew at a faster rate from the 1790s and earlier acquired a global nature – with respect to exports from the 1820s and imports from the 1840s or 1850s. Much of continental European trade remained intra-European, and became even more so over the mid-century, so that geographical diversification was not a marked feature until the 1880s. Previously, British re-exports had largely supplied continental Europe with the raw materials of the New World and the Orient.

The contrast between Britain and continental Europe in overseas trade was evident in other areas of international commerce and finance. The global multi-branch mercantile and banking house was a feature almost unique to British trading activity during the first three-quarters of the nineteenth century. Continental commercial firms tended to restrict their networks of branch houses to Europe. During the late 1840s, according to a contemporary British survey, there were about 1500 British mercantile houses overseas compared with 500 French, while about half the latter were located in the Mediterranean and the Levant. However, that survey overlooked German commerce, which in 1845 had 340 extra-European mercantile houses, almost exclusively based in the New World – 170 in the United States and 100 in Latin America. A further difference between British and continental European international commerce was that a significant proportion of the British houses had begun to combine banking business with dealings in goods to the extent of providing credits to other merchants.

London's rise as Europe's financial centre from the eighteenth century and the development of the global multi-branch 'mercantile' banking house contributed to the earlier development of British overseas corporate banks. However, as indicated above, French banks from the mid-nineteenth century opened extra-European offices, so becoming 'universal' in a rather different sense to that which is normally implied. German banks, for example the Deutsche, followed the same strategy and combined with overseas affiliates, and likewise Belgian banks. Among the major economies of Northern and Central Europe the only major exception was Austrian banks. These, by and large, stayed at home, a reflection of the much lesser role that foreign trade played in the development of the Habsburg economy and the greater importance of the large domestic market constituted by the post-1848 internal customs union. Despite rising competition from the mid-century, London remained the major European international market, pointed up here by the London & River Plate (20th) and the Standard Bank of South Africa (25th) being among the largest 25 commercial banks in Northern and Central Europe in c. 1914 (see Table 10.5).

Table 10.6, drawn from the *Almanac*, provides something of an extreme test of the extent of internationalisation by 1914 (in terms of overseas commercial corporate banking) as no suitable way could be devised of incorporating London foreign/merchant bankers and their continental European peers. Furthermore, in its upper portion the overseas interests of banks such as the Crédit Lyonnais and the Deutsche are not fully reflected. To some extent these impediments counterbalance each other. The overwhelming importance of London is displayed in the upper half of Table 10.6. The table also indicates that London's premier position was due to the number of locally based corporate overseas banks, a development that gathered pace from the 1830s, together with the branches of foreign banks attracted to London, the openings of which grew significantly from the 1870s. Paris's international role derived from the same developmental processes and was further augmented by the overseas networks of the Comptoir National d'Escompte de Paris, the Crédit Lyonnais and the Société Générale, absent from the table.

The data displayed in the upper portion of Table 10.6 also point to the still relative infancy of Berlin as a centre of international corporate banking in 1914, especially in terms of the relatively few branches of foreign banks in contrast to either London or Paris.

The lower part of Table 10.6 was devised as a test of the responsiveness to new opportunities of British, French and German international banking based in Europe. China, Russia and Japan constituted in various ways the new international economic frontier by the 1910s. Some of their major cities and ports – St Petersburg, Shanghai and Tokyo/Yokohama – had become secondary, or tertiary, centres of international

Table 10.6   Number of branches of corporate international banks in various banking centres, *c.* 1914

Nationality of branches in:	Berlin	London	Paris	Total, by nationality
Locally based overseas banks	7	37	15	59
American	3	8	5	16
Austrian	–	2	2	4
Belgian	–	2	–	2
British	–		9	9
Dutch	–	3	–	3
French	2	8		10
German		3	–	3
Other	–	35	12	47
Total	12	98	43	153

Nationality of branches in:	St Petersburg	Shanghai	Tokyo and Yokohama	Total, by nationality
Locally based overseas banks	3	–	5	8
American	–	–	–	–
Austrian	–	–	–	–
Belgian	–	1	–	1
British	2	3	3	8
Dutch	–	1	–	1
French	3	1	–	4
German	–	1	1	2
Other	2	4	1	7
Total	10	11	10	31

Source: *Banking Almanac*, 1914

banking, in the process attracting branches of European international banks. When considered together, branches of British, London-based, banks were the dominant migrants, although the 'national balance' varies between each individual centre. The test was devised in these terms, as with practically any other extra-European economic/financial urban centre, the different international developmental paths of the major European economies would have had a distorting effect.

The First World War revealed the delicate nature of the fabric of the world economy. In spite of the long historical roots of international European banking, it was gravely disrupted by the outbreak of hostilities. Peace in 1918 brought further, new challenges. Some American bankers saw Britain's international network of branches as a prime reason for the maintenance of global British economic power. Morgans, an Anglo-American private house dating from the mid-nineteenth century, argued that the most appropriate strategy was to 'Americanise' the British system. This could be accomplished by continuing transatlantic cooperation in which the American pole would inevitably become greater and more significant as a result of the momentum of growth of the United States economy. However, Vanderlip of National City decided upon open competition. In 1916 his bank lent to Russia, a country which Morgans acknowledged to be a solely British preserve, and, at the same time, opened branches there. In order to develop the necessary expertise, Vanderlip established a training school in Brooklyn to provide the staff for offices which had been opened in Denmark, Italy, Spain and Switzerland by the close of 1916. The National City gained an affiliate – the International Banking Corporation – and also opened branches in Brazil and Argentina. The Morgan group had no choice but to follow, although deciding that they would only directly challenge their British partners in Latin America and China. These different approaches within the New York banking community became further evident with the formation of the 'Edge Banks' from 1920. Unlike the American & Foreign Banking Corporation and the Mercantile Bank of the Americas (both affiliated to the Morgan group and having outlets only in Latin America), the International Acceptance Bank under P. M. Warburg involved European capital and based its provision of acceptance credits not on foreign branches but a network of European correspondents. The Morgan group's presence in Europe – in London and Paris (the associated private partnerships) – was augmented by its affiliated banks – Guaranty Trust, Equitable Trust and Farmer's Loan & Trust – having English and French offices, and was further developed through other partnerships involving both American and European banks. In the case of the French American Banking Corporation, this directly utilised the existing branch network of the Comptoir National.

The high tide of what proved to be the precocious development of American international branch banking was reached in 1920 when there were 181 American overseas offices. The ebb then rapidly set in with the worldwide slump of the early 1920s. From 1921 National City closed branches and wound up subsidiaries. In 1924 the Morgan-owned Asia Banking Corporation was liquidated, with the remaining assets passed to the International Banking Corporation, an affiliate of National City. During 1925 the Bank of Central & South America was transferred by Morgans to the Royal Bank of Canada. These retrenchments and reconstructions undercut the attempt that had been mounted in various ways since 1920 to substitute dollar acceptances for sterling international trade bills. As the retreat progressed, American bankers recognised that the postwar boom had not provided a propitious context in which to create an American system abroad; in particular the acceptance market had been disrupted by unstable foreign exchanges (Parrini, 1969: 58, 61–96, 100, 109, 112–18, 122).

At the same time there were some significant changes in the configuration of the British system. From 1918 the major English commercial banks became British institutions through acquiring affiliates in Ireland and Scotland. Not all the managements of the members of the 'Big Five' were content to be solely major national institutions. Some – Lloyds and the Westminster – had begun to develop a European presence before 1914, but the management of Midland, although it conjured with opening a branch in St Petersburg, decided to stick to its last. Midland had acquired an interest in the provision of international acceptances through the acquisition of the City Bank in 1898, and its management decided to open a Foreign Bank Department in London in 1902, which had 132 overseas correspondents during the 1910s and 850 such connections by 1918. Others of the 'Big Five', with some official encouragement, decided to develop directly European or even international banking. Acting together, Lloyds and the National Provincial opened branches in Northern and Central Europe, while a partnership of Lloyds and the Westminster invested in the Banca Italo-Britannica. In the case of the Westminster, this ran in conjunction with developing offices in Belgium, France and Spain. Likewise, Barclays opened in France, Germany and Algeria in the early postwar years and during the second half of the 1920s acquired an interest in a Belgian bank and established an Italian branch. However, these attempts to construct direct British presences in Europe proved to be as ill-fated as American postwar global branch expansion.

Despite the continuing hostility of Governor Norman towards what he regarded as the dangerous intermixing of domestic and international banking, both Lloyds and Barclays began to establish major global networks during the 1920s. Managers at Lloyds have subsequently admitted that this development of their bank lacked any rationale. It involved acquiring British international banks operating in Latin America which led to the creation of the Bank of London & South America in 1923. This was coupled with acquiring interests in the National Bank of New Zealand and the British Bank of West Africa. These were immediate, postwar steps in the internationalisation of this domestic clearer, but Lloyds' overseas presence was further augmented by its rescue of Cox & Kings. This was undertaken at the request of the Bank of England and, as a result, Lloyds developed a sizeable branch network in India from the mid-1920s, despite the chagrin of Montagu Norman who had considered that the clearer's role was simply one of liquidation. Barclays' parallel internationalisation arose from the personal mission of its chairman, Goodenough, to create a 'British Empire Bank'. In part Goodenough's energies were diverted overseas by the informal dictates from 1918 which barred further expansion at home through the acquisition of another major clearer. The realisation of Goodenough's overseas initiative built upon an existing interest in the Colonial Bank, to which were added the National Bank of South Africa and the Anglo-Egyptian Bank, to form in 1925 Barclays (DCO). This imperial subsidiary was further developed through the founding in 1929 of Barclays Bank (Canada).

French banking over the 1920s participated in what Soutou has called 'the imperialism of poverty' (Soutou, 1976), but a very different form of internationalisation affected the inflation-ravaged banks of Central Europe. Their position was assisted by the old ties of the European private banking community, connections invigorated by the way that the business of the London international credit market was altered by the postwar growth of American overseas branch banking. This is particularly evident with Schroders and Kleinworts, both Anglo-German acceptance houses, which used their long-standing continental European links to redevelop their businesses. As a result, in the case of Kleinworts over the 1920s, the United States' share of their acceptances fell from 15 per cent (of £15.9m) to 3.5 per cent (of £19.6m), while the German proportion rose from 5.2 per cent to 28.9 per cent. The necessary extra security for Central European credits was thought to arise from the increasing use of reimbursement credits which carried the guarantee of a local bank. It was only with the German situation in November 1923 that Kleinworts preferred 'not to extend our commitments on the continent at the present' and this proved to be short pause (Diaper, 1986; Cottrell and Stone, 1992).

Within Germany, private banks almost regained their former, nineteenth-century relationships with industrial clients during the mid-1920s on the basis of their international connections, thus dethroning for a while the Berlin 'great' banks. In the wake of stabilisation, the great banks were unable to meet industry's demand for finance to rationalise and reorganise. Private banks utilised their long-standing foreign links to stimulate an inward flow of funds. Hirschland of Essen obtained sterling and dollar credits and, above all, the Krupp loan, negotiated during 1924 and 1925 and supplied by Goldman, Sachs and Paul

Warburg, provided the entrée for German industry to the International Acceptance Bank. Sal. Oppenheim gave access to the Paris market, while Mendelssohns used their connections with Amsterdam and New York. However, this proved to be a short interlude, because the Berlin 'great' banks were able to rebuild their deposit bases, whereas those of the private banks never regained their prewar levels (Wixworth and Ziegler, 1994).

The major banks in East Central Europe sustained their capital bases in part by a series of inflation-induced share issues, which frequently attracted Western participations. These capital increases occurred during the inflation but continued after stabilisation and involved not only participations from American, British and French banks, but also Belgian, Dutch and Swiss institutions and even German private banks. In the case of the Boden-Credit-Anstalt, the personal links of Baron Bruno Schröder of the London acceptance house played some part in the necessary prior negotiations, as did the international network of the Mendelssohns with regard to the Ceská Eskomptní Banka. Comparable personal networks stemming from the Rothschilds facilitated the Credit-Anstalt's creation of the Amstelbank in 1919 and the 'Dutch company of Credit and Finance' in mid-1928 (Cottrell, 1983; 1994).

A further aspect of the internationalisation of European banking over the 1920s was the placing by Western institutions of deposits denominated in foreign currencies with major banks in Central and East Central Europe. Total foreign liabilities of the Berlin banks rose from Rm 3.5bn at the end of 1926 to Rm 9.2bn by mid-1930 (Balderston, 1994). It is frequently presumed that the largest proportion of these claims were held by American banks, but this was not always the case. The Wiener Bank-Verein, for instance, from early 1925 held not only dollar deposits, but also deposits denominated in sterling, French francs and Swiss francs. Furthermore, its dollar deposits, which peaked at $7.475m in late 1927 but still amounted to $6.86m in July 1930, largely originated from West European banks. Indeed, during the mid-1920s $3 out of every $4 deposited with the Bank-Verein came from a European bank (and not a European branch of an American bank) as a result of recycling dollars domiciled in New York. Most of these inflows came from Belgian, British and Swiss banks. Five years later, following the Wall Street crash, British, Dutch and Swiss institutions were the main placers, while American banks hardly featured in the Bank-Verein's list of foreign depositors of dollars during the early 1930s.

The close intra-European connections of European banking during the second half of the 1920s, especially those that linked the west and the east of the continent, proved ultimately to be a major source of weakness. The collapse of Austrian, then German, banking over the spring and summer of 1931 affected financial institutions in every European market, as well as their American peers. London was the most embarrassed by the illiquidity of its institutions' claims upon Berlin and Vienna, arising through acceptance credits and sterling- and dollar-denominated deposits. The consequent standstills and creditors' committees, established in the wake of the 1931 crises, occupied Western bankers' energies for nearly half a decade, whereas the all-enveloping world depression hardly provided the context for a rapid resumption of banking internationalisation. Reconstruction of the banking system at home went hand in hand with liquidating foreign claims, while the 1931 crisis had cast doubt upon the world monetary order so that to many domestic self-sufficiency appeared the only route forward.

V. Conclusion

The parallel rise of banking concentration within the systems of Northern and Central Europe from the 1880s is suggestive of a single cause in operation. Yet an examination of the various ways by which Northern and Central Europe's largest banks reached their size in 1914, measured by balance sheet total, shows that a wide variety of developmental forces had been in operation. In the case of English domestic commercial banks, amalgamation brought about concentration, but only from 1910, so that it was only the climax of the banking combination movement that had this effect. Within Europe's other major economies, the increasing size of a few commercial banks was offset, in France, by the vitality of regional and local banking, and in Germany particularly by the competition offered by the savings banks. The further development of concentration after 1914 was shaped by forces which had a wider effect: the rise of the state as an economic power during the hostilities and the extreme volatility of the price level, especially of asset prices, over the 1920s. None the less, surveys of banking conducted during the 1950s commented on the continuing hybrid nature of many of Northern and Central Europe's national banking systems, attributed to the sustained strength of local and regional banking, and the role played by savings banks. Even in England, mutual institutions have played a part within banking, particularly coming to the fore in retail banking from the 1960s.

Although internationalisation is frequently regarded as the last stepping stone in a progression running from local bank to regional bank to national financial institution to 'global banking player', it has been maintained here that internationalisation has been an enduring characteristic of the development of modern European banking. Furthermore, there were various aspects of internationalisation and these were very evident during both the nineteenth century and the first three decades of the twentieth century. Although internationalisation was a source of strength, because it brought with it an opportunity to diversify risk, during the 1920s it proved ultimately to be a source of danger. In particular the 1931 crisis considerably weakened the London market, which had previously been the world's financial centre for a century and a half.

Notes

1. I am grateful to Youssef Cassis for inspiration, to Edwin Green and Sara Kinsey of Midland Bank for allowing such ready access to *The Banking Almanac* and to my colleagues, Dr Sally Horrocks and D. M. Williams, for their valuable commentaries during the first drafting of this chapter. Practical help in its production was given by Dr Lucy Newton and G. Austen. There is of course the normal disclaimer.
2. On Hobson see for example Lloyd (1972) and, more generally, Cain (1980).
3. On Hilferding see Winkler (1974) and Wellhoner (1989).
4. For further development of this point see Ashworth (1974).
5. As this contribution was drafted, it was recognised that this section was somewhat self-indulgent, being a return by the author to the literature that provided his own introduction to banking studies. In revision, it has taken on further implications through bringing forward the contribution of Professor J. S. G. Wilson who, sadly, died on 5 June 1996. I greatly benefited from his introductory lectures to economics and his seminar on 'Comparative Banking'.
6. An obvious exception is Germany, while the Dutch study (Wilson) notes the rapid expansion of branches over the decade 1945–55.
7. The clearest instance is Johnson and Sayers's observation that 'Belgian bankers [are] keenly aware of the problems of organisation inherent in a system of branch banking' (Johnson and Sayers, 1962: 240).
8. There is only one passing reference to internationalisation on p. 425, where the process is regarded implicitly as being of great significance, but not needing substantial comment within the discussion and analysis.
9. Wilson also includes in this group of national economies with hybrid banking systems Austria, India, Italy, Japan and Switzerland.
10. The only other near contemporary study is P. B. Whale (1930).
11. See also Donabauer (1988).
12. One consequence is the absence of savings banks, the importance of which will become evident later.
13. The group abstracted consists of those listed in the *Almanac* with regard to Northern and Central Europe, with the exception of, first, proto-/quasi-central banks (despite their involvement with commercial business) and, second, institutions concerned only with transactions within the financial sector, such as the London discount houses, so far as it was

possible to identify them. The data have also been augmented to some degree by information contained within Pohl and Freitag (1994).

14. The data set was manipulated by using the sort facility within Microsoft Word, version 5.1 and 6. Although in many respects this is only one remove from shuffling index cards, it none the less proved to be, within the time available, a very effective procedure.

15. Rates used: £1 = 25 francs of France and the Latin Monetary Union (mint par = 25.221fcs); = 18 krones of Denmark and the Scandinavian Union (mint par = 18.159 kr); = 20 German marks (mint par =20.429 mks); =12 Dutch florins (mint par =12.107 fl); = 24 Austrian krones (mint par =24.027 ök).

16. Respectively, the Société Générale Alsacienne de Banque, Banque Balkanique, Société Française de Banque et de Depôts, Banque Hongroise d'Escompte et de Change, Banque de Salonique, Banque Russo-Asiatique, Banque Française et Italienne pour l'Amerique du Sud and Société Suisse de Banque et de Depôts.

17. For a recent discussion of the shaping forces at work see Da Rin (1996).

18. For other aspects see Motschmann (1915).

19. See also Ziegler (1997) which considers in particular the effect of IGs on customer relations.

20. Excluding the Duisborg-Ruhroter Bank and the Oberrheinische Bank for which data could not readily be found.

21. Dr D. Ziegler kindly supplied me with the necessary data to overcome this very serious omission but, unfortunately, there was insufficient time available to enable the inclusion of the results.

References

Ashworth, W. (1974), 'Industrialisation and the economic integration of nineteenth century Europe', *European Studies Review*, 4.

Bairoch, P. (1973), 'European trade in the XIXth century: the development of the value and volume of exports (Preliminary results)', *Journal of European Economic History*, 2.

Bairoch, P. (1976), 'Europe's Gross National Product: 1800–1975', *Journal of European Economic History*, 5 (2).

Balderston, T. (1994), 'The banks and the gold standard in the German financial crisis of 1931', *Financial History Review*, 1 (1).

Baster, A. S. J. (1929), *The Imperial Banks*, London, King.

Baster, A. S. J. (1935), *The International Banks*, London, King.

Cain, P. J. (1980), *Economic Foundations of British Overseas Expansion 1815–1914*, London.

Cameron, R. et al. (1967), *Banking in the Early Stages of Industrialisation: A Study in Comparative Economic History*, Oxford, Oxford University Press.

Cameron, R. (ed.), (1972), *Banking and Economic Development: Some Lessons of History*, New York.

Cameron, R. and Bovykin, V. I. (eds) (1991), *International Banking 1870–1914*, Oxford.

Capie, F. (1988), 'Structure and performance in British banking', in Cottrell, P. L. and Moggridge, D. E. (eds), *Money and Power*, London, Macmillan.

Capie, F. and Rodrik-Bali, G. (1982), 'Concentration in British banking 1870–1920', *Business History*, 24.

Carter, A. C. (1959), 'Financial activities of he Huguenots in London and Amsterdam in the mid-eighteenth century', *Proceedings of the Huguenot Society of London*, 19.

Chandler, G. (1964), *Four Centuries of Banking, I, The grasshopper and the liver bird: Liverpool and London*, London, Batsford.

Chapman, S. (1984), *The Rise of Merchant Banking*, London, Allen and Unwin.

Chapman, S. (1992), *Merchant Enterprise in Britain from the Industrial Revolution to World War One*, Cambridge, Cambridge University Press.

Clayton, G. (1962a), 'Denmark', in Sayers, R. S. (ed.), *Banking in Western Europe,* Oxford.

Clayton, G. (1962b), 'Sweden', in Sayers, R. S. (ed.), *Banking in Western Europe,* Oxford.

Cottrell, P. L. (1983), Appendix to 'Aspects of western equity investment in the banking systems of east central Europe', in Teichova, A. and Cottrell, P. L. (eds), *International Business and Central Europe, 1918–1939*, Leicester/New York, Leicester University Press.

Cottrell, P. L. (1985), 'The business man and financier', in Lipman, S. and V. D. (eds), *The Century of Moses Montefiore*, Oxford.

Cottrell, P. L. (1992), 'The domestic commercial banks and the City of London 1870–1939', in Cassis, Y. (ed.), *Finance and Financiers in European History 1880–1960*, Cambridge, Cambridge University Press.

Cottrell, P. L. (1994), 'Mushrooms and dinosaurs', in Teichova, A., Gourvish, T. and Pogany, A. (eds), *Universal Banking in the Twentieth Century*, Aldershot, Edward Elgar Publishing Ltd.

Cottrell, P. L. and Stone, C. J. (1992), 'Credits, and deposits to finance credits', in Cottrell, P.L., Lindgren, H. and Teichova, A. (eds), *European Industry and Banking between the Wars: A Review of Bank–Industry Relations*, Leicester, Leicester University Press.

Da Rin, M. (1996), 'Understanding the development of the German Kreditbanken, 1850–1914: an approach from the economics of information', *Financial History Review*, 3 (1).

Diaper, S. (1986), 'Merchant banking in the inter-war period. The case of Kleinwort Sons & Co', *Business History*, 28.

Donabauer, K. (1988), *Privatbankiers und Bankenkonzentration in Deutschland von der Mitte des 19 Jahrhunderts bis 1932*, Frankfurt am Main.

Gall, L. (1995), 'The Deutsche Bank from its founding to the Great War 1870–1914', in Gall, L. et al., *The Deutsche Bank 1870–1995*, London, Weidenfeld & Nicolson.

Gerschenkron, A. (1952), 'Economic backwardness in historical perspective', in Hoselize, B. (ed.), *The Progress of Underdeveloped Areas*, Chicago, Reprinted in Gerschenkron, A. (1965), *Economic Backwardness in Historical Perspective*, New York.

Gueslin, A., (1992), 'Banks and the state in France from the 1880s to the 1930s' in Cassis, Y. (ed.), *Finance and Financiers in European History 1880–1960*, Cambridge, Cambridge University Press.

Hannah, L. and Kay, J. A. (1977), *Concentration in Modern Industry*, London.

Hart, P. E. (1979), 'On bias and concentration', *Journal of Industrial Economics*, 27.

Hilferding, R. (1910), *Das Finanzkapital*, Vienna. Translated as *Finance Capital. A Study of the Latest Phase of Capitalist Development*, London, 1981.

Hobson, J. A. (1902), *Imperialism: A Study*, London.

Holmes, A. R. and Green, E. (1986), *Midland. 150 Years of Banking Business*, London, Batsford.

Inglis Palgrave, Sir R. H. (1914), *The Banking Almanac*, London, Waterlow.

James, H. (1992), 'Banks and economic development: comments', in Cassis, Y. (ed.), *Finance and Financiers in European History 1880–1960*, Cambridge, Cambridge University Press.

Johansen, H. C. (1991), 'Banking and finance in the Danish economy', in Cameron, R. and Bovykin, V. I. (eds), *International Banking 1870–1914*, Oxford.

Johnson, S. M. and Sayers, R. S. (1962), 'Belgium' in Sayers, R. S. (ed.), *Banking in Western Europe*, Oxford.

Jones, G. (1993), *British Multinational Banking*, Oxford, Clarendon Press.

Jonker, J. (1995), 'Spoilt for choice? Banking concentration and the structure of the Dutch capital market, 1900–1940' in Cassis, Y., Feldman, G. D. and Olsson, U. (eds), *The Evolution of Financial Institutions and Markets in Twentieth-Century Europe,* Aldershot, Scolar Press.

Knutsen, S. (1995), 'Phases in the development of the Norwegian banking system, 1880–1980', in Cassis, Y., Feldman, G. D. and Olsson, U. (eds), *The Evolution of Financial Institutions and Markets in Twentieth-Century Europe*, Aldershot, Scolar Press.

Kurgan van Hentenryk, G. (1992), 'Finance and financiers in Belgium 1880–1940', in Cassis, Y. (ed.), *Finance and Financiers in European History 1880–1960*, Cambridge, Cambridge University Press.

Larrson, M. (1992), 'Government susidy or internal restructuring? Swedish commercial banks during the crisis years of the 1920s', in Cottrell, P. L., Lindgren, H. and Teichova, A. (eds), *European Industry and Banking between the Wars: A Review of Bank–Industry Relations*, Leicester, Leicester University Press.

Lenin, V. I. (1916), *Imperialism, the Highest Stage of Capitalism*, written in Zurich; subsequently published as *Notebooks on Imperialism*, St Petersburg, 1917; English translation, *Selected Works* 1.2, Moscow, 1952: 31.

Lloyd, T. (1972), 'Africa and Hobson's imperialism', *Past and Present*, 55.

Luthy, H. (1961), *La banque protestante en France*, Paris.

Motschmann, G. (1915), *Das Depositengeschaft des Berlin Grossbanken*, Munich.

Nishimura, S. (1995), 'The French provincial banks, the Banque de France, and bill finance, 1890–1913', *Economic History Review*, 43 (3).

Nougaret, R. (1995), 'The Crédit Lyonnais historical archives', *Financial History Review*, 2 (1).

Opie, R. G. (1962), 'Western Germany', in Sayers, R. S. (ed.) *Banking in Western Europe*, Oxford.

Parrini, C. P. (1969), *Heir to Empire. United States Economic Diplomacy 1916–1923*, Pittsburgh.

Pohl, M. (1982), *Konzentration im deutschen Bankwesen,* Frankfurt am Main.

Pohl, M. and Freitag, S. (eds) (1994), *Handbook on the History of European Banks*, Aldershot, Edward Elgar Publishing Ltd.

Prais, S. J. (1976), *The Evolution of Giant Firms in Britain*, Cambridge, Cambridge University Press.

Riesser. J. (1905), *Die deutschen Grossbanken und ihre Konzentration im Zusammenhange mit der Entwicklung der Gesamtwirtschaft in Deutschland*, Rome. Translated by Jacobson, M. (1911), *The German Great Banks,* Washington, DC: National Monetary Commission, 14; Senate Document 593.

Sayers, R. S. (ed.) (1962a), *Banking in Western Europe*, Oxford.

Sayers, R. G. (1962b), 'Norway', in Sayers, R. S. (ed.), *Banking in Western Europe,* Oxford.

Sayers, R. S. (1976), *The Bank of England 1891–1944, I*, Cambridge, Cambridge University Press.

Seizenzahl, F. (1970), *100 Jahre Deutsche Bank 1870–1970*, Frankfurt am Main.

Soutou, G. (1976), 'L'imperialisme du pauvre', *Relations Internationales*, 7.

Sykes, J. (1926), *The Amalgamation Movement in English Banking, 1825–1924*, London.

Teichova, A., Gourvish, T. and Pogany, A. (eds) (1994), *Universal Banking in the Twentieth Century*, Aldershot, Edward Elgar Publishing Ltd.

Tilly, R. (1991), 'International aspects of the development of German banking' in Cameron, R. and Bovykin, V. I. (eds), *International Banking 1870–1914*, Oxford.

Tilly, R. (1992), 'An overview on the role of the large German banks up to 1914', in Cassis, Y. (ed.), *Finance and Financiers in European History 1880–1960*, Cambridge, Cambridge University Press.

Wellhoner, V. (1989), 'The relationship between banks and industry in the "Finanzkapital of Ralph Hilferding"', *Uppsala Papers in Economic History*, 4.

Whale, P. B. (1930), *Joint Stock Banking in Germany*, London.

Wilson, C. (1941), *Anglo-Dutch Commerce and Finance in the Eighteenth Century*, Cambridge, Cambridge University Press.

Wilson, J. S. G. (1962), 'France', in Sayers, R. S. (ed.), *Banking in Western Europe*, Oxford.

Wilson, J. S. G. (1986), *Banking Policy and Structure: A Comparative Analysis*, London/Sydney.

Winkler, H. A. (1974), *Organisierter Kapitalismus. Voraussetzunger und Anfange*, Gottingen.

Wixworth, H. and Ziegler, D. (1994), 'The niche in the universal banking system: the role and significance of private bankers within German industry, 1900–1933', *Financial History Review*, 1 (2).

Yogev, G. (1978), *Diamonds and Coral. Anglo-Dutch Jews in Eighteenth Century Trade*, Leicester.

Ziegler, D. (1997), 'The origins of the Macmillan Gap: comparing Britain and Germany in the early twentieth century', in Cottrell, P. L., Teichova, A. and Yazawa, T. (eds), *Finance in the Age of the Corporate Economy*, Aldershot/Leicester, Scolar Press.

CHAPTER ELEVEN

Concentration and Internationalisation in Banks after the Second World War

Geoffrey Jones

This chapter will survey the main trends in the internationalisation of banking over the last fifty years. It will deal primarily with developments in the three main banking markets of Europe, the United States and Japan. The focus will be to try to explain the radical changes which have occurred in international banking in this era. Within the general theme of internationalisation, the issues of size, nationality and risk will also be addressed.

The place to begin is with the immediate postwar decade. A number of key features stand out in the world banking system in the late 1940s and early 1950s. The first was the low level of innovation. In most respects, the products and services offered by banks were similar to those seen in nineteenth-century banking. This is especially evident in international banking. The finance of international trade was primarily undertaken using the same kinds of bill finance and correspondent networks inherited from earlier generations. Even the currency used in international trade had a familiar look. Despite the emergence of the United States as the world's largest economy by the early twentieth century, the US dollar had failed to establish itself as the major international reserve currency even by the interwar years. As the US used its current account surpluses chiefly to buy gold in this period, the supply of dollars would have been inadequate for any such role, even had the Americans sought it. As a result, at least 40 per cent of world trade was still being financed in sterling during the late 1940s. This percentage was not that much less than in the pre-1914 period.

Innovation in banking was extremely difficult in the early postwar period because the industry had become cocooned in a web of regulation designed to prevent a repetition of the banking disasters of the 1930s, and to aid governments in their management of the economy. The influence of regulation was all-pervasive. In the US, Japan and elsewhere, commercial and investment banking were kept apart by regulations. All over Europe central banks and governments intervened to curb product innovation. Exchange controls and restrictions on currency convertibility provided few opportunities for international banking.

A second striking feature of the late 1940s and early 1950s was the segmentation of national markets. The banking system of the United States was almost entirely separated from the world economy. Although in the late nineteenth century foreign banks had been able to build up a presence in the US, by the post-1945 period federal and state regulations excluded them from all but the most limited representative roles in the American economy. The Japanese financial system was reconstructed by the US Occupation Forces after 1945 and emerged with a highly compartmentalised and regulatory structure. Until the later 1960s it was virtually impossible either for foreign banks to establish a presence in the Japanese market, or for Japanese banks to go abroad.

There was a broadly similar picture in Europe. Although foreign banks were sometimes able to occupy a niche role in a particular market, European banking markets were in general dominated by locally owned institutions, although the structure of individual markets differed radically from one another. Governments were active in preventing penetration by foreign banks. Even in the ostensibly liberal United Kingdom, foreign banks could open branches in the 1950s, but their exclusion from the clearing house cartel greatly curtailed their business opportunities in the British market. Although there was no law preventing a foreign acquisition of a British bank, in reality the Bank of England blocked the attempts of US banks to acquire British banks. The *de facto* prohibition of foreign acquisitions remained in force until the 1980s.

In this world of low innovation and market segmentation, multinational banking was very restricted. In part this reflected the pattern of multinational investment as a whole. Foreign direct investment grew rapidly before the First World War, and by 1914 had reached a size compared to overall world output which it was not to regain until the 1990s. In the 1930s high levels of political risk and economic depression had encouraged alternatives to multinational enterprise, such as the formation of international cartels. Subsequently, from the late 1940s, multinational investment in manufacturing and petroleum recovered and grew rapidly, but the banking sector saw no equivalent growth. Although US multinationals accounted for around 85 per cent of new direct investment between 1945 and 1960, US banks rarely went abroad. At the end of the 1950s a mere seven US banks had any overseas branches. In Europe, the powerful Swiss and German banks also chose not to venture abroad. Through the 1950s and 1960s Germany's expanding foreign trade was financed through correspondent relationships. The internationalisation of the German banks was slow. During the 1950s they opened their first representative offices. The foundation of subsidiaries, especially in Luxembourg, followed in the late 1960s, along with participation in banking consortia. Finally, from the late 1970s, came the opening of branches in foreign financial centres.

The major exceptions from this pattern were the overseas banks established in European countries with large empires in the nineteenth century, notably Britain and France. By the 1950s British-owned banks operated over 3500 overseas branches, mainly in the Southern Hemisphere and Asia, where they both conducted trade finance and held large shares of local banking markets. The British overseas banks had originated as wholly autonomous institutions with no equity or other relationship with the domestic banks. Each overseas bank specialised in a particular geographical region. This structure only began to break down in the interwar years when two large domestic banks, Barclays and Lloyds, took shareholdings in a number of the overseas banks, but through the 1950s and 1960s the domestic and overseas banking sectors remained rather separate. There was a long and difficult process of merger, which strong corporate cultures and geographical specialisation made difficult to achieve. The British overseas banks, like their French and other European counterparts, faced growing political difficulties as Latin American countries and newly independent colonies in Africa and Asia sought to restrict foreign banks. Nevertheless some of these banks held powerful franchises in major growth centres in the Middle East and Asia and proved very adaptable. One example of this genre – the Hongkong and Shanghai Banking Corporation – was destined not only to survive, but to become one of the world's largest banks. It is currently the fourteenth largest bank in the world in terms of total assets, the third largest European bank after Deutsche Bank and Crédit Agricole, and larger than any US bank, including the Chemical Banking/Chase Manhattan merger.

From the late 1950s this structure of world banking began to disintegrate. The key development was the re-creation of the integrated international money and capital market which had been lost after 1914. The emergence of the Eurodollar markets was both to undermine the national regulatory systems which restricted innovation, and to provide enormous growth opportunities for multinational banking. A key development was the return to convertibility of European currencies in the late 1950s. The Eurodollar market owed its birth in the late 1950s to restrictions on interest paid on deposits (Regulation Q) within the United States. The unwillingness of Eastern European governments to hold their dollars in the United States, and British government restrictions on sterling lending by its banks, helped to create the conditions where a market for dollars outside the United States emerged in London. The market grew in London, partly because of the large financial infrastructure associated with its traditional role as an international financial centre, but especially because of the lightness of regulatory controls. There were no liquidity ratios, and there was freedom of entry and exit in London's Euromarkets. This made London an attractive location compared to the other more tightly regulated European financial centres such as Paris and Frankfurt, as well as Tokyo. London's ability to attract transactions in non-sterling currencies enabled it to become and remain the world's largest international financial centre. Although London's growth has tended to be treated as inevitable, it was in fact encouraged and orchestrated by a number of key figures, such as Sir George Bolton. In the 1950s Bolton, while at the Bank of England, perceived how London could be reborn as a financial centre for non-sterling transactions, and at the end of the decade the bank of which he had become Chairman – the Bank of London and South America – became one of the first movers in the Eurodollar market.

The Eurodollar market captured a rising share of financial intermediation from sheltered and conservative domestic banking markets. It was regulated neither by the host country nor according to the currencies being transacted. In large transactions for corporations and governments – wholesale banking – multinational banks could offer higher deposit and charge lower loan rates on business transacted in London. The emergence of Eurobonds in 1963 resulted in a similarly unregulated capital market. The nature of international banking was transformed. Formerly it had been closely tied to international trade flows and related exchange operations. Over time, the Eurocurrency, Eurobond and foreign exchange markets became largely uncoupled from international trade. Multinational banks became the dominant players in these new financial markets, while lending to multinational enterprises (MNEs) and to governments was undertaken on a dramatically enhanced scale. This lending was especially centred on a number of international financial centres. This 'hierarchy' of financial centres had London as its apex, followed by New York and later Tokyo, and extended down to major regional centres such as Singapore and Hong Kong in Asia, while at its base there were 'offshore' centres such as the Cayman Islands and Panama, through which transactions were passed mainly for fiscal reasons.

Figure 11.1 shows the growth of foreign banks in New York since the 1970s. A striking feature of this new era of global banking was that, despite the growing deterritorialisation of the credit system, 24 hours a day, global markets continued to require a physical manifestation.

There were a number of reasons why particular locations developed as international financial centres after 1960. Except in the cases of New

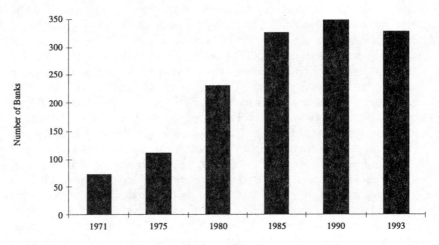

11.1 Growth of foreign banks in New York since 1971
Source: *City Research Project* (1994), Subject Report X1

York and later Tokyo, the size and strength of the domestic economy
was not a factor. Confidence in political stability was a prerequisite.
Regulatory policies had to be sufficiently competent and transparent to
convince bankers that their funds would be safe and, at all times,
accessible and mobile, while at the same time regulations had to be
sufficiently liberal and flexible to allow the freedom for entrepreneurial
banking activities to be pursued. Countries which operated extensive
exchange controls which sought to exclude or closely regulate foreign
banks, and which tightly restricted work permits to foreign bankers,
lawyers and accountants, did not develop as international financial
centres. It was critically important for London's growth from the 1960s
that major continental European financial centres, such as Frankfurt
and Paris, remained tightly regulated. Accessibility was a further important factor. Financial centres developed where there were good communications, ports, airports and, often, an English-speaking workforce.
Given the size of the economies of scale and agglomeration which arise
from a concentration of banking and financial activity, once a centre
had begun to grow, its growth became self-perpetuating. It took a major
and catastrophic security crisis to destroy a well-established financial
centre. The elimination of Beirut as the leading Middle Eastern financial
centre in the 1970s as a result of the Lebanese Civil War is the prime
example.
    A distinguishing characteristic of the global markets was their contin-
ued growth even after the original causes of their emergence were

removed. During 1973 and 1974 the United States abolished Regulation Q and controls against capital outflows, but the oil price rises of the period provided a further stimulus to the system. There was a massive inflow of funds into the Eurodollar market from the oil-producing countries, while many non-oil-producing countries borrowed from the market to finance their deficit balance of payments. The world debt crisis, which began in 1982 when Mexico announced its inability to service its large debt, revealed the poor quality of much of this international bank lending.

The Eurodollar markets triggered an unprecedented expansion in the internationalisation of banking. While in 1960 only seven US banks had any overseas branches, Table 11.1 shows that by 1986 US banks owned 899 branches outside the US. All seven US banks had London branches in 1960. By 1975, 55 US banks had London branches, and a decade later 68 US banks. Of non-US banks, 65 had London branches in 1960, but by 1985 the figure was 312. In the new era of multinational banking, the number of branches abroad was not a good proxy for the size of international banking activity, but other indicators pointed in the same direction. If we look at the real value of the foreign assets of deposit banks, these increased in real terms by a factor of 45 between 1960 and 1980. While before 1960 multinational banking had focused on the markets of the Southern Hemisphere and Asia, subsequently it increasingly took the form of cross-investment between developed markets.

Table 11.1   US bank MNEs, 1960 and 1986

	1960	1986
Number of banks with foreign branches and subsidiaries	8.0	151.0
Number of:		
foreign branches	131.0	899.0
foreign subsidiaries	2.0	860.0
Assets ($ bn) of:		
foreign branches	3.5	285.1
foreign subsidiaries	–	132.2
total foreign offices	3.5	417.3
Foreign assets of US bank MNEs relative to total assets of:		
US bank MNEs (%)	–	25.0
all US banks (%)	1.0	14.0

Source: Huertas (1990) p. 253

There are various explanations for the rapid internationalisation of banking after 1960. The new opportunities provided by the Euromarkets and the progressive liberalisation of regulatory regimes were clearly of major significance. There was a correlation with foreign trade expansion. Between 1950 and 1980 world exports increased in real terms by about 8 per cent per annum. There was also a delayed correlation with the growth of multinational investment in the manufacturing sector, as banks followed their clients abroad. In truth, after 1960 multinational banking became a complex activity involving different products for which different explanations are necessary. The reasons why a bank opened a branch in an international financial centre were quite different from those which prompted an investment in a foreign retail market.

During the 1970s and early 1980s the pursuit of asset growth and a global presence became central features of the international strategies of banks. The large US banks which dominated the growth of syndicated sovereign loans in the 1970s sought to achieve an accelerated growth of their assets through lending strategies which emphasised wide margins and large volumes of loans. Other US and non-US banks either shared the same strategy, or were the victims of 'herd behaviour', fearing to be left behind if they did not follow the leaders. There were, however, strong national variations in international bank lending strategies. US and British banks retained the lead in syndicated lending. By the end of 1985, US banks had 61 per cent of their total loans with developing countries and British banks 45 per cent, but Swiss banks, for example, had a mere 18 per cent. It was striking that in this matter, as in others, the British banks – despite their long international experience – often sought to follow the lead of US banks. This strategy was especially unfortunate as their staff usually had a lower level of professional competence than US banks.

Globalisation was also a key feature in bank strategies in these years. It became widely held among the world's major banks that large corporate customers needed a bank's presence in all the countries in which they operated. The desire to go global became so strong that concern about the profitability of particular branches or services became a secondary consideration. It was established as an article of faith that a large US presence was a prerequisite of being taken seriously as a global bank. As a result, from the 1970s the leading British banks began acquiring large US banks. The Midland Bank's acquisition of Crocker National, the eleventh largest US bank in 1981, entered the annals of banking history. By the time Midland divested itself of Crocker in 1986, the British bank had lost an estimated one billion dollars in its American foray. This was an extreme example of a more general problem experienced by foreign banks acquiring US banks. There was a tendency to pay too dearly for banks which turned out to have serious problems.

The post-1960 surge in multinational banking came to an end in the mid-1980s, since when retrenchment has occurred. While US overseas bank assets expanded rapidly during the 1970s, both in absolute terms and as a proportion of total overseas assets, Figure 11.2 shows that from the early 1980s bank assets fell as a proportion of the total US private assets abroad. The number of overseas branches of US banks declined sharply from the mid-1970s to reach just over 700 in 1992. The number of US banks with London branches declined from 68 to 49. There were several related factors in this slowdown. At its heart was the problem of deteriorating asset quality. In addition to the large provisions against LDC loans in the late 1980s, US, UK, Japanese and Scandinavian banks had also become seriously exposed to property-related lending, the full dangers of which were revealed when property values fell in major conurbations such as Tokyo, London and Toronto. Through international lending, foreign banks were in many cases exposed to property loans. At the same time the problems of acquiring foreign banks and operating in foreign markets had become all too apparent. Global ambitions began to be qualified by the need to be profitable in all the activities undertaken abroad, with subsequent disposal of 'non-core' activities in foreign markets. It is worth stressing, however, that the overall deceleration in multinational banking over the

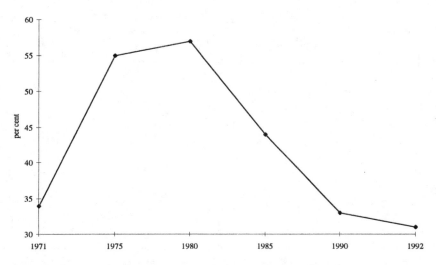

11.2   US banking assets abroad as a percentage of private assets
Source: *City Research Project* (1994), Subject Report X1

last decade has in part reflected a decline in the relative international importance of banks from English-speaking countries, while continental European and Asian multinational banking activity continued to grow.

The declining importance of banks from English-speaking countries was visibly reflected in rankings of size in world banking. As Table 11.2 shows, there were some striking changes between 1956 and 1992. American, British and Canadian banks had contributed 38 banks to the world's largest 50 (as measured by deposit size) in 1956, but by 1992 they only contributed nine banks. Japanese and, to a lesser extent, German and French banks had replaced them. Listings of the world's largest banks came to be dominated by Japanese institutions. Table 11.3 provides a ranking of banks by asset size in 1994. This was before the Chemical/Chase Manhattan merger and other consolidations in the United States, though even then the largest US bank could only make it into the bottom of such a table. In parentheses, however, it needs to be stressed that all such tables raise acute problems of interpretation. The denomination of deposit size in US dollars in Table 11.2 means that the figures are heavily distorted by exchange rate movements, while this kind of measure fails to include the growth of off-balance-sheet activities.

The internationalisation of banking helped progressively to undermine the segmentation of national markets. The most remarkable devel-

Table 11.2 Nationality of the world's largest banks, ranked by deposit size (number of banks in the top 50)

	1956	1960	1970	1979	1988	1992
USA	25	19	13	6	2	4
UK	7	5	4	4	4	3
Canada	6	5	5	4	1	2
France	3	3	3	4	4	6
Germany	0	3	4	7	7	8
Italy	3	5	4	2	1	1
Japan	3	8	11	16	25	16
Australia	1	1	1	0	0	0
Netherlands	0	0	1	3	2	2
Switzerland	0	0	3	3	3	3
Others	2	1	1	1	1	5

Source: Tickell, Adam (1993), 'Banking on Britain: The changing role and geography of Japanese banks in Britain', School of Geography, University of Leeds Working Paper 93/8

Table 11.3   The world's top 20 banks by assets, 1994

Rank	Bank	Country	Assets ($bn)
1	Bank of Tokyo/Mitsubishi	Japan	701.3
2	Fuji	Japan	507.2
3	Dai-Ichi Kangyo	Japan	506.6
4	Sumitomo	Japan	497.8
5	Sakura	Japan	496.0
6	Sanwa	Japan	493.6
7	Norinchukin	Japan	429.2
8	Industrial Bank of Japan	Japan	386.9
9	Crédit Lyonnais	France	338.8
10	Industrial & Commercial Bank of China	China	337.8
11	Deutsche Bank	Germany	322.4
12	Tokai	Japan	311.4
13	HSBC Holdings	UK	305.2
14	Long-Term Credit Bank of Japan	Japan	302.2
15	Crédit Agricole	France	282.9
16	Asahi	Japan	262.0
17	Société Générale	France	260.2
18	ABN-Amro	Netherlands	253.0
19	Banque Nationale de Paris	France	250.4
20	Barclays	UK	245.9

Source: 'Size isn't everything', *Financial Times*, 29 March 1994.

opment was the end of the isolation of the United States from world banking. As US banks expanded abroad, foreign banks penetrated the American market. In the 1960s foreign banks held an insignificant share of the American market. By 1983 they had acquired 18 per cent of the commercial and industrial loan market. While some acquisitions went disastrously wrong, a long-term and major change was under way. By 1992 non-US banks accounted for 45 per cent of the loan market, which made commercial bank lending a more foreign-dominated business sector in the United States than the automobile industry.

In Europe, the internationalisation of national markets was less clear-cut. During the 1970s German, French, Italian and other European banks began to expand abroad on a large scale. Their strategies tended to be more incremental than the British, and as a result they were somewhat less exposed to major accidents in foreign markets. Within the European market, wholesale activities became progressively internationalised. Retail banking was another matter. Although regulatory barriers to foreign acquisitions of banks were dismantled from the 1970s, other barriers remained. Individual European retail markets remained idiosyncratic. Although important examples of multinational retail banking occurred – by French, German and British banks in Spain, and by Australian banks in Britain – foreign penetration of European retail markets remained easier said than done. The penetration of niche markets, such as credit cards and the formation of strategic alliances, appeared a more rewarding strategy. The overall foreign penetration of European banking markets differed enormously between countries. In the United Kingdom, the US banks that opened branches to participate in the Euromarkets began to diversify into domestic business in the 1960s, tempting British corporate customers with long-term loans and aggressive marketing campaigns. They were able to build up a large share of domestic, sterling lending. Between 1980 and 1990 foreign banks increased their share of UK bank lending from 26 per cent to 35 per cent. In Germany, on the other hand, local banks retained a much stronger domestic franchise because of traditional bank–industry relationships.

Japan remained the odd one out in the internationalisation of banking. It was only from the late 1960s that the Ministry of Finance permitted Japan's city banks, long-term credit banks, trust banks and securities houses to establish branches in foreign countries. Their international growth began substantially only in the 1980s. The result was dramatic, especially after the yen–dollar realignment in 1985. The Japanese share of international bank assets rose from 23 to 35 per cent between 1984 and 1990, while the US share fell from 26 to 12 per cent over the same short period. Two city banks, Bank of Tokyo and Sanwa, made major US acquisitions and acquired a substantial share of the Californian retail market. Yet it was never clear that Japanese banks held the kind of advantage over their European and US competitors that Japanese automobile and consumer electronics firms possessed. On the one hand, the foreign expansion of Japanese banks in the 1980s was motivated in part by a desire to evade continuing domestic regulatory constraints by shifting some commercial lending and inter-bank trading activities to London and New York. On the other hand, the growth of Japanese foreign bank assets was driven by the disastrous 'bubble economy' of the late 1980s. The history of the last twenty years showed Japanese banks as more often followers than leaders in product innovation; prone to poor lending decisions and ill-judged acquisitions; and generally experiencing acute problems in incorporating foreign employees into Japanese-style management systems.

The experience of Japanese banking over the recent past demonstrated clearly that size was no substitute for strategy. By the mid-1990s the bad debts of Japanese banks were probably equivalent to between 11 and 17 per cent of Japanese gross domestic product, while it was Japan's largest banks which accounted for around 60 per cent of the total bad loans. The problem of poor lending was made much worse because the profitability of Japanese banks was amongst the lowest in the world as a result of extremely thin margins between lending and borrowing rates.

Even leaving aside the debt problem, Japanese banks have yet to achieve the significance in international banking which their sheer size would imply. Table 11.4 gives a ranking of the leading banks in foreign exchange dealing in 1995. Like other data of this kind, such a ranking is crude and subject to very considerable margins of error. Yet it is significant that even the largest Japanese banks did not appear in such listings, as their significance remained confined to certain niche and regional markets.

Table 11.4   The world's top 20 banks' share in foreign exchange dealing, 1995

Rank	Bank
1	Citibank
2	Chase Manhattan
3	HSBC Markets/Midland
4	Chemical
5	Union Bank of Switzerland
6	Bank of America
7	NatWest
8	JP Morgan
9	Swiss Bank
10	Standard Chartered
11	Barclays
12	First Chicago
13	BNP
14	SE Banken
15	Indosuez
16	Crédit Suisse
17	Bankers Trust
18	ABN-Amro
19	Royal Bank of Canada
20	Svenska Handelsbanken

Source: 'Citibank maintains top foreign exchange rank', *Financial Times*, 8 May 1995

The Japanese market remained peculiarly resistant to foreign penetration from the 1960s until the present day. Banking proved one of the sectors most resistant to liberalisation and deregulation. By 1970 only 18 foreign banks were licensed to operate branches in Japan. By 1990 the number had reached 83, but this revealed more about their enthusiasm to be represented in Japan than their success in that market. The Ministry of Finance continued to restrict foreign penetration of the retail market. Through the 1980s acquisitions of Japanese banks were blocked, leaving foreign banks no alternative but the slow and extremely expensive strategy of opening greenfield branches. Unable to enter retail banking, foreign banks were unable to access low-cost yen deposits. The only profits to be made were in activities the Ministry of Finance thought suitable for foreign banks – foreign currency lending and foreign exchange operations.

A remarkable characteristic of multinational banking from the 1960s was the progressive divorce of the location of international banking activity and the ownership of that activity. The role of London as the world's leading international financial centre was the most striking example of this phenomenon. London's importance was, unlike that of New York or Tokyo, unrelated to the size of its domestic economy. Sterling's use as a reserve currency was abandoned by the 1970s and the UK's share of world trade fell from 25 per cent in 1950 to 5 per cent in the 1980s, but London flourished as never before as an international financial centre. However, its character changed from being a sterling-based banking centre to a multi-currency one.

While the decline in the international use of sterling did not weaken London as a centre, it helped to diminish the part played by British institutions. At the beginning of the 1990s London was the world's leading Eurocurrency lending centre, accounting for perhaps 30 per cent of the total, but British-owned institutions accounted for less than 7 per cent of this total. London had flourished as a financial centre in the nineteenth century because of the activities of the foreign entrepreneurs who settled there, but the control of financial activities in London by foreign institutions based abroad was a new phenomenon. The decline of British ownership of financial activity continues. The year 1995 saw a remarkable series of acquisitions of the UK's remaining independent merchant banks, including ING's acquisition of the ruined Barings, and the sale of Warburg to Swiss Bank Corporation. The interpretation of this trend is debatable. It certainly implied that London would continue to flourish as Europe's leading financial centre. It also suggested that the bankers and financiers who worked in the City continued to possess many desirable skills which, however, seemed to function best if placed under the firm discipline of foreign control. The revival of Morgan Grenfell's fortunes under Deutsche Bank ownership since 1988 stands in contrast to the collapse of Barings as the result of an incompetent senior management's pursuit of speculative profits.

By the 1990s the cosy world of segmented markets and government regulation of forty years previously had largely disappeared in the developed market economies, with only the partial exception of Japan. The development of the global currency and capital markets outside the control of governments had given banks and their products an unprecedented importance in the world economy, though at the same time the very concept of a 'bank' had blurred. Banking had become an industry driven by innovation, deregulation and technological advance. In some senses the pace of internationalisation had slowed after the frenetic 25 years of expansion after 1960. Yet in the fast-growing Asia/Pacific region, international banking activities continued to boom.

Internationalisation, deregulation and innovation have been the major themes in world banking since the 1960s. The opportunities and achievements have been remarkable. What about the dangers? In what ways had banking also become a riskier industry than in the past? Risk, of course, lies at the heart of banking. Poor decisions and their consequences litter the history of banking. The poor lending judgements which led up to the outbreak of the world debt crisis in 1982 were part of a long tradition when apparently sober and conservative bankers had made gross misjudgements and paid the consequences with bad debts. The policy response was encouraging. The world financial system was not permitted to collapse, even though Latin America and Africa lost a decade of growth. There was no repetition of the banking collapses of the 1930s. None the less the internationalisation of banking widened the opportunities for the bankers of the US, Japan and Germany to make poor lending decisions on an international scale, while forty years previously they were effectively confined to their domestic, and familiar, market.

There were new opportunities also in international banking for making really gross misjudgements with major financial consequences. The phenomenon of buying and selling foreign banks was novel, and – as the experience of foreign banks in the United States showed – it offered the opportunity to lose huge sums of money in a short space of time. The pace of innovation in banking products, so different from the early postwar period, was potentially even more serious. The Euromarkets were inherently risky and, because much of the market was inter-bank, the danger of chain risk was considerable. Since 1975 a great deal of international regulatory effort has gone into identifying and responding to such risks, but acute problem areas arguably remain. These include the implications of the dismantling of regulatory barriers (and the consequent sight of once safe deposit-taking institutions engaging in risky proprietary trading) and of government safety nets designed to prevent depositors losing money in the event of a bank failure. The growth in the 1990s in scale and significance of international transactions in derivative instruments such as futures, swaps and options has revealed a further layer of danger. At its heart lies the problem of highly skilled young bankers inventing and selling products which their senior managers, regulators and customers do not understand. Over the last thirty years international banking has been uncoupled from international trade finance and, in part, from regulation. The dynamic consequences are obvious, but so are – or should be – the risks.

References

Aliber, Robert Z. (1984), 'International banking: a survey', *Journal of Money, Credit, and Banking*, 16 (4).

Goldberg, Laurence G. and Johnson, Denise (1990), 'The determinants of US banking activity abroad', *Journal of International Money and Finance*, 9.

Hirtle, Beverly (1991), 'Factors affecting the competitiveness of internationally active financial institutions', *Federal Reserve Bank of New York Quarterly Review*, New York.

Huertas, Thomas F. (1990), 'US multinational banking: history and prospects', in Jones, Geoffrey (ed.), *Banks as Multinationals*, London, Routledge.

Jones, Geoffrey (1995), *British Multinational Banking 1830–1990*, London, Clarendon Press.

Jones, Geoffrey (1996), *The Evolution of International Business*, London, Routledge.

King, Frank H. H. (1991), *The History of the Hongkong and Shanghai Banking Corporation*, vol. 4, Cambridge, Cambridge University Press.

'London as an International Financial Centre' (November 1989), *Bank of England Quarterly Bulletin*, London.

London Business School (1994), *The City Research Project*, 3 vols, London, Corporation of London.

Tschoegl, A. E. (1987), 'International retail banking as a strategy: an assessment', *Journal of International Business Studies*, 19 (2).

CHAPTER TWELVE

Panel Discussion: European Banking in the Past, Present and Future

Lionello Adler, Hilmar Kopper, Alexandre Lamfalussy and Pedro Martinez Mendez

Lionello Adler

During recent years the evolution of the European banking market has shown a remarkable trend in helping the concentration of market power, together with increased competition among intermediaries belonging to foreign countries. The latter phenomenon may be seen mainly as an outcome of the liberalisation process in the European financial services sector which had its cornerstone in the 1992 programme promoted by the second European banking directive. Such a process is likely to gain more strength in the near future as long as the creation of the single market continues. A variety of factors which influence the success, or otherwise, of concentration and merger activity will be examined below.

In an assessment of concentration in banking, consideration should be given to the fundamental economic forces linked to economies of scale and diversification. Economies of scale are often asserted to be at the origin of the concentration process, although it must be recognised that such economies have so far received little empirical support, mainly due to the enormous difficulties in their measurement. There are indeed some advantages linked to concentration, for example, the increase of market share and the expansion of territorial presence. Moreover, reaching a critical dimension often combines with the creation of a diversified intermediary.

Diversification may take different forms. First, it may be linked to banking through traditional intermediation activity. In this respect, diversification may be realised through mergers between banks possessing different features, for example long-term versus short-term lending; indirect versus direct funding; different loan deposit ratios; different contributions of service fees; and larger or smaller presence abroad. Second, at the periphery, diversification may be realised with the result that the provision of services is less directly linked to a bank or business

– that is, merchant banking, insurance products and investment services. Thus the diversified intermediary has the opportunity of exploiting
'diversification economies' resulting from the joint production of several financial services. As a consequence, the cost of joint production
may ultimately be less than the cost of producing such services sepa-
rately. This may be the result of cost savings in the production of
information about customers, savings, marketing and other expenses;
the more efficient use of the branch network; or by making the customer relationship easier.

The complementary features of different banking institutions, and the
target of achieving a critical mass, have been the two driving forces
behind mergers that have taken place in Europe in recent years. In
reality, the cost savings due to scale economies have turned out to be
very difficult to implement. Typically, the rigidity of the labour market
has prevented mergers involving significant cuts in personnel and general expenses. However, the complementary nature of merging institutions has been a crucial factor for success in concentration, giving the
opportunity to put together banks with different features, such as the
type of services offered and the geographical distribution of branches.
One of the many aspects arising from the concentration process has
been the creation of value in a new institution, produced through
merger, and this has resulted in benefits such as increases in gross sales
of product and the acquisition of new customers for each of the merging banks.

Finally, it must be stressed that one crucial factor in an amalgamation
operation is the compatibility between the information and operating
systems of the merging institutions. The difficulties inherent in the
merger of different information systems and different procedures may
generate high transition costs which may, in turn, significantly reduce
the benefits of the merger operation in the initial phase.

In conclusion, the concentration process will continue to characterise
the evolution of the European banking market in the near future. However, each merger operation will have to be carefully evaluated before
implementation in order to ensure its success.

Hilmar Kopper

The topic under consideration is 'European banking in the past, present
and future'. This contribution will consider the present situation of
banking in Europe and, more particularly, in Germany.

In present-day Germany just under 3800 banking institutions exist,
that is 42 per cent of all banking institutions in the European Commu-

nity. Germany has the highest density of banking outlets in Europe: 1600 inhabitants per banking outlet, whilst the European Community average is slightly above 2000. Thus it could be argued that Germany is not only over-banked, it is also over-branched, but this is a debatable issue. However, another more definite assertion is that at present the majority of financial institutions are looking at their networks (in as much as they have networks) to decide whether they can, or should, continue to offer all things to all people in all places. Some restructuring is already visible and has taken place over the last few years. This process is reinforced by technology or, to be more precise, by information technology. The first effects of this may be witnessed in the markets and such developments will become increasingly significant over time.

What of the structure of German banking or of the German banking industry? Germany has a very peculiar banking structure which is often overlooked. If we measure market shares by total deposits or total lending, the result is that in Germany over 50 per cent of market share is held by 'government-owned' institutions or municipally owned institutions: the huge block of savings banks and Landesbanken.

A further 15 per cent of market share is held by cooperative banks which are growing rapidly. Private banks account for a declining market share. The Deutsche Bank is the biggest bank in Germany, having a market share of 5 per cent. In comparison with any other Western European country, the situation in Germany is unique. There is no other European country where the three biggest commercial banks combined have under 20 per cent of the total market. Indeed, in some European countries the three biggest banks have over 50 per cent of the total market share. In Germany the corresponding figure is just 13 per cent. What do these figures illustrate? They show that there is a tremendous degree of competition in Germany, and competition is good for the clients. However, banks in Germany are not pleased by this situation and the structure of the banking system has been the cause of much debate. Banks and bankers in Germany have a major task: they have to be prepared to defend their legitimacy and defend their role as members of the German economy. This situation is little understood outside Germany and appears to be one which is unique to this country.

The types of banks within the German banking system and the possibilities for mergers among them should also be considered. As previously stated, there are three types of banks in Germany, the savings banks, the cooperative banks and the private banks, and within this system trans-segment mergers or takeovers are highly unlikely. Mergers between different types of banks are rare. Some have been attempted but they have failed, regardless of regional or political structures, and they are not viewed favourably in Germany, at least for the time being.

However there have been many mergers within the savings bank sector and amongst cooperative banks.

When examining the German banking system in an international context, three factors stand at the forefront of such a discussion. First, it is important to consider the corporate and individual tax burden. Tax is, of course, an issue for business in any country. In Germany, the high tax burden means that returns on equity after tax are lower because a higher tax burden exists than elsewhere. Such a comparison has disadvantages for Germany, particularly when looking for international money to bolster equity resource: German banks are not very attractive in this sense. Second, Germany possesses a rather inflexible labour market, and wage costs are high. Third, the country has a tightly knit regulatory network in the banking sector. This may be viewed as a positive characteristic. Indeed, tight regulations may be seen as a contributory factor to the stability of the German banking system, by international standards, during the last fifteen years. However, there is one factor in the regulatory network which may be viewed in a negative fashion: this is the requirement for high minimum reserves. Because of this feature the German banking sector has always lacked an international flavour, since German banks were forced to do most of their international business outside their domestic geographical boundaries, as Geoffrey Jones has already highlighted (Chapter 11). German banks went to Luxembourg, London or elsewhere to carry out international business. Such actions may be viewed as disadvantageous: taxes may have been generated for the German government and more domestic jobs created if such a strategy had not been pursued. What factors influence the attractiveness of international financial deals and the regulatory framework? Germany cannot be viewed as a front-runner in this context.

Finally, consideration should be given to the expansion of banking in Germany. Branches in Germany are referred to as 'outlets', and indeed operate as such, yet they were originally operated as 'inlets': the German word for them was *Depositenkassen*. Their task was to collect money in the form of deposits, but consequently they slowly transformed into outlets. If they are to be maintained, branches will have to become better outlets, that is, increasing the sale of services through them. In this context, the experience of the Deutsche Bank may provide a useful example. The bank entered into the insurance business because it was viewed as a wonderful tool with which to push more business into existing 'bricks and mortar' outlets and to generate provision and commission in doing so. More steps could be undertaken to develop business in this direction: time will tell.

Alexandre Lamfalussy

This discussion intends to look to the future and to the introduction of a single European currency. This event will no doubt cause some interesting problems and banks will face a number of challenges during the transition process. The heads of state or government have requested the European Commission, the finance ministers and the European Monetary Institution (EMI) to present their views on the currency changeover scenario. It is likely that in the near future the heads of state or government will give their seal of approval to it. Such approval is essential for the preparation not only of the banks but all market participants, economic agents, private individuals, corporations and governments.

The EMI is in the middle of finalising its view on the introduction of a single European currency but has already established a certain number of points. What are the cornerstones of the scenario as seen by the EMI? First, there is the assumption that the monetary union will start on 1 January 1999. This involves the locking of exchange rates and the beginning of the single monetary policy operations by the European System of Central Banks (ESCB). It is likely that the decision to select the countries that are fit to lock exchange rates and the decision to go ahead will have to be taken sometime around March 1998, the same year that the European Central Bank will be established. Once the exchange rates are locked, the European Central Bank will start operating. It will announce and conduct its monetary policy in the European currency, but the banks which have not been able to equip themselves appropriately will be provided with conversion facilities. This policy will allow the latter institutions to carry out banking operations in national currencies for their customers but to deal with the ESCB in the European currency. This will mean that, in practice, the inter-bank market will start operating predominantly in the European currency from the beginning of the new system, and that foreign exchange transactions between the member countries of the union *vis-à-vis* outside currencies will be conducted in the European currency.

It is likely that the ESCB will require up to three years before banknotes in the single currency can be introduced. The timing of the introduction of banknotes is imprecise as it is impossible to know exactly how long it will take. Moreover, the decision regarding the exact duration of this intermediate period should be taken by the European Central Bank once it is established in 1998.

When the banknotes are introduced, all banking operations will have to switch over into the European currency. Businesses and households will be free to open accounts in the European currency right from the beginning, but they cannot be obliged to do so. In practice, it is unlikely that a large number of private individuals will wish to open their accounts in the European currency as long as they do not have banknotes. They will also have a second reason for waiting until the end of the transition period: it is at this time, that is three years later, that all normal operations of the public authorities will begin to be conducted in the European currency. These normal operations do not include the issuing of bonds, new debt, or re-denomination of the existing debt (where the changeover may take place earlier), but rather tax payments, payments of salaries, pension payments, social security payments, and so on. Considering that the contribution of the public sector to GDP is 40 to 50 per cent in most European countries, this massive change will be perceived by private individuals as the real change.

During the three-year transition period, national banknotes will still be legal tender. Private agents should be free to operate in the single currency but should not be compelled to do so. Therefore, a choice will exist as to the use of the currency. It is likely that corporations will open European currency accounts – especially for their treasury operations – at a relatively early stage, according to their requirements, but, as mentioned above, it is unlikely that private individuals will do so.

This is a very simplified summary of the main points of the changeover scenario. What are the challenges and problems it raises for the banking industry?

The first major challenge is the time needed for preparing the process of changeover. Some banks might be tempted to delay their active preparatory work until the decision to lock exchange rates and the countries participating in this process are known, that is, until March 1998. This approach would appear to be sensible, but it is in reality a risky one because the lead time needed to implement the preparatory process may be quite long. Preparation involves not simply the adjustment of organisation, information technology and business strategy but, even more fundamentally, the mental adjustment of management and staff. Whatever the probability of monetary union effectively starting on 1 January 1999, bank managements would be wise to take precautionary measures to insure themselves against the risk of monetary union happening. Insurance is not costless, but the alternative is a loss of market shares in favour of more enterprising competitors. The introduction of the single currency amounts to a major step towards a truly competitive European banking market. A cost–benefit calculation of early versus delayed preparation cannot be avoided.

As to the business areas most likely to be affected immediately after 1999, the following points can be made. The key feature of the changeover will be that monetary policy will be announced and conducted in the European currency right from the beginning of the changeover. This will have a far-reaching and almost instantaneous impact on the money market and on the inter-bank market, and the effects will probably also spread quickly to the financial sphere – especially if the governments decide (as they probably will) to issue new debt in the European currency right at the beginning. Thus the changeover will be the quickest in capital markets, financial markets and money markets. The daily life of the ordinary citizen will change little until three years later, but all those institutions which will either play, or hope to play, an important role in the financial markets will have to be ready with their preparatory work much earlier.

The second main challenge is to foresee the end of the transition period and be ready to switch over to the single currency at the end of this process on all banking accounts, including the large number of retail accounts. This will be a very large-scale operation. Banks may find it relatively easy to operate in multiple currencies, or make changeovers, for specific projects; to quote an example, banks may have portfolio management services that already use a number of currencies. However, a complete changeover of all the accounts into the single currency is a massive move and will, almost inevitably, be left to the end of the process. Therefore, in terms of organisation, this is a very major challenge to all banks.

The third challenge concerns the timespan between the beginning and the end of the changeover process – life during the period of transition. How will banks respond to the growing desire of corporate customers to use the single European currency during this period? Large corporate customers will be the leaders, and they will be followed by the medium and then the smaller customers. How fast, and by how many of them, is anybody's guess. Competition between banks is likely to be fierce and it is in this area that the handling of the whole process will present a genuinely difficult task. Flexibility in responding to business needs will be the key to success.

Pedro Martinez Mendez

The issues of internationalisation and concentration in banking are linked by the subject of competition, a topic that will be highlighted in the following discussion.

First, the issue of concentration will be considered with reference to the experience of a Southern European country, Spain, which is similar to the experience of Northern and Central European countries, as discussed by the previous contributors. Starting from a number of small local banks, progressive concentration was achieved by absorptions and mergers. The history of banking in Spain shows that many banks have disappeared, but that there have been very few explicit bankruptcies. In most cases, banks with difficulties were absorbed by other banks. It is no surprise that these mergers have accelerated in times of crisis; the timing of a takeover or a merger has usually coincided with a stage of poor performance or financial difficulties of the absorbed banks. This may be viewed as competition of a sort. In many cases it was not the result of aggressive competition, but rather depended on the differing abilities of banks in designing the balance of their assets and liabilities. The failure to get this balance right over time proved to be the stumbling block for banks disappearing in the concentration process.

Throughout the history of banking in Spain, especially in the 1920s, the process of concentration has also taken more gradual forms, often supported by the absence of a money market. The role of the money market was replaced by the development of special direct inter-bank relationships. These led over time to growing dependent relationships and controlling interests, which were not always highly apparent, as the controlled institutions retained their formal personality and identity and explicit mergers only took place many years after a full controlling interest had been established. As a result, implications may not be drawn concerning the concentration process merely by looking at changes in the number of banks or the volume of their assets.

The role of savings banks must also be considered in the process of concentration, as these institutions are very important in Spain. Here the same pattern may be found as in Northern and Central Europe: concentration continued in non-savings banks, whilst savings banks remained largely outside this process. This is a good example of the influence of regulation referred to by Geoffrey Jones in Chapter 11. Savings banks in Spain were subject to a large number of limitations on their activities and were limited to very specific markets. Since the 1980s these restrictions to competition have been lifted and consequently the Spanish savings banks may now undertake exactly the same functions as commercial banks, the only difference being their ownership status. Higher competition and poor relative performance of some savings banks have sparked concentration forces in this area. Very recently the psychological barrier of a savings bank owning a proportion of the equity of a commercial bank has been broken, as several instances of such a participation have now been observed. By definition it is still legally impossible for the reverse to occur. However, it is just a matter of time before an inevitable breakdown in regulations removes this last barrier to competition. As a result, the process of concentration in the future will, it is hoped, involve both commercial and savings banks on an equal footing.

Regarding the subject of capital flows, the Spanish experience will again be considered, in an attempt to highlight the difference between accidental and sustained developments. As an example of the former, the consequences of the First World War may be mentioned. As a result of neutrality, Spain experienced very high current account surpluses, which are well documented, and very significant capital inflows, on which there is a lack of quantitative evidence. However, two developments may be stated with certainty. First, a huge amassing of gold and foreign assets by the Central Bank occurred, and, second, a large number of foreign banks were established in Spain. These developments lasted throughout the war and for a few years beyond. After the war the situation gradually reverted to its previous state. Foreign assets were kept, because the Central Bank refused to sell them to counteract a depreciation of the exchange rate, but foreign banks, little by little, disappeared from the Spanish market.

In contrast, sustained changes have taken place in recent years in the internationalisation of Spanish financial markets and, contrary to the past, there is now ample statistical information on the process. Looking at the relevance of total foreign assets and liabilities as a percentage of GDP, it can be observed that total foreign liabilities, which between 1970 and 1983 had remained rather stable at about 18 per cent of GDP, had increased by 1993 to 68 per cent of GDP. Total foreign assets had risen from about 8 per cent of GDP between 1970 and 1983 to almost 50 per cent of GDP in 1993. Looking at the detail by sectors between 1970 and 1993, the following observations can be made: a largely balanced position of commercial and savings banks assets, increasing however in gross terms from 4 to 25 per cent of GDP; a small increase of non-bank foreign assets from 6 to 9 per cent of GDP; and a very large increase of non-bank foreign liabilities from 14 to 43 per cent of GDP, with a significant contribution, since 1990, of foreign investment in the Spanish market for government securities, which has become, within its category, one of the most successful European markets.

In examining figures for other countries, the same pattern of sustained changes emerges. If a comparison is made of total foreign assets in the economy to GDP between 1983 and 1992, the figures for Japan show an increase from 30 per cent in 1983 to 42 per cent in 1992; in France from 35 per cent to nearly 70 per cent; and Italy displays an increase from 22 per cent to approximately 40 per cent. The USA shows a similar trend, but at strikingly lower levels. Total foreign assets increased from 9 per cent of GDP in 1983 to 21 per cent in 1992, while in the same period foreign liabilities rose from 15 per cent to 21 per cent of GDP. The breakdown of these figures between banks and non-banks will not be discussed here in detail, but it can be pointed out that, broadly speaking, the upward trend is applicable to both sectors.

These figures also show a striking feature: when the balance of foreign assets and liabilities is drawn, the net balance does not change radically in the period under discussion. This net balance, depending on the country, has moved between 5 and 15 per cent of GDP over the period from the late 1970s to early 1990s. Thus, while gross assets and liabilities are on a clearly upward trend, macroeconomic constraints appear to be operating which result in the relative stabilisation of their net balance. The similarity between these trends, and trends in international trade (also with gross volumes as a percentage of GDP on an upward path, while net trade balances remain constrained within a narrow band) is noticeable. In the short run, of course, net current transactions must match net capital movements. But the figures on foreign assets and liabilities indicate that a constraining influence limits the build-up of persistent balances, either credit or debit, something understandable in the case of net debtor countries, but less easy to explain in the case of net creditor countries.

When discussing the internationalisation of banking, it is important to examine both the banking and the non-banking sector. There are two aspects to this subject. First, when looking at domestic financial markets in several developed countries, the balance sheets of banks, as a percentage of GDP, show very rapid growth, whereas the figures for outstanding domestic inter-bank lending (as a percentage of GDP) look rather flat. It has not been possible to ascertain whether the same pattern prevails in international bank lending. It would be interesting to know systematically how much of the growth of international banking is explained by international inter-bank lending and how much by international bank lending to, or borrowing from, the non-banking sector. A situation similar to that prevailing in domestic markets, as is likely to be the case, would enhance the relevance of the following observation.

Second, when considering the portfolios of multinational banks, it is not enough to look at them from a purely banking perspective. It is also important to have a clear picture of what economic forces are at work in the counterpart non-banking sector, and influencing the banks. Trends and patterns of international trade, direct investment and portfolio investment should be brought into the picture. This leads back to the distinction between accidental and sustained developments. To draw clear lines between non-economic and economic factors for the internationalisation of banking may be difficult and not entirely necessary. However, as in the case of Spain during the First World War, there have been, in recent economic experience, many other episodes of capital movements associated with special circumstances, some short-lived but some more persistent. Political instability has existed in a number of countries with obvious effects on international banks. In some countries, as has been rightly mentioned, regulations may block the process of internationalisation, but in others they have stimulated it. Differences in tax rules have, for instance, been a persistent source of capital movements and of international banking intermediation. These factors have been neglected and deserve further attention. It is important to know the particular developments which have been in force at a particular time, country or banking system.

In addition to these factors, there are also those peculiar to banks. International banking has been characterised by higher competition and innovation than domestic banking systems. The types of products that international banks have offered and the pricing of these products has allowed them to carve out a niche in countries where regulations and isolation from external influence have reduced the ability or willingness of domestic banks to compete and innovate. Occasionally, success in influencing domestic banks to share such attitudes may have, in turn, inhibited the possibilities of further expansion of foreign banks in a domestic market. Spain would again offer a good example. It would be useful, where possible, to ascertain to what extent the growing internationalisation of banking has been due to such a competitive impulse, what the influence of the higher performers has been, and what impact international banks have had on changing the attitudes of domestic banks and their regulators.

Finally, it may be important to attempt to distinguish more forcefully between two meanings of internationalisation in the banking sector. Philip Cottrell in Chapter 10 is correct to assert that there are many different meanings of this term, but here just two interpretations will be focused on. The first definition of internationalisation, as mentioned above, may be associated with the size of external financial assets and liabilities as a percentage of GDP or as a percentage of bank assets. The second interpretation may be associated with the presence of banks abroad. The issue may appear to be just a matter of location – whether, for instance, a Deutsche Bank loan to an Argentinean borrower is booked in the Frankfurt head office or is booked in a branch in Argentina. In some cases the distinction may be a formality, but on the whole many relevant differences (sources of funds, overall influence on domestic banks, statistical measurement, etc.) are likely to be involved.

In conclusion, it is possible to draw another link between the issues of internationalisation and concentration. The topic falls into the second definition of internationalisation mentioned: the presence of banks abroad. Thus, the question may be asked: is it inevitable for concentration to occur at the international level? Does the process of concentration, which has been witnessed in almost every national economy, have to proceed at a European level for banks to be better able to face their future challenges? My belief is that we shall see this process of concentration continuing at an international level. It may be a very slow process; historically, the same process also took place at a slow rate in domestic economies, but it took place. It might be even slower on a European scale, for various obvious reasons. However, it is difficult to imagine why such an evolution should now stop at national borders.

Banks in Northern and Central Europe, *c.* 1913

Philip L. Cottrell

Explanatory notes

Columns

(i)   Date of formation
(ii)   Location of head office
(iii)   Nationality
(iv)   Number of branches
(v)   Balance sheet total (in local currency)
(vi)   Local currency
(vii) Balance sheet total in sterling

Column abbreviations and notes

(i)   Where space is limited B. = Bank or Banque; Oe. = Oesterreichische
(iii)   a = Austrian; b = Belgian; d = German; den = Danish; f = French; gb = British; gbf = British foreign bank; nl = Netherlands; nor = Norwegian; swe = Swedish
(vi)   fcs = French francs; fcsb = Belgian francs; fl = Dutch florins; kr = krones of Denmark and the Scandinavian Union; m = German marks; ök = Austrian krones. Where this space is empty it indicates that the local currency is sterling.
(vii) £1 = 25 francs of France and the Latin Monetary Union (mint par = 25.221 fcs); £1 = 18 krones of Denmark and the Scandinavian Union (mint par = 18.159 kr); £1 = 20 German marks (mint par = 20.429 mks); £1 = 12 Dutch florins (mint par = 12.107 fl); £1 = 24 Austrian krones (mint par = 24.027 ök)

NB   An entry of a dash (–) in any column shows that no data were available under this heading in the *Almanac*.

Source: Inglis Palgrave, Sir R. H., *The Banking Almanac and Directory*, 1914.

Bank	(i)	(ii)	(iii)	(iv)	(v)	(vi)	(vii)
Aachner Bank für Handel und Gewerbe	1874	Aachen	d	0	7 799 862	m	389 993
Aakirkeby Bank	1902	Aakirkeby	den	0	790 827	kr	43 935
Aalesund Kreditbank	1877	Aalesund	nor	0	5 711 347	kr	317 297
Aalesunds Landmansbank	–	Aalesund	nor	0	3 414 521	kr	189 696
Aarhus Privatbank	1870	Aarhus	den	0	28 421 018	kr	1 578 945
Adler, D. B. & Co.	1850	Copenhagen	den	0	–	–	–
Adriatische Bank	–	Trieste	a	0	33 899 763	ök	1 412 490
African Banking Corp.	–	London	gbf	43			6 723 334
Agricultural Bank of Egypt	1902	Cairo/London	gbf	0			11 905 412
Aktiebolaget Mälareprovinsernas Bank	1847	Stockholm	swe	11	79 774 099	kr	4 431 894
Aktiebolaget Göteborgs Bank	1847	Gothenburg	swe	20	152 834 869	kr	8 490 826
Aktiebolaget Göteborgs Folkbank	1871	Gothenburg	swe	2	8 806 137	kr	489 229
Aktiebolaget Göteborgs Handelsbank	1897	Gothenburg	swe	27	61 483 993	kr	3 415 777
Aktiebolaget Stockholms Diskontobank	1891	Stockholm	swe	0	38 024 901	kr	2 112 494
Aktiebolaget Stockholms Folkbank	–	Stockholm	swe	0	–	–	–
Aktiebolaget Stockholms Handelsbank	1871	Stockholm	swe	6	143 775 059	kr	7 987 503
Aktiebolaget Nordiska Kreditbank	1896	Stockholm	swe	8	36 564 735	kr	2 031 374
Aktiebolaget Norrlansdbanken	1911	Stockholm	swe	35	103 829 887	kr	5 768 327
Aktiebolaget Skånska Handelsbank	1896	Malmö	swe	29	101 223 211	kr	5 623 511
Aktie-Kreditbanken I. Sandefjord	1893	Sandefjord	nor	0	6 920 200	kr	384 455
Aktieselskabet Fredrikshalds Kreditbank	1897	Fredrikshalds	nor	0	4 554 360	kr	253 020
Aktieselskabet Trondhjems Handelsbank	1885	Trondhjem	nor	0	21 643 394	kr	1 202 410
Allegemeine Deutsche Credit-Anstalt	–	Leipzig	d	0	471 875 873	m	23 593 793
Allgemeine Oe. Boden-Credit-Anstalt	1864	Vienna	a	1	877 013 044	ök	36 542 210
Amsterdamsche Bank	1871	Amsterdam	nl	6	70 815 941	fl	5 901 328
Amsterdamsche Handelsbank	1912	Amsterdam	nl	0	2 173 513	fl	181 126
Andresens B. Aktieselskabank	–	Oslo	nor	0	–	–	–
Anglo-Levantine Banking Co.	1908	London	gbf	1		gbf	87 076

Bank	Year	City					
Anglo-Austrian Bank	1863	Vienna	a	50	–		27 415 958
Anglo-Egyptian Bank	1864	London	gbf	11			5 467 877
Anglo-Palestine Co.	–	London	gbf	1			481 624
Anglo-South American Bank	–	London	gbf	21			19 017 494
Armstrong & Co.	–	London	gb	0	–	–	–
Arndts Herzog & Co.	–	Hamburg	d	0	–	–	–
Agdesidens Bank	1887	Ariendal	nor	0	9 144 691	kr	508 038
Ayrton, F. S. (the English Bank)	1850	Pau	f	0	–	–	–
Banque Argentine et Française	1909	Paris	f	0	24 906 561	fcs	996 262
Banque Centrale Anversoise	1878	Antwerp	b	0	106 689 187	fcsb	4 267 567
Banque Continentale de Paris	1911	Paris	f	0	16 433 917	fcs	657 356
Banque d'Alsace & de Lorraine	1871	Strasbourg	d	17	121 813 804	m	6 090 690
Banque d'Outremer	1899	Brussels	b	0	242 644 165	fcs	970 576
Banque de Gand	–	Ghent	b	0	67 690 429	fcs	2 707 617
Banque de l'Union Anversoise	1910	Antwerp	b	0	120 115 702	fcs	48 046 308
Banque de Metz	–	Metz	d	0	17 967 144	m	898 357
Banque du Hainaut	1872	Mons	b	2	67 713 405	fcs	2 708 536
Bank für Oberösterreich und Salzburg	1869	Linz	a	5	58 515 294	ök	2 438 137
Bank für Thuringen, vormals B. M. Strupp AG	1905	Meiningen	d	0	71 200 040	m	3 560 002
Banque Française d'Egypte	–	Paris	f	1	10 015 373	fcs	400 615
Banque Franco-Japonaise	1912	Paris	f	1	57 979 010	fcs	2 319 160
Banque Générale Belge	1860	Antwerp	b	2	130 442 958	fcs	5 217 718
Banque Générale d'Ostende (SG)	1913	Ostend	b	0	–	–	–
Banque Générale de Liège	1882	Liège	b	0	62 150 481		2 486 019
Banque Internationale de Bruxelles	–	Brussels	b	0	98 146 198		3 925 847
Banque Nationale de Crédit	1913	Paris	f	62	–	–	–
Bank of British West Africa	1894	London	gbf	58			2 660 232
Bank of Ireland	1783	Dublin	gb	99			22 916 229
Bank of Whitehaven	1837	Whitehaven	gb	9			760 807
Banque Regionale du Nord	–	Roubaix	f	0	–	–	–
Banque Suisse et Française	1894	Paris	f	0	189 541 299	fcs	7 581 651

Bank	(i)	(ii)	(iii)	(iv)	(v)	(vi)	(vii)
B. & Wechselstuben-Actien-Gesellschaft 'Mercur'	1887	Vienna	a	33	266 943 202	ök	11 122 633
Banque Adam	1784	Boulogne-sur-mer	f	14	–	–	–
Banque Belge pour l'Etranger	1902	Brussels	b	5	–	–	–
Banque Centrale d'Escompte de Bruxelles	–	Brussels	b	0	–	–	–
Banque Centrale de la Lys	1911	Courtrai	b	2	–	–	–
Banque Centrale Gantoise	1906	Ghent	b	0	62 23 303	fcs	24 893
Banque Ch. Noel & Cie	1850	Paris	f	0	–	–	–
Bank Commandite Baden-Baden, Meyer & Diss	1872	Baden-Baden	d	0	–	–	–
Banque d'Anvers	1826	Antwerp	b	0	279 445 129	fcs	11 177 805
Banque de Bordeaux	1899	Bordeaux	f	11	49 036 917	fcs	1 961 476
Banque de Bruxelles	1871	Brussels	b		602 597 578	fcs	24 103 903
Banque de Charleroi	–	Charleroi	b	0	22 471 320	fcs	898 852
Banque de Commerce		Antwerp	b	0	–	–	–
Banque de Crédit Commercial	1865	Antwerp	b	0	92 952 935	fcs	3 718 117
Banque de Flandre	–	Ghent	b	0	–	–	–
Banque de l'Union Parisienne	1904	Paris	f	0	334 471 811	fcs	13 378 872
Banque de Mulhouse	1872	Mulhouse	f	8	201 111 788	fcs	8 044 471
Banque de Paris et des Pays Bas	1872	Paris	f	3	715 984 674	fcs	28 639 386
Banque de Reports de Fonds-Publique et de Dépôts	1900	Antwerp	b	0	236 387 630	fcs	9 475 505
Banque de Verviers		Verviers	b		50 260 362	fcs	2 010 414
Banque du Midi	–	Carcassonne	f	0	–	–	–
Bank für Chile und Deutschland	–	Hamburg	d	8	57 671 612	m	2 883 580
Bank für Handel und Gewerbe	1880	Bremen	d	0	16 097 362	m	804 868
Bank für Handel und Industrie	1853	Berlin/Darmstadt	d	48	894 529 783	m	44 726 489
B. Française et Italienne pour l'Amerique du Sud	1910	Paris	f	12	535 568 677	fcs	21 422 747
Banque Française pour le Brésil	1911	Paris	f	2	–	–	–
Banque Française pour le Commerce et l'Industrie		Paris	f	1	328 981 757	fcs	13 159 270
Banque Industrielle de Bohême	1898	Prague	a	23	160 173 514	ök	6 673 896

Name	Year	City	Code	No.	Amount	Unit	Value
B. J. Allard & Co. (SA)	1857	Paris	f	0	50 123 725	fcs	2 004 949
Bank of British North America	1836	London	gbf	95	–	–	13 256 423
Bank of Liverpool	1831	Liverpool	gb	138	–	–	21 754 004
Bank of Mauritius	1894	London	gbf	2	–	–	555 982
Bank of Roumania	1866	London	gbf	1	–	–	1 672 694
Bank of Scotland	1695	Edinburgh	gb	176	–	–	27 342 554
Banque Privée	1898	Lyons	f	72	178 378 993	fcs	7 135 159
Banque Transatlantique	–	Paris	f	0	–	–	–
Banque Vasseur	–	Paris	f	0	–	–	–
B. W. Serruys	1911	Ostend	b	38	–	–	–
Bankaktiebolaget Sodra Sverige	–	Helsingborg	swe	0	130 711 403	kr	7 261 744
Badische Bank	1870	Mannheim	d	0	–	–	–
Badon-Pascal, Pommier et Cie (Sen C.)	–	Paris	f	0	16 790 404	fcs	671 616
Baelde Frères	–	Antwerp	b	0	–	–	–
Barber, J. Lionel, & Co.	1899	London	gb	0	–	–	–
Barclay & Co. Ltd	1896	London	gb	598	–	–	62 960 616
Baring Brothers Ltd	1762	London	gb	0	–	–	16 415 796
Barmer Bank Verein	1867	Barmen	d	25	298 874 046	m	14 943 702
Barnard, Thomas & Co.	1799	Bedford	gb	0	–	–	412 296
Baschwitz, C. W.	–	London	gbf	0	–	–	–
Bayerische Disconto und Wechsel-bank	1905	Nürnberg	d	19	81 906 154	m	4 095 307
Bayerische Handelsbank	1869	Munich	d	28	550 388 434	m	27 519 171
Bayerische Hypotheken und Wechsel Bank	1835	Munich	d	0	1 337 052 064	m	66 852 603
Bayerische Vereinsbank	1869	Munich	d	12	651 979 807	m	32 598 990
Beckett & Co.	1750	Leeds/York	gb	34	–	–	7 251 104
Behrens, L., & Sohne	–	Hamburg	d	0	–	–	–
Belfast Banking Co.	1827	Belfast	gb	77	–	–	8 138 547
Bellairs, H., & Co. (British & International Bank)	1871	Biarritz	f	1	–	–	–
Benas, L., & Son	1819	Liverpool	gb	0	–	–	–
Benson, Fredk. J. & Co.	–	London	gb	0	–	–	–
Berenberg, Joh., Gossler & Co.	1730	Hamburg	d	0	–	–	–

Bank	(i)	(ii)	(iii)	(iv)	(v)	(vi)	(vii)
Bergens Kreditbank	1876	Bergen	nor	1	56 257 335	kr	3 125 407
Bergens Privatbank	1855	Bergen	nor	0	60 559 407	kr	3 364 411
Bergisch Markische Bank	1871	Elberfeld	d	35	380 472 275	m	19 023 613
Berle, Marcus & Co.	1829	Wiesbaden	d	0		-	-
Berliner Handelsgesellschaft	1856	Berlin	d	0	574 586 065	m	28 729 303
Bernhard, Scholle & Co.	-	London	gbf	0		-	-
Bethmann, Gebrüder	1748	Frankfurt	d	0		-	-
Biggerstaff, W. & J.	-	London	gb	2		-	-
Bignon & Co.	-	Abbeville	f	0		-	-
Blandy Brothers & Co.	-	London	gb	0		-	-
Blydenstein, B. W. & Co.	1858	London	gbf	0		-	6 760 279
Blyth, Greene, Jourdain & Co. Ltd.	1837	London	gb	0		-	-
Böhmische Escompte Bank	1863	Prague	a	15	159 874 093	ök	6 661 420
Böhmische Union Bank	1872	Prague	a	24	337 624 768	ök	14 067 698
Boissevain, Adolph, & Co.	1875	Amsterdam	nl	0		-	-
Bonn & Co.	1910	London	gbf	0		-	-
Bougère, Vve, & Fils	-	Angers	f	0			
Boulton Brothers	-	London	gbf	0		-	-
Boyle, Low, Murray & Co.	1833	Dublin	gb	0		-	-
Bradford & District Bank	1862	Bradford	gb	15			6 238 967
Brandt's, Wm. Sons & Co.	-	London	gbf	0		-	
Brasilianische Bank für Deutschland	-	Hamburg	d	0	134 476 078	m	6 723 803
Braunschweigische Bank und Kreditanstalt	1853	Braunschweig	d	0	54 877 526	m	2 743 876
Brees-Janssens	-	Antwerp	b	0		-	-
Bremer Bankverein	1869	Bremerhaven	d	0	8 082 930	m	404 146
British & Foreign Banking Corp.	1909	London	gbf	0		-	15 509
British Bank for Foreign Trade	1911	London	gbf	0		-	4 070 276
British Bank of Northern Commerce	1912	London	gbf	0		-	-

	Founded	City					
British Bank of South America	1863	London	gbf	13	–		20 005 331
British International Bank	1912	London	gb	0	–		2 280 467
British Linen Bank	1746	Edinburgh	gb	148	–		17 673 603
British Mutual Banking Co.	1857	London	gb	0	–		69 343
British Oriental Bank	1909	Smyrna/London	gb	0	–		34 636
British, Foreign & Colonial Corp.	1910	London	gbf	0	–		399 260
Brown Shipley & Co.	–	London	gbf	0	–	–	–
Bunge & Co.	–	Amsterdam	nl	3	–	–	–
Caisse Commerciale de Dieppe	–	Dieppe	f	0	4 764 106	fcs	190 564
Caisse de Crédit de Nice	–	Nice	f	0	31 465 032		1 258 601
Caisse Générale de Reports et de Dépôts	1874	Brussels	b	0	594 797 770	fcs	23 791 910
Caisse Privée du Nord	1912	Brussels	b	0	–		–
Capital & Counties	1834	London	gb	480	–		43 671 404
Carlone & Co.	–	Nice	f	0	–	–	–
Cassel & Co.	–	Brussels	b	0	–	–	–
Cattaui, J. M., Fils & Co.	–	Paris	f	0	–	–	–
Centralbanken fur Norge	–	Oslo	nor	0	118 021 398	kr	6 556 744
Centralbank der Deutschen Sparkassen	–	Prague	a	13	–	–	–
Chalmers, Guthrie & Co. Ltd.	–	London	gbf	0	–	–	–
Chaplin, Milne, Grenfell & Co. Ltd.	1899	London	gb	35	–		2 820 515
Chartered Bank of India, Australia & China	1853	London	gbf	2	–		27 477 477
Chartered Commercial Bank	1855	Hamburg	d	12	9 622 630	m	481 113
Cheminitzer Bank Verein	1871	Cheminitz	d	0	40 661 960	m	2 033 098
Child & Co.	1673	London	gb	4	–		2 914 758
Christiania Bank & Kreditkasse	1848	Oslo	nor	0	59 635 744	kr	3 313 096
Civil Service Bank	1892	London	gb	0	–		85 987
Clare (George) & Co.	–	London	gbf	1	–	–	–
Claude-Lafontaine, Prevost & Co.	–	Paris	fcs	148	–	–	–
Clydesdale Bank	1838	Glasgow	gb	0	–		18 251 517
Cocks, Biddulph	–	London	gb	20	–		1 146 984
Colonial Bank	1836	London	gbf		–		4 012 740

169

Bank	(i)	(ii)	(iii)	(iv)	(v)	(vi)	(vii)
Commercial Bank of Spanish America	1904	London	gbf	10			394 853
Commercial Bank of London	1906	London	gbf	0		–	–
Commercial Bank of Scotland	1810	Edinburgh	gb	170			19 926 663
Commerz-und-Disconto Bank	1870	Hamburg/Berlin	d	5	466 447 041	m	23 322 352
Commerz Bank in Lübeck	–	Lübeck	d	0	26 211 179	m	1 310 558
Compagnie Algérienne	–	Paris	f	64	303 565 643	fcs	12 142 625
Compagnie Commerciale Belge	–	Antwerp	b	0		–	–
Comptoir d'Escompte de Bruxelles	–	Brussels	b	0	45 756 678	fcs	1 830 267
Comptoir d'Escompte de Mulhouse	1848	Mulhouse	f	3	219 991 142	fcs	8 799 645
Comptoir Lyon Alemand	–	Paris	f	0		–	–
Comptoir National d'Escompte de Paris	1848	Paris	f	273			74 555 737
Cook, Thomas	–	London	gbf	85		–	–
Cossart, Gordon & Co. Ltd.	–	London	gbf	0		–	–
Coulon, Bethoud & Co.	–	London	gbf	0		–	–
Courtois & Co.	–	Toulouse	f	0		–	–
Courvoisier Berthoud & Co.	1785	Paris	f	0		–	–
Coutts & Co.	1892	London	gb	0			9 748 067
Cox & Co.	1909	London	gbf	5			4 673 327
Credietvereeniging	1853	Amsterdam	nl	13	18 276 621	fl	1 523 051
Crédit Anversois	–	Antwerp	b	2		–	–
Crédit des Flandres	–	Bruges	b	0		–	–
Crédit du Nord	1866	Lille	f	36	171 532 599	fcs	6 861 303
Crédit Française	–	Paris	f	0		–	–
Crédit Général de Paris	1903	Paris	f	1		–	–
Crédit Général Liégeois	–	Liège	b	7	298 735 396	fcs	11 949 415
Crédit Industriel et Commercial, SG	1859	Paris	f	49			12 618 805
Crédit Lyonnais	1863	Paris	f	373	2 758 317 860	fcs	110 332 716
Crédit Mobilier Français	1852	Paris	f	0	215 129 911	fcs	8 605 106

Name	Location	Year					
Crédit Nantais	Nantes	1912	f	0	–	–	–
Crompton & Evans' Union Bank	Derby	1877	gb	47	–	–	6 094 093
Cunliffe, Roger & Sons	London	1830	gb	0	–	–	–
Danon, Joseph & Cie	Paris	–	f	0	–	–	–
Danske Landmandsbank Hypothek & Vekselbank	Copenhagen	1871	den	29	397 524 723	kr	22 084 706
Dantzig, S. van, & Co.	Rotterdam	1872	nl	0	–	–	–
Danziger Privat-Aktien-Bank	Danzig	1856	d	15	61 359 016	m	3 067 950
Davillier & Co.	Paris	–	f	0	–	–	–
De Neuflize et Cie	Paris	1667	f	0	–	–	–
de Neufville, D. & J.	Frankfurt	–	d	0	–	–	–
de Pury, Gautschi & Co.	London	1902	gbf	0	–	–	–
Deichmann & Co.	Cologne	1858	d	0	–	–	–
Delbruck Schickler & Co.	Berlin	1854	d	0	–	–	–
Delhi & London Bank	London	1844	gbf	7	–	–	2 299 328
Den Norske Arheid Boigbank	Oslo	–	nor	0	–	–	–
Deutsch–Westafrikanische Bank	Berlin	1904	d	2	10 008 222	m	5 004 111
Deutsch–Südamerikanische Bank AG	Berlin	1906	d	7	126 434 975	m	6 321 748
Deutsche Bank	Berlin	1870	d	14	–	–	112 998 222
Deutsche Afrika-Bank AG	Hamburg	–	d	3	7 386 141	m	369 307
Deutsche Effecten und Wechsel Bank	Frankfurt	–	d	0	88 593 272	m	4 429 663
Deutsche National KG	Bremen	1906	d	20	164 876 853	m	8 243 842
Deutsche Orientbank	Berlin	1906	d	15	103 702 888	m	5 185 144
Deutsche Palastina Bank	Berlin	1898	d	7	87 745 634	m	4 387 281
Deutsche Überseeische Bank	Berlin	1886	d	25	–	–	15 588 018
Deutsche Vereinsbank	Frankfurt	1871	d	2	85 468 546	m	4 273 427
Deutsch–Ostafrikanische Bank	Berlin	1905	d	0	10 335 129	m	516 756
Dingley & Co.	Launceston	1855	gb	9	–	–	–
Dingley, Pearse & Co.	Okehampton	1856	gb	4	–	–	–
Disconto-Maatschappij	Rotterdam	–	nl	0	9 636 251	fl	803 020
Disconto-, Laane-og Sparebanken	Aalborg	1854	den	0	10 017 322	kr	556 517
Disconto-Gesellschaft	Berlin	1851	d	13			58 013 331

Bank	(i)	(ii)	(iii)	(iv)	(v)	(vi)	(vii)
Dobree, Samuel & Sons	–	London	gbf	0	–	–	–
Donner, Conrad Hinrich	–	Hamburg	d	0	–	–	–
Dordtsche Bank	–	Rotterdam	nl	4	6 924 689	fl	577 057
Drammens Og Oplands Kreditbank	1875	Drammen	nor	0	26 978 016	kr	1 498 778
Drammers Privatbank	1867	Drammen	nor	0	24 397 404	kr	1 355 411
Dresdner	1872	Dresden	d	50			72 275 403
Dreyfus, J., & Co.	1868	Frankfurt	d	0	–	–	–
Drummonds	1717	London	gb	0	–	–	–
Ducoing, Loiselle & Co.	–	Paris	f	0	–	–	–
Dumail, C. & Boujassy, E.	–	Lyons	f	0	–	–	–
Eastern Bank	1909	London	gbf	3	14 622 849		3 566 636
Elberfelder Bankverein	–	Elberfeld	d	2		m	731 142
English, Scottish & Australian Bank	–	London	gbf	133			10 146 152
Enskilda Banken i Wenersborg	1865	Wenersborg	swe	3	29 576 952	kr	1 643 164
Equitable Bank	1900	Halifax	gb	3			206 964
Erlanger, Emile, & Co.	1859	London	gbf	0	–	–	–
Essener Credit-Anstalt	1872	Essen	d	22	270 936 195	m	13 546 809
Evekink, D. & Son	1812	Zutphen	nl	0	–	–	–
Farrow's Bank	–	London	gb	67			1 277 533
Forbes, Forbes, Campbell & Co. Ltd	1790	London	gbf	3	–	–	–
Fox, Fowler & Co.	1787	Wellington	gb	39	–	–	–
Frankfurter Bank	1854	Frankfurt	d	0	58 378 785	m	2 918 939
Frankfurter Gewerbekasse	1862	Frankfurt	d	0	17 620 791	m	881 039
Fredriksstad Privatebank	1891	Fredriksstad	nor	0	14 659 602	kr	814 422
Frege & Co.	1739	Leipzig	d	0	–	–	–
Friedburg, Martin & Co.	–	Hamburg	d	0	–	–	–
Fuld & Co.	–	Pforzheim	d	0	–	–	–
Fyens Disconto Kasse	1846	Odense	den	0	25 587 106	kr	1 421 505

	Founded	Place	Country				
Fyen Landmansbank	–	Odense	den	0	–	–	–
Galizische Volksb. für Landwirtschaft und Handel	–	Lemberg	a	0	–	–	–
Gans, Alfred et Cie	1896	Paris	f	0	–	–	–
Geertsema, Feith & Co.	1876	Groningen	nl	0	–	–	–
Geestemunder Bank	–	Geestemunder	d	0	–	–	–
Gilbert & Co.	–	Avranches	f	5	–	–	–
Gillett & Co.	1784	Banbury	gb	8	–	–	–
Gillett & Co.	–	Oxford	gb	0	–	–	–
Glyn, Mills	1753	London	gb	0	–	–	19 015 784
Gouin Frères	–	Tours	f	0	–	–	–
Goldschmidt, Gebr.	1868	Gotha	d	0	–	–	–
Gosselin, Huret et Cie	1804	Boulogne-sur-mer	f	1	–	–	–
Gontard, Heinrich, & Co.	1815	Frankfurt	d	0	–	–	–
Grace Brothers & Co. Ltd	–	London	gbf	0	–	–	–
Graverend, Metenier & Co.	–	Dieppe	f	0	–	–	–
Grindlay & Co.	–	London	gbf	0	–	–	–
Grosvenor's Bank	1913	London	gb	0	–	–	–
Guerin, Vve, et Fils	–	Lyons	f	6	–	–	–
Guernsey Banking Co.	1827	St Peter Port	gb	1	–	–	432 581
Guernsey Commercial Banking Co.	1835	St Peter Port	gb	0	–	–	–
Guinness Mahon & Co.	1836	Dublin/London	gb	0	–	–	2 291 000
Gunner & Co.	1809	Bishop's Waltham	gb	1	–	–	–
Haarbleicher & Schumann	–	London	gbf	0	–	–	–
Haarlemsche Bankvereeniging	1864	Haarlem	nl	3	fl	7 509 553	625 796
Haes & Sons	–	London	gbf	0	–	–	–
Halifax & District Permanent Banking Co.	1909	Halifax	gb	3	–	–	29 396
Halifax Commercial Banking Co.	1810	Halifax	gb	17	–	–	2 258 346
Hallescher Bankverein	–	Halle/Saale	d	0	m	43 961 890	2 198 094
Hammer & Schmidt	1821	Leipzig	d	0	–	–	–
Hannoversche Bank	1856	Hanover	d	6	m	113 632 303	5 681 615
Hardy & Hinrichsen	1879	Hamburg	d	0	–	–	–

Bank	(i)	(ii)	(iii)	(iv)	(v)	(vi)	(vii)
Harris, Bulteel & Co.	1774	Plymouth	gb	15	–	–	–
Harris, Winthrop & Co.	–	London	gbf	0	–	–	–
Haugesunds Privatbank	1907	Haugesund	nor	0	5 547 715	kr	308 206
Heine et Cie	–	Paris	f	0	–	–	–
Helsinglands Enskilda Bank	1874	Söderhamn	swe	18	46 405 177	kr	2 578 065
Hesse, Newman & Co.	1777	Hamburg	d	0	–	–	–
Heude, Vitu & Co.	–	Fougères	f	0	4 785 353	fcs	191 414
Heydt & Co., E., Von der	1910	London	gbf	0	–	–	–
Heydt, Von der, & Co.	1895	Berlin	d	0	–	–	–
Heydt-Kersten, Von der, & Sohne	1754	Elberfeld	d	0	–	–	–
Hibernian Bank	1825	Dublin	gb	82	–	–	4 765 852
Hoares	1771	London	gb	0	–	–	3 155 835
Holt & Co.	1809	London	gb	0	–	–	–
Hope & Co.	1732	Amsterdam	nl	0	–	–	–
Hotinguer & Co.	–	Paris	f	0	–	–	–
Huth, Fredk	1808	London	gbf	0	–	–	300 424
Imperial Bank of Persia	1889	London/Tehran	gbf	16	–	–	3 229 767
Incasso-Bank	–	Amsterdam	nl	2	38 757 208	fl	2 729 204
Ionian Bank	1839	London	gbf	15	–	–	958 029
Isle of Man Banking Co.	1865	Douglas	gb	0	–	–	–
Jackson, J.	1866	Liverpool	gb	0	–	–	–
Jacobson, Ferdinand	1848	Hamburg	d	0	–	–	–
Jacquier & Co.	–	Lyons	f	0	–	–	–
Japhet, S. & Co.	1896	London	gbf	0	–	–	–
Jenssen & Co.	1818	Trondhjem	nor	0	–	–	–
Jonas, H. A., Sohne & Co.	–	Hamburg	d	0	–	–	–
Jordaan & Co.	–	Paris	f	0	–	–	–
Journel & Co.	–	Paris	f	0	–	–	–

Name	Year	City					
Kas-Vereeniging	1865	Amsterdam	nl	0	23 128 555	fl	1 927 379
Keizer, N. & Co.	–	London	gb	0	–	–	–
Keller's, G. H., Sohne	–	Stuttgart	d	0	–	–	–
Keyser, A. & Co.	–	London	gbf	0	–	–	–
King & Foa	1886	London	gb	0	–	–	–
King, Henry	–	London	gbf	0	–	–	–
Kirchberger, L. J.	–	Ems	d	0	–	–	–
Kjobenhavns Grundejerbank	1898	Copenhagen	den	0	28 365 488	kr	1 575 860
Kjobenhavns Handelsbank	1873	Copenhagen	den	0	175 237 778	kr	9 735 432
Kjobenhavns Laane-og-Diskontobank	1895	Copenhagen	den	0	67 510 917	kr	3 750 606
Kleinwort, Sons & Co.	1855	London/Liverpool	gbf	0	–	–	–
Koch Lauteren & Co.	–	Frankfurt	d	5	–	–	–
Kohn, Anton	1878	Nuremberg	d	0	–	–	–
Konig Brothers	1899	London	gbf	0	–	–	–
Königl. Wurtt. Hofbank Gmbh	1906	Stuttgart	d	0	–	–	–
Königliche Seehandlung	–	Berlin	d	0	–	–	–
Königsberger Vereins-bank	1871	Königsberg	d	0	29 457 704	kr	1 636 539
Kopparbergs Enskilda Bank	1836	Falun	swe	14	46 321 717	kr	2 573 428
Krebs, J. A.	–	Freiburg/Baden	d	0	–	–	–
Kroatische Escompte Bank	–	Agram	a	0	–	–	–
Kugelmann, David	–	Hissigen	d	0	–	–	–
Laane, Firma W.	1860	Roosendaal	nl	4	–	–	–
Ladenburg, W. & Co.	–	London	gb	0	–	–	–
Lancashire & Yorkshire Bank	1872	Manchester	gb	130	–	–	12 838 431
Landry, P. J.	1842	Hague	nl	0	–	–	–
Laurvigs Privatbank	1885	Larvik	nor	0	5 672 594	kr	315 144
Lazard Brothers & Co.	–	London	gbf	0	–	–	–
Lazard Frères & Cie	1854	Paris	f	0	–	–	–
Le Grelle, J. J.	–	Antwerp	b	0	–	–	–
Lehideux & Co.	–	Paris	f	0	–	–	–
Levy, Eugene & Co.	–	Paris	f	0	–	–	–

Bank	(i)	(ii)	(iii)	(iv)	(v)	(vi)	(vii)
Lippmann, Rosenthal & Co.	-	Amsterdam	nl	0	-	-	-
Lloyds	1765	London	gb	651			101 846 765
Lobbecke Brothers & Co.	1761	Brunswick	d	0	-	-	-
Loewenherz, J.	-	Berlin	d	0	-	-	-
London & Brazilian Bank	1862	London	gbf	16			2 230 754
London & Hanseatic Bank	1873	London	gbf	0			7 822 273
London & Liverpool Bank of Commerce	1871	London	gbf	0			2 960 774
London & Provincial Bank	1864	London	gb	343			21 604 014
London & River Plate Bank	1862	London	gbf	30			38 193 519
London & South Western Bank	1862	London	gb	194			24 407 370
London Bank of Central America	1888	London	gb	0			45 152
London Bank of Australia	1852	London	gbf	87			7 388 938
London County & Westminster Bank	1836	London	gb	358			101 079 034
London Joint Stock Bank	1836	London	gb	301			41 395 548
London Metal Banking Co.	1907	London	gb	0			101 885
London, City & Midland Bank	1836	London	gb	845			105 951 247
London, Singapore & Java Bank	1912	London	gbf	0			90 442
Lübecker Private Bank	1820	Lübeck	d	0	10 948 651	m	547 432
Magdeburger Bankverein	1867	Magdeburg	d	12	66 137 127	m	3 306 856
Mahrische Escomptebank	1862	Brunn	a	1	29 499 736	ök	1 229 155
Mallet Frères & Co.	-	Paris	f	0	-	-	-
Manchester & County	1862	Manchester	gb	114			12 664 162
Manchester & Liverpool District Bank	1829	Manchester	gb	205			28 943 953
Marcuard, Meyer-Borel et Cie	-	Paris	f	0			-
Marcus & Volkmar	1874	Berlin	d	0			-
Martin's Bank	-	London	gb	12			-
Marx & Co's Bank	1869	Rotterdam	nl	0	8 313 655	fl	4 236 264
Matthieu, J. & Fils	-	Brussels	b	0	-	-	692 804

Name	Year	City	Code	No.	Amount 1	Unit	Amount 2	
McGrigor, Sir Charles	–	London	gb	1	254 736 012	m	12 736 800	–
Mecklenburgische Hypotheken und Wechsel Bank	1871	Schwerin	d	1	–	–	–	–
Mees, R., & Zoonen	–	Rotterdam	nl	0	–	–	–	–
Meissner, F., & Co., nachf.	–	Berlin	d	0	–	–	–	–
Mendelssohn & Co.	–	Berlin	d	0	–	–	–	–
Mercantile Bank of London	1891	London	gb	0	–	–	54 253	–
Mercantile Bank of India	1892	London	gbf	18	–	–	8 368 314	–
Mercantile Bank of Scotland	1889	Glasgow	gb	13	–	–	177 372	–
Merck, Fink	–	Munich	d	0	–	–	–	–
Merck, H. J., & Co.	1800	Hamburg	d	0	–	–	–	–
Messein, Fisson & Co. – Comptoir de Lorraine	–	Paris	f	0	39 464 787	fcs	1 578 591	–
Metropolitan Bank	1866	London	gb	165	–	–	12 347 261	–
Meyer & Co.	1814	Leipzig	d	0	–	–	–	–
Meyer, Adolph	1835	Hanover	d	0	–	–	–	–
Middlesex Banking Co.	1885	London	gb	0	–	–	33 243	–
Miller Brothers & Co.	–	London	gb	0	–	–	–	–
Mirabaud & Co.	1820	Paris	f	0	–	–	–	–
Mitteldeutsche Creditbank	1856	Frankfurt/Berlin	d	18	223 851 933	m	11 192 596	–
Mitteldeutsche Privat-Bank AG	1856	Magdeburg	d	59	281 099 386	m	14 054 969	–
Mittelrheinische Bank	1873	Coblenz	d	4	68 976 171	m	3 448 808	–
Morgan, Grenfell	1838	London	gbf	0	–	–	6 834 119	–
Morgan, Harjes & Co.	–	Paris	f	0	–	–	–	–
Moss Privatbank	1897	Moss	nor	0	–	–	208 396	–
Munroe & Co.	1851	Paris	f	0	–	–	–	–
Munster & Leinster	1885	Cork	gb	91	–	–	6 830 983	–
National Bank	1835	London/Dublin	gb	140	–	–	17 335 039	–
National Bank of New Zealand	1872	London	gbf	57	–	–	6 641 961	–
National Bank of India	1863	London	gbf	26	–	–	18 469 011	–
National Bank of Scotland	1825	Edinburgh	gb	123	–	–	20 013 244	–
National Provincial Bank of England	1833	London	gb	418	–	–	72 310 905	–
Nationalbank für Deutschland	1881	Berlin	d	21	456 376 546	m	22 818 827	–

Bank	(i)	(ii)	(iii)	(iv)	(v)	(vi)	(vii)
Nederlandsche Bank voor Zuid Afrika	1888	Amsterdam	nl	7			813 023
Nederlandsche Handel Maatschappij	1824	Amsterdam	nl	28	246 261 446	fl	20 521 787
Nederlandsche–Indische Handelsbank	1863	Amsterdam	nl	15	71 238 325	fl	5 936 527
Neumann, Luebeck & Co.	–	London	gbf	0	–	–	–
Neumann, P. & Co.	–	London	gbf	0	–	–	–
Niederlausitzer B. AG	–	Cottbus	d	0	9 216 385	m	460 819
Niederösterreichische Escompte-Gesellschaft	1853	Vienna	a	0	388 975 214	ök	21 609 734
Norddeutsche Creditanstalt	1897	Königsberg	d	19	101 722 278	m	5 086 113
Nordenfjeldske Kreditbank	1868	Trondhjem	nor	0	25 858 466	kr	1 436 581
Norddeutsche B. in Hamburg (Disconto-ges 1895)	1856	Hamburg	d	0	295 832 515	m	14 791 625
Nordisk Resebureau	–	Gothenburg	swe	4	–	–	–
Nordlands Privatbank	1893	Bodo	nor	1	6 392 923	kr	355 162
Norrköpings Enskilda Bank	–	Norrköping	swe	1	28 957 200	kr	1 608 733
Norske Creditbank	1857	Oslo	nor	1	94 477 963	kr	5 248 775
North Eastern Banking Company	1872	Newcastle	gb	99			5 142 117
North of Scotland	1836	Aberdeen	gb	149			10 467 091
Northern Banking and Town & County Bank	1824	Belfast	gb	105			7 344 308
Nottingham & Nottinghamshire Banking Co.	1834	Nottingham	gb	37			5 066 167
Oberlausitzer Bank zu Zittau	–	Zittau	d	2	12 635 743	m	631 787
Oberndoerffer, J. N.	–	Munich	d	0	–	–	–
Oe. Credit-Anstalt für Handel und Gewerbe	1855	Vienna	a	20	1 195 107 440	ök	49 796 143
Oe. Länderbank	1880	Vienna	a	33			32 698 478
Offroy, Guiard & Co.	–	Paris	f	0	–	–	–
Oldenburgischen Spar- & Leih-Bank	–	Oldenburg	d	9	67 149 638		3 357 481
Ontvang en Betaalkas	1813	Amsterdam	nl	0	14 222 252	fl	1 422 264
Oppenheim, Hugo & Sohn	–	Berlin	d	0			–
Oppenheim, Sal. jr & Cie	1789	Cologne	d	0			–
Oppenheimer, Lincoln Menny	–	Frankfurt	d	0			–

Name	Year	City	Country	No.	Amount	Cur.	Amount
Orebo Enskilda Bank	1837	Orebo	swe	9	32 223 577	kr	1 790 198
Osnabrucker Bank	–	Osnabruck	d	12	73 883 900	m	3 694 195
Ostbank für Handel und Gewerbe	1857	Königsberg	d	33	126 657 057	m	6 332 852
Ostergotlands Enskilda Bank	1837	Linköping	swe	15	46 913 094	kr	2 606 283
Oyens, H. & Zonen	1800	Amsterdam	nl	0	–	–	–
Palatine Bank	1899	Manchester	gb	8	–	–	462 132
Parr's Bank	1865	London	gb	276	–	–	52 409 246
Parry & Co.	–	London	gb	0	–	–	–
Perier & Co.	1800	Paris	f	0	–	–	–
Petyt, A. et Cie	–	Dunkerque	f	0	–	–	–
Pfalzische Bank	1867	Ludwigshafen	d	21	258 852 131	m	12 942 606
Pfeiffer & Co.	1876	Wiesbaden	d	0	–	–	–
Pfeiffer, L.	1846	Cassel	d	3	–	–	–
Pforzheimer Bankverein AG	1872	Pforzheim	d	0	21 226 212	m	1 061 310
Phillppson, F. M., & Co.	–	Brussels	b	0	–	–	–
Pinto Leite & Nephews	–	London	gbf	0	–	–	–
Plaut, H. C.	–	Leipzig	d	0	–	–	–
Plump, Carl F. & Co.	–	Bremen	d	0	–	–	–
Pool, Edward, E. & Co.	–	London	gb	0	–	–	–
Porges, E., & Co.	–	Paris	f	0	–	–	–
Preußische Central-Genossenschafts Kasse	1895	Berlin	d	5	27 951 125	m	1 397 55(
Privatbank zu Gotha	1856	Gotha	d	8	150 614 377	kr	8 367 465
Private Bank of Copenhagen	1857	Copenhagen	den	3	–	–	–
Prost, Maurice	–	Lons-le-Saunier	f	88	–	–	–
Provincial Bank of Ireland	1825	London	gb	0	–	–	7 792 068
Provinciale B.	1900	Hertogenbosch	nl	0	946 122	fl	78 843
Provinciebank, The	1898	Hague	nl	0	4 394 320	fl	366 193
Quin (Gerald), Cope & Co.	–	London	gb	0	–	–	–
Raymond, Pynchon & Co.	1895	London	gbf	0	–	–	–
Ree, Wilhelm, jr	1872	Hamburg	d	0	–	–	–
Reeves, Whitburn & Co.	–	London	gb	0	–	–	–

Bank	(i)	(ii)	(iii)	(iv)	(v)	(vi)	(vii)
Reid & Co., Neville	1780	Windsor	gb	1	-	-	-
Reliance Bank	-	London	gb	0			326 303
Reuter's Bank	1913	London	gb	28			665 345
Revionsbanken I Kjobenhavn	-	Copenhagen	den	0	12 315 238	kr	684 179
Rheinische Bank	1897	Mulheim a.d Ruhr	d	7	93 257 731	m	4 662 886
Rheinische Creditbank	1870	Mannheim	d	24	427 254 611	m	21 362 730
Rheinische–Westfalische Disconto-Gesellschaft	1872	Aachen	d	21	328 496 995	m	16 424 849
Richards & Co.	1854	Llangollen	gb	0		-	-
Richardson & Co.		London	gb	0		-	-
Richer, Felix, & Co.	1845	Le Havre	f	0		-	-
Robarts, Lubbock	-	London	gb	0			4 318 533
Rodocanachi, Sons	1830	London	gbf	0		-	-
Rosenberg, O. A., & Co.	1906	London	gbf	0		-	-
Rothschild, N. M., & Sons	1804	London	gb	0		-	-
Rotterdamsche B. Vereeniging	1911	Rotterdam/Amsterdam	nl	0	83 801 453	fl	69 834 54
Royal Bank of Ireland	1836	Dublin	gb	12			2 554 675
Royal B. of Scotland	1727	Edinburgh	gb	164			20 555 727
Ruffer, A. & Sons	-	London	gbf	0		-	-
Sachs & Hochheimer	1840	Frankfurt	d	0		-	-
Sachs, Moritz	-	Frankfurt	d	0		-	-
Sächsische B. zu Dresden	-	Dresden	d	8	197 754 124	m	9 887 706
Sale & Co.	-	London	gbf	0		-	-
Samuel Montagu & Co.	-	London	gbf	0		-	-
Samuel, M., & Co.	1831	London	gbf	0		-	-
Sasson, David	-	London	gbf	0		-	-
Scala & Co.	-	London	gbf	0		-	-

Name	Year	City					
Schaaffhausen'scher, A., Bankverein	1848	Cologne	d	30	709 499 671	m	35 474 833
Schill en Capadose	-	Hague	nl	0	-	-	-
Schlesischer Bankverein	1856	Breslau	d	19	214 446 329	m	10 722 316
Schleswig-Holsteinische Bank	1876	Husum	d	15	68 194 832	m	3 409 741
Schlutow, Wm.	-	Stettin	d	1	-	-	-
Schraidt & Hoffmann	1860	Coburg	d	0	-	-	-
Schroder, J. Henry	1804	London	gbf	0	-	-	-
Schuhmann, Robert	-	Paris	f	0	-	-	-
Schuster, Gebrüder	-	Frankfurt	d	0	-	-	-
Seligman Brothers	1864	London	gbf	0	-	-	-
Seligman Frères & Co.	-	Paris	f	0	-	-	-
Senlecq, C. M.	-	Ardres	f	0	-	-	-
Seyd & Co. Ltd.	1858	London	gbf	0	-	-	-
Sheffield Banking Co.	1831	Sheffield	gb	26	-	-	4 421 108
Shilson, Coode & Co.	-	St Austell	gb	0	-	-	-
Skandinaviska Kreditaktiebolaget	1864	Gothenburg, Stockholm	swe	19	363 053 273	kr	20 169 626
Skaraborgs Enskilda Bank	1864	Sköfde	swe	18	59 294 825	kr	3 294 156
Skiens og Oplands Privatbank	1898	Skien	nor	0	-	-	-
Skiensfjordens Kreditbank	1882	Skien	nor	4	25 653 394	kr	1 425 188
Smålands Enskilda Bank	1837	Jönköping	swe	14	49 868 140	kr	2 770 452
Société Belge de Crédit Industriel et Commercial	-	Brussels	b	2	57 018 344	fcs	4 751 528
Société Centrale des Banques de Province	1911	Paris	f	0	142 666 725	fcs	5 706 669
Société Commerciale Française au Chili	1893	Paris	f	1	8 333 044	fcs	333 321
Société de Dépôts et de Crédit	1896	Brussels	b	1	87292396	fcs	7 274 366
Société Française de Banque et de Dépôts	-	Antwerp	b	5	-	-	-
Société Française de Reports et Dépôts	1881	Paris	f	0	162 840 954	fcs	6 513 638
Société Generale Alsacienne de Banque	1881	Strasbourg	d	24	104 146 613	m	5 207 330
Société Générale	1864	Paris	f	1031	2 176 571 703	fcs	87 062 868
Société Générale de Belgique	1822	Brussels	b	0	1 797 106 442	fcs	71 884 257
Société Lyonnais de Dépôts	1865	Lyons	f	0	76 801 312	fcs	3 072 952

Bank	(i)	(ii)	(iii)	(iv)	(v)	(vi)	(vii)
Société Marseillaise de Crédit	–	Marseilles	f	0	187 972 210	fcs	7 518 888
Société Torlades	1719	Paris/Lisbon	f	0	9 561 170	fcs	382 446
Sodermanlands Enskilda Bank	1865	Nyköping	swe	11	41 712 991	kr	2 317 388
Sondenfjeldske Privatbank	1890	Christianssand	nor	0	9 586 619	kr	532 589
Spangler, Carl & Co. (NOEG)	1855	Salzburg	a	0	–	–	–
Speyer Brothers	1861	London	gbf	0	–	–	–
Speyer-Ellissen, Lazard	1818	Frankfurt	d	0	–	–	–
Stahl & Federer AG	–	Stuttgart	d	0	–	–	–
Standard Bank of South Africa	1862	London	gbf	216	–	–	29 724 123
Stavanger Handels-Og Industribank	1898	Stavanger	nor	0	8 466 919	kr	470 384
Stavanger Privatbank	1879	Stavanger	nor	1	15 239 412	kr	846 634
Steen Frères & Cie	–	Paris	f	0	–	–	–
Steen Frères & Cie	1889	Antwerp	b	0	–	–	–
Steiermarkische Escompte-bank	1864	Graz	a	2	84 145 807	ök	3 506 075
Stein, J. H	1790	Cologne	d	0	–	–	–
Stilwell & Sons	–	London	gb	0	–	–	–
Stockholms Enskilda Bank	1856	Stockholm	swe	12	160 096 443	kr	8 894 246
Stockholms Intecknings Garanti Aktiebolaget	–	Stockholm	swe	0	180 879 920	kr	10 048 884
Stuart, John & Co. Ltd.	1834	Manchester	gb	0	–	–	40 864
Suddeutsche Disconto-Gesellschaft AG	–	Mannheim	d	9	186 286 361	m	9 314 318
Sundsvalls Enskilda Bank	1864	Sundsvall/Stockholm	swe	7	77 633 923	kr	4 312 995
Sundsvalls Handelsbank	1874	Sundsvall	swe	3	32 064 166	kr	1 781 342
Sydsvenska Kredit Aktiebolaget	1896	Malmö	swe	33	116 340 893	kr	6 463 382
Thomas, Luke & Co. Ltd	–	London	gbf	1	–	–	–
Tönsbergs Privatbank	1870	Tönsberg	nor	0	8 109 687	kr	450 538
Tönsbergs Handelsbank	1899	Tönsberg	nor	0	4 274 225	kr	237 456
Trägårdh & Co.	1911	Stockholm	swe	0	–	–	–

Name	Year	City	Country	No.	Value	Currency	Value
Transvaalsche Banken Handels-Vereeniging	1898	Amsterdam	nl	2	6 020 861	fl	501 738
Tubb & Co.	1793	Bicester	gb	0	-	-	-
Twentsche Bankvereeniging	1861	Amsterdam	nl	2	116 520 426	fl	9 710 035
Twentsche Bank	1908	London	gbf	0	-	-	-
Ulster Bank	1836	Belfast	gb	196			12 131 291
Union Bank	1870	Vienna	a	2	352 808 339	ök	14 700 347
Union Bank of Australia	1837	London	gbf	176			27 118 975
Union Bank of Manchester	1836	Manchester	gb	88			7 450 247
Union Bank of Scotland	1830	Glasgow	gb	162			19 496 080
Union of London & Smiths Bank	1839	London	gb	214			49 284 778
United Counties	1836	Birmingham	gb	206			16 303 185
Uplands Enskilda Bank	1865	Uppsala	swe	15	42 732 133	kr	2 374 007
Valckenberg, P. J., Ltd	1786	Worms	d	0	-	-	-
Vereinsbank in Kiel	1865	Kiel	d	0	14 132 746	m	706 637
Vereinsbank in Nürnberg	1871	Nürnberg	d	0	43 665 588	m	2 183 279
Vereinsbank in Hamburg	1856	Hamburg	d	18	178 429 739	m	8 921 486
Verley, Decroix & Co.	-	Lille	f	0	-	-	-
Vermeer & Co.	1825	Amsterdam	nl	0	-	-	-
Vernes & Co.	1824	Paris	f	0	-	-	-
Verschoore, P. & Co.	-	Courtrai	b	0	-	-	-
Vienna Giro- und Cassen-Verein	1872	Vienna	a	0	53 764 478	ök	2 240 186
Vogtlandische Bank	-	Plauen	d	4	45 750 777	m	2 287 538
Warburg, M. M.	-	Hamburg	d	0	-	-	-
Wermslands Enskilda Bank	1832	Karlstad	swe	23	116 574 851	kr	6 476 380
Wertheim & Gompertz	1834	Amsterdam	nl	0	-	-	-
West Yorkshire Bank	1829	Halifax	gb	32			6 730 485
Westendorp & Co.	1828	Amsterdam	nl	0	-	-	-
Weyhausen, E. C.	1865	Bremen	d	0	-	-	-
White & Shaxson	-	London	gb	0	-	-	-
Wiegman's Bank	1903	Amsterdam	nl	0	-	-	-
Wiener Bank-Verein	1869	Vienna	a	58	34 252 488	ök	1 427 187

Bank	(i)	(ii)	(iii)	(iv)	(v)	(vi)	(vii)
Wiener, Levy & Co.	1880	Berlin	d	0	–	–	–
Williams Deacon's	1836	Manchester	gb	113			19 356 287
Wilts & Dorset Banking Co.	1835	Salisbury	gb	181			14 031 618
Wissel-en Effectenbank	1879	Rotterdam	nl	0	9 858 344	fl	821 528
Wogau & Co.	1839	London	gbf	2	–	–	–
Woodhead & Co.	1816	London	gb	1	–	–	–
Wurttembergische Vereinsbank	1869	Stuttgart	d	10	188 200 463	m	9 410 023
Wurttembergische Bankanstalt, vormals Pfluam	1881	Stuttgart	d	0	30 039 064	m	1 501 953
Yorkshire Penny Bank	1859	Leeds	gb	116			21 233 951
Zip, J. A. & van Teylingen	–	Middelburg	nl	0	–	–	–
Zivnostenská Bank	1868	Prague	a	20	386 750 826	ök	16 114 617

Index

(X) 15/5/10

~~6795~~

4400

107130-BUS